THE ECONOMICS OF
New England

THE ECONOMICS OF
New England

CASE STUDY OF AN
OLDER AREA

SEYMOUR E. HARRIS

HARVARD UNIVERSITY PRESS
Cambridge, Massachusetts

1952

Library of Congress Catalog Card Number 52–5031
Printed in the United States of America

TO ROBERT HAMMOND HAYNES

Assistant Librarian of the Harvard College Library,
whose kindly helpfulness in serving scholars — fer-
reting out materials, saving them time and energy
— has contributed much to American scholarship

ABOUT THIS BOOK

The present volume is primarily about New England. But in some measure it applies to the Middle Atlantic States and to the East North Central States. A generation from now the same problems may apply to the Southeast, just as similar problems have troubled England since World War I. These problems are indigenous to older regions.

The question of New England's future is not new. Frequently, in the 35 years I have lived in New England, I have heard, and participated in, discussions on this subject. I recall that as long ago as the middle 1920's, as a junior member of the Harvard Faculty, I had frequent luncheon discussions of New England's economic problems with other junior members, including Edward Mason, now Dean of the Graduate School of Public Administration, and Crane Brinton, now Professor of History at Harvard. One recurrent subject of our almost daily luncheon debates was: "Would Harvard decline with New England?" Although I have no way of knowing whether President Conant had in mind the less favorable economic prospects for New England than for the country generally *(inter alia)* when he decided upon his program of national scholars and of tapping other regions more aggressively for Harvard's students, we can see how wise a program it was in view of New England's *relative* economic decline.

It was in 1947 that I first published material on New England's economic prospects. That article, "The Economic Decline of New England," appeared in the *Harvard Business Review.* It was frank, outspoken, and perhaps overly pessimistic, possibly a necessary antidote to the ostrich-like behavior and booster-smugness of some of the region's leaders.

It was soon after that the financial community began to examine the region's economy more intensively; and the Federal Reserve Bank of Boston to spend much larger sums on research, and, though at times their appraisals were overoptimistic, the Bank, under the leadership of Dr. Neal and more recently with the encouragement of President Erickson, has performed a real service in producing the facts upon which the required analysis might be made. The *Boston Herald* and the *Boston Globe*, and even the *New York Times*, became more interested in these problems and broadcast the issues widely. At times John Crider, then the able editor of the *Herald*, was unduly optimistic; nevertheless, his interest has helped rather than injured the region. There are relatively few financial writers anywhere in the country as able and objective as Mr. John Harriman of the *Globe*; he has listed courageously and objectively both the pluses and minuses for the New England economy. He is one of the relatively few economic writers who realize that the greatest service they can render is not to slant the analysis from the viewpoint of business, financial, or any other interest, but to write from the viewpoint of the community as a whole.

Following a serious recession in New England in 1948–49, much of interest to the region has happened. The President's Council of Economic Advisers organized a New England Committee (its report to President Truman was issued on July 2, 1951, with proposals of the Council for a careful study of the Committee's recommendations); the Joint Congressional Committee on the Economic Report has set up a Committee on New England's Economy under the guidance of the National Planning Association; finally, President Truman appointed a New England – New York Inter-Agency Committee to explore the problem of exploitation of resources. I am fortunate to have served (or now to be serving) with all three committees. Soon after the completion of the present book, I was appointed chairman of the New England Textile Committee by the Conference of New England Governors.

The present volume is the outgrowth of further investigation on my own of the New England problem, and permits wider treatment of the issues involved. Regional economics is only in its infancy: the United States is a continent and not merely a country. Interregional competition of the states raises all the problems of international trade, but in a much more intense and more important form. The battle of the regions and the states goes on in a most ruthless manner.

In all these discussions of New England, one of the crucial issues has been: Shall we speak in truth or shall we speak with tact and conceal the truth? I am aware that frankness may accelerate the loss of industry; nevertheless, I contend that the region will fare better the quicker its diseases are diagnosed and therapy applied, even though the truth may hurt initially. I have, it is true, been critical of some businessmen in New England who broadcast far and wide the heavy burden of taxes in this area and their putative effects. My criticism stems not from a dislike of candor but from a dislike of exaggeration and bad analysis.

As mentioned above, the Report of the Council's Committee on the New England Economy, of which I was a member, was released July 2, 1951, before the present book went to press. A word about the relation of my book and the Report. I have drawn upon my own contributions to this report, as they were originally submitted, before revisions were made by the Committee in order to present a composite view. But my book nevertheless is a new product.

Where I had little to add to the treatment in the Report, I have remained silent or, better, summarized an issue very briefly — e.g., stability. I subscribe generally to the report to the President. I believe it to be the best official analysis of the New England economy yet made available. The present volume, however, deals with many topics much more fully than does the report: history, the general problems of older areas, South-North competition, federal relations, regional balance of payments, power, the St. Lawrence Seaway, industrial structure, taxation, wage costs, unionization, local and state differences, and other problems also, often with different emphasis and even to some extent in disagreement with the Report's conclusions.

My book necessarily reflects an individual's views which of course an official committee report seldom does. A single author can take a stronger position than can be presented in an official report, in part because his views may differ from the average position, and in part because of the greater degree of frankness possible in an unofficial document.

After much thought and study on New England's problems, I am far from convinced that New England need suffer an absolute decline. Its climb has been steady for 150 years, with the notable exception of the twenties, of the thirties, and of 1948–49. I *am* convinced that federal expenditures and deficits, which account, more than any other factors, for the unparalleled national prosperity of the last ten to twelve years, have to some extent obscured the underlying weaknesses of the New England economy. The most concentrated industrial area in the country, as measured by the proportion of workers in industry, necessarily gains disproportionately from military outlays.

The main conclusion I would stress at the outset is that New England can have a healthy and prosperous economy. The region suffers especially from more favorable labor conditions in the South and a social climate there favorably oriented towards business and against the worker; from the paucity of raw materials (a very significant and underestimated factor); from the shifting of markets (an item of less importance than generally assumed); from weaknesses in management which are indeed serious; and from unsatisfactory relations with federal government. Deficiencies of management, labor attitudes, relations with federal government, and several other handicaps lend themselves to treatment. New England businessmen resent especially the lack of interest and even (as it seems to them) hostility here in contrast to the enthusiastic support given by Southern states and communities.

At last we are getting the facts, and we are suggesting therapy. We have moved beyond second base. There are many signs that New England's leaders are becoming aroused both to the dangers and to the prospects.

As a resident of this area for most of my life, as a member of the faculty of one of its great institutions for thirty years, and as one who loves the region, I am anxious to contribute towards the solution of its economic problems. I want to be able to tell my students that, other things being equal, there is no strong economic reason for migrating to the South or West. This is advice that could not have been honestly given during the last few decades.

My obligations are many. From my colleagues on the Council's New England Committee (Messrs. George Ellis, Charles Gragg, John Hogan, John Miller, Alfred Neal, Philip Taft), I learned much. The services of the Boston Federal Reserve Bank have been invaluable to the community, as have their studies to the writer. New England owes much to Messrs, Keyserling, Clark, and Blough, the members of the President's Council of Economic Advisers, and especially their two staff members, Bertram Gross and Joseph Fisher, who worked on our problems. In preparing material for Governor Paul Dever, I had the privilege of envisaging at first hand some of the problems as viewed by those responsible for government. In the course of writing this volume, I have learned much from several Ph.D. theses recently submitted at Harvard and Radcliffe: Dr. W. A. Krause on "Regional Shifts in Industry"; Dr. Penelope Hartland on the "New England Regional Balance of Payments"; Dr. J. A. Morris on the "Woolen and Worsted Industry in the Southern Piedmont States"; Dr. J. A. Cumberland on the "Locational Structure of the East Coast Steel Industry," etc., and Morton Schussheim on "Massachusetts' Fiscal Problems" (in preparation). Mr. Orville Poland, Assistant to Governor Dever, has helped me greatly.

I also acknowledge my indebtedness to Miss Jeanne Pearlson and Mrs. Daniel Cheever for research help, to Dr. Carolyn Shaw Solo for valuable editorial and research help, to Miss Lillian Buller for secretarial help, and to Mrs. Anna Thorpe for typing. I have discussed many matters with my wife and as usual have had the benefit of her good sense. She also gave editorial help and read the proofs.

Seymour E. Harris

Cambridge, Massachusetts
December, 1951

Contents

PART ONE
GENERAL PROBLEMS

CONTENTS

PART FOUR
FISCAL POLICY

PART FIVE

FUEL COSTS AND RESOURCE DEVELOPMENT

PART SIX

MARKETS, TRANSPORTATION, AND RAW MATERIALS

PART SEVEN

INDUSTRIAL STRUCTURE

CONTENTS

CHARTS

PART I

GENERAL PROBLEMS

INTRODUCTION

In the first six chapters, the objective is concentration on some broad issues raised by the New England problem.

The first chapter will give the reader in the shortest space possible, the diagnosis, prognosis, and suggested therapy. (On the last, however, see the concluding remarks.) I hope that the reader will return to Chapter 1, once he (she) has finished reading the book. In fact, one of my critics suggested that I transfer Chapter 1 to the end.

Older Areas is the problem of Chapter 2. My purpose here is to show that the New England problem is not unique; that the aging process raises problems for the region in the same sense that it does in the human body. Lack of venturesomeness, excessive search for security, the competition of youth, worship of the past, and unreceptiveness to the new — these are some of the earmarks of age. Yet it is revealed in this chapter that backsliding is not a necessary process for the older region. In Chapter 3, we trace the emergence of New England as a problem area.

Over the last 150 years, pessimism concerning New England's future has prevailed, and can be traced in the many surveys, public and private, of the region's economy. In Chapters 4 and 5, we examine some of these surveys and reproduce many of the pessimistic statements. The problems raised over the last 50 to 100 years are similar to those being discussed today: shortage of labor supplies, poverty of resources, distance from markets, lack of venturesomeness. With the advance of industrialization, these handicaps are of increasing importance; and, of late, poor management, the lack of raw materials, low wages in newer areas, the loss of natural advantages arising from tidewater location, the structure of taxes, and costly fuel and power are receiving more attention.

It is well to stress the fact that, though New England is a region, the problems of parts of this region are not always similar, nor has the development of the different parts been equal (Chapter 6). Southern New England has left Northern New England far behind; and Connecticut, oriented towards New York and not heavily dependent on declining industries, has had a much more favorable economic history than Massachusetts and Rhode Island.

For New England, a major problem is the intense competition of the South (Chapter 7). No better index of the extent of this competition is to be found than a comparison of the *proportion of persons in manufacturing* in the Northeast and South. Note that in the last 100 years, the South's proportionate advance in manufacturing on this basis has been 400 per cent as against about 15 per cent for the Northeast.

Proportion of Persons in Manufacturing

	Northeast	South
1850–60	1 to 8	1 to 82
1900	1 to 7	1 to 33
1947	1 to 7	1 to 16

Source: J. A. Morris, "The Woolen and Worsted Industry in the Southern Piedmont States," Doctorate Thesis Deposited in Harvard University Library (1951), p. 10.

Unfortunately for New England the intensification of Southern competition has been especially costly. In Chapter 7 (and later ones also), we seek to discover the reasons for the gains of the South, the extent to which they are supportable by underlying advantages in the South, and the extent to which they are to be associated with underbidding for the factors of production by the South about which we ought not to be indifferent.

This general issue of unfair competition among states and regions is an important one and continues to gain in significance. Our states' rights tradition makes control of this battle of the states and regions very difficult. Yet there can be no doubt but that resources are being squandered if skilled labor is displaced in the North, plants are closed down, and public services wasted in response to *excessive* migrations to the South. The case is strong for greater control of industrial location by central government; and as the United States Government expands its control over the economy through increased spending, social security programs, resource development, wage legislation, and the like, the federal government will increasingly influence location and reduce the waste and deterioration of standards involved in excessive migration.[1]

[1] An excellent statement of the possibilities of public control of this waste will be found in Political and Economic Planning, *Report of Location of Industry in Great Britain* (1939), chap. I.

This general part of the book might well have included chapters on New England in a defense economy, the problem of stability, and perhaps a chapter on the theory of location of industry. I have not, however, included such chapters, in part because the President's Council's *Report on the New England Economy* (1951) includes chapters on stability (3) and defense (4), mainly because I preferred a briefer treatment here. Here I note that as New England advances in the output of durable goods, the region will lose one of its advantages, namely, a greater degree of stability than has prevailed in the nation generally. This past stability is all the more surprising since, over part of the period under consideration, the cyclical decline was aggravated by a secular decline.

New England's defense problem is, in no small part, that of obtaining a fair share of government contracts and of federally subsidized plants. Both in World War II and in 1950–51, this region has failed to participate adequately in the procurement of new plants financed in whole or in part with federal funds. This failure has aggravated a disadvantage in the quality of the capital plant and equipment which plagues New England. Another defense problem is that of decentralization in response to vulnerability to military attack, the solution of which is bound greatly to affect New England's economic future.

In many respects, the theme of this book is localization of industry. Why does New England, for example, concentrate on shoes and textiles, and why are these industries growing more rapidly elsewhere? Throughout we are concerned with problems of location, though, unfortunately, space does not permit a systematic and extended discussion of location theory. I can only refer to the excellent treatments by the United States National Resources Planning Board,[2] Edgar M. Hoover,[3] Carter Goodrich,[4] G. E. McLaughlin,[5] and Political and Economic Planning,[6] volumes which greatly aided me in the writing of this book.

The availability of labor and of capital, the quality of manage-

---

[2] *The Structure of the American Economy* (1939).

[3] *The Location of Economic Activity* (1948).

[4] *Migration and Economic Opportunity* (1936).

[5] *Growth of Manufacturing Areas* (1938).

[6] *Report on the Location of Industry in Great Britain* (1939); also see Great Britain: *Report of the Royal Commission on the Distribution of the Industrial Population* (1940).

ment, proximity to markets and to raw materials (inclusive of power), and the relative prices of factors of production will determine what is produced in a particular region, and the nature of interregional competition. But through taxes, subsidies, and spending policies generally, government policy has an increasing influence on location. This volume especially stresses labor costs; but, though management and raw materials receive less attention, they are also vital aspects of the problem. The detailed treatment of taxes and power rests upon the space given them in public discussions rather than upon their actual importance. Again, they are presumed to be more subject to public treatment than other costs.

CHAPTER 1

FUNDAMENTAL ISSUES

1. THE ESSENCE OF THE PROBLEM

Candor. As we shall presently see, the decline of New England is an old problem. Our interest in it is not in order to proclaim the weaknesses of the region and thus stimulate an exodus of capital and brains. Rather we are striving to diagnose the situation with as complete objectivity as is possible, pointing to strength as well as weakness, to signs of impending advances as well as declines, and then to suggest therapy. We insist upon candor. We do not agree with viewpoints expressed at times, for example in the *Boston Herald,* and by the Federal Reserve Bank of Boston during the Whittemore regime, which reflected an unwillingness to face facts. As *Time* expressed it (July 26, 1948, commenting on Mr. Whittemore): "He likes to preach the greatness of New England industry, and pooh-poohs statistics which sometimes tell a different tale." Much more sensible is the statement made to me in 1951 by the president of a New England bank, one of the largest in the country, that he would not support a research project for New England unless the truth were told.

We ought to be clear concerning what we mean by the decline of New England. Over the last 200 years, New England has climbed to new heights, generation after generation, with interruptions indeed, the most serious one being the decline of the twenties and thirties. The miracle of New England is not how badly she has performed, but, in the face of barren natural resources and unfavorable location relative to raw materials and markets, how remarkably she has moved ahead. With an area of 12,000 square miles, Southern New England alone produces $7 billion of manufactured goods and is one of the great manufacturing "nations" of the world.

By New England's decline, we generally mean the reduction in

New England's share of the nation's population, manufacturing, or income, and possibly the *relative* decline of per capita income. No one should be the least surprised that New England does not grow as rapidly as the rest of the country. The New England problem is not that New England fails to keep pace with the Middle West, or the South, or the West, but that losses are larger than they need be. Indeed, one may too easily conclude that an older area must fall behind. That this is not necessarily so is suggested by the rise of New York's manufacturing output from 10 per cent of the nation's 150 years ago to 13 per cent today. (New England's decline was from 30 to 9 per cent in these 150 years, a percentage record 1/4–1/5 as favorable as New York's: 30 per cent of the 1800 level against 130 per cent.)

In reply to my article on the "Decline of the New England Economy," published in the *Harvard Business Review*, in 1947, the Boston Federal Reserve Bank, the New England Council, and the *Boston Herald* stated that of course New England cannot be expected to grow as rapidly as the newer parts of the country. I agree.

The Problem Is the Rate of Expansion of New Employments. The number one problem is that New England may be losing ground too rapidly, that as employment is lost in some industries, new industries or expanding old ones do not adequately absorb displaced workers and new employees. In the twenties and thirties, this was the problem, and the decline of 1948–49 as well as the textile depression of 1951–52 reminds us that it still exists.

Another symptom of decline is the tendency of incomes in New England to fall relative to the rest of the country, although in absolute terms, incomes rise. If, in relative terms, they decline, the explanation may well be that industrialization is proceeding elsewhere. Many ask, why be upset by that?

Again, this is not the whole explanation. In part, the relative decline in incomes also reflects the capturing of the most productive (i.e., mass production) industries by other sections of the country. It may well be, as Mr. Edward Filene insisted almost twenty years ago, that one of the weaknesses of New England is its unwillingness to use mass-production techniques.

The evidence is clear that wages are declining in New England. In a refutation of my article, the economists of the Boston Federal Reserve Bank tried to show that wages were not so low, relatively, as I had claimed. Actually, this is not the vital point. What is significant is the fact that, under pressure of unemployment in New England and rapid growth elsewhere, wages have been depressed in our area relative to wages elsewhere. (In some years, there were actual declines here.) Would anyone deny that of all the major industrial areas (i.e., New England, Middle Atlantic, Southeast, Middle West, and Far West) wages are lowest in New England, with the exception of the South? Or that the wage structure vis-à-vis the nation is lower than it was twenty-five or fifty years ago?

In the discussion of this problem of setbacks in manufacturing, the optimists have stressed the importance of the tertiary (service) industries. As manufacturing became less important, excess labor tends to move into the tertiary industries. Since the latter are supposed to be the high-paying industries, the shift is generally considered a net gain. But this approach is an oversimplification of the problem. The tertiary industries of an area will not support large numbers at high rates of pay unless they in turn are supported by productive agricultural and manufacturing industries. Those employed in the services (e.g., selling, professional, and clerking) can maintain a high standard of living only if their pay can buy manufactured goods, foods, etc., at reasonable prices. Hence the need for productive primary and secondary industries which yield plentiful supplies of goods — otherwise the high pay in tertiary industries will be dissipated in high prices; or with prices determined at national levels, wages will be depressed in accordance with restricted supplies. The only other means to high pay in the service industries would be increased sales of services to outside regions.

That the expansion of tertiary employment may be a sign of economic distress, as well as of economic health, is suggested by the fact that Massachusetts' tertiary employment is relatively about 20 per cent higher than Connecticut's. Yet the latter has had a much more favorable economic history in the last generation. To some extent, at least, the advance of tertiary employment in Massachusetts reflects the pressure of unabsorbed workers to seek outlets in nonfactory jobs.

In the discussion of the New England problem, it has been held by some (inclusive of the Boston Reserve Bank) that the relative per capita gains of the nation vis-à-vis New England should be interpreted as a favorable rather than as an unfavorable factor.

Gains in other areas mean increased markets for New England. Moreover, a narrowing of income differentials will dull the incentive to move industries out of New England. These arguments carry some weight. But New Englanders should not gloat over the fact that their income advantage is disappearing. They should not accept without some misgivings the fact that from 1929 to 1948 per capita income rose 2¼ times as much in the South as in New England. The remarkable fact about this progress has been that, despite large migrations from the South, the population gains of the South exceed those of New England by almost one-half. In this period of twenty years (1929–1949), New England's gains of population were but 15 per cent of those of the Pacific Southwest and 21 per cent of those of the Pacific Northwest. In these latter areas, however, the rise of per capita income was only equal to that in New England. In these years, the rise of population in the Middle Eastern States exceeded that in New England by almost 30 per cent, and the rise in the East North Central exceeded New England's by more than 40 per cent.

A series of charts present graphically the main issues.

1. The first gives the growth of population, 1929–1949.

2. The second gives the net change of population in relation to natural increase, 1930–1948.[1] What is of particular interest here is the large rise of population in relation to natural increase in the Pacific states and large losses for the Southeast — with gains of but 0.5 for each unit of natural increase. In general, the agricultural areas retained only part of the natural growth in population. The industrial areas gained more than is explicable by natural factors; but the net gains on migration were small for the three important industrial areas in the Northeast. Large variations occurred within regions. Thus Connecticut gains 2 for every unit of natural increase (net) and Vermont loses 9 out of every 10 of net natural increase.

3. In the growth of manufacturing workers in the population, New England's position was next to last. In relation to her most important competitors, New England's gains of manufacturing workers in the years 1939 to 1947 were 65 per cent of the increase in the Middle East, 59 per cent of that in the South Atlantic, and 46 per cent of that in the East North Central.

4. New England's rise of total income payments from 1929 to

---

[1] Natural increase equals the excess of births over deaths; net change reflects also population shifts.

CHART 1. GROWTH OF POPULATION, 1929–1949

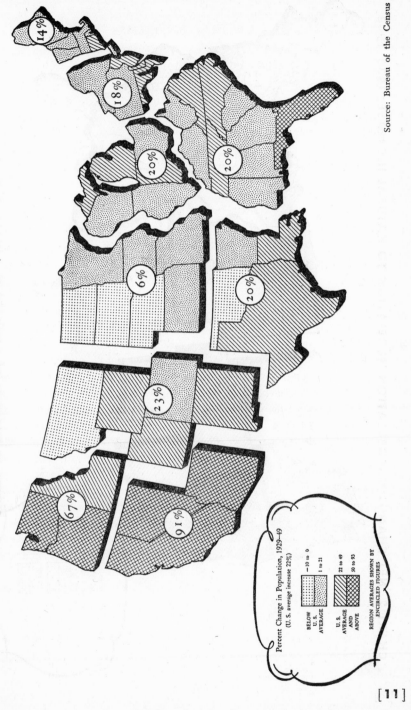

Source: Bureau of the Census

Percent Change in Population, 1929–49
(U. S. average increase 22%)

BELOW
U.S.
AVERAGE

−10 to 0

1 to 21

U.S.
AVERAGE
AND
ABOVE

22 to 49

50 to 93

REGION AVERAGES SHOWN BY
ENCIRCLED FIGURES

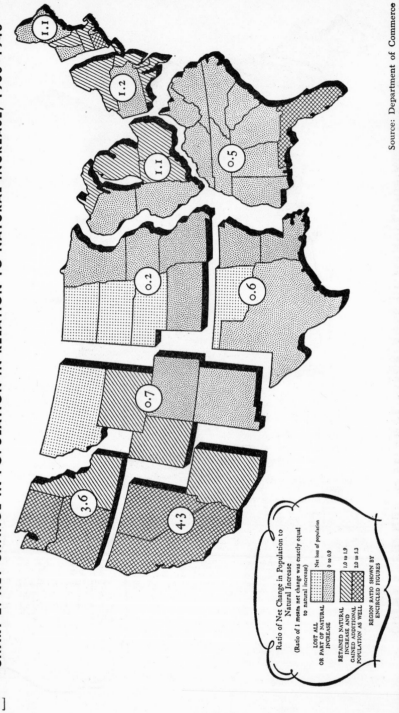

CHART 2. NET CHANGE IN POPULATION IN RELATION TO NATURAL INCREASE, 1930–1948

Ratio of Net Change in Population to Natural Increase

(Ratio of 1 mean net change was exactly equal to natural increase)

LOST ALL OR PART OF NATURAL INCREASE

Net loss of population

0 to 0.9

RETAINED NATURAL INCREASE AND GAINED ADDITIONAL POPULATION AS WELL

1.0 to 1.9

2.0 to 5.3

REGION RATIO SHOWN BY ENCIRCLED FIGURES

Source: Department of Commerce

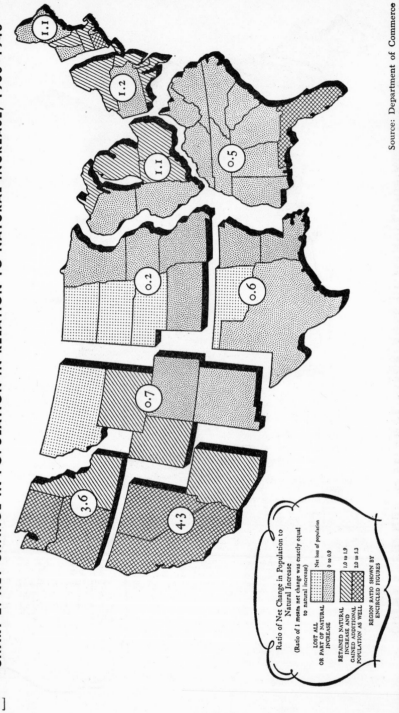

CHART 3. CHANGE IN RELATIVE IMPORTANCE OF MANUFACTURING, 1939–1947

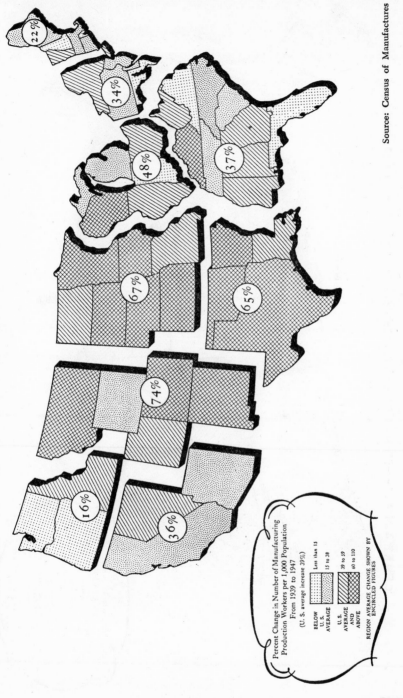

Percent Change in Number of Manufacturing
Production Workers per 1,000 Population
From 1939 to 1947
(U. S. average increase 39%)

BELOW
U. S.
AVERAGE — Less than 15

U. S.
AVERAGE — 15 to 38

U. S.
AVERAGE
AND
ABOVE — 39 to 59 / 60 to 110

REGION AVERAGE CHANGE SHOWN BY
ENCIRCLED FIGURES

Source: Census of Manufactures

[13]

CHART 4. INCREASE IN PER CAPITA INCOME PAYMENTS, 1929–1948

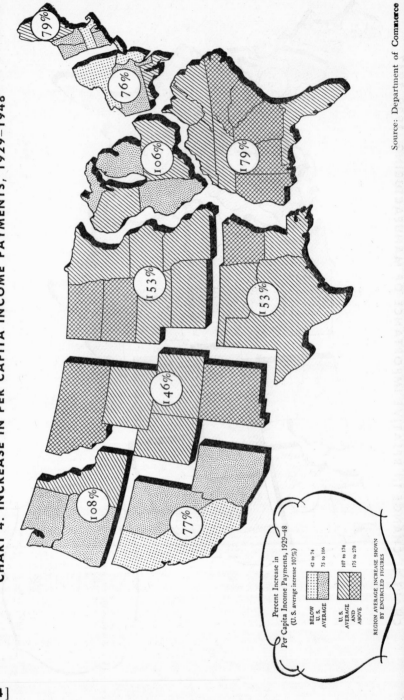

Percent Increase in
Per Capita Income Payments, 1929–48
(U. S. average increase 107%)

BELOW
U. S.
AVERAGE
42 to 74
75 to 106

U. S.
AVERAGE
AND
ABOVE
107 to 174
175 to 278

REGION AVERAGE INCREASE SHOWN
BY ENCIRCLED FIGURES

Source: Department of Commerce

CHART 5. RELATIVE IMPORTANCE OF MANUFACTURING, 1947

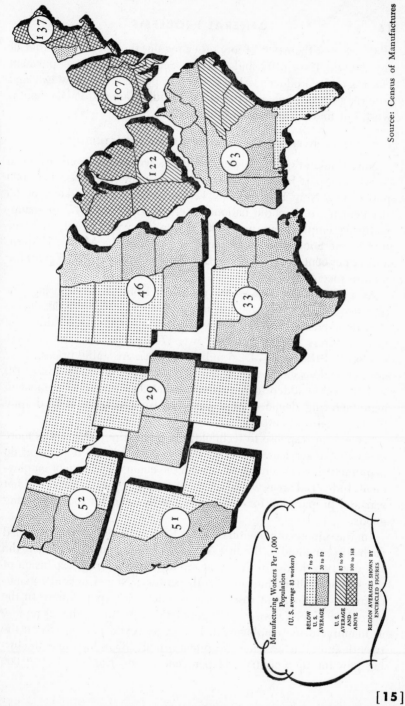

Manufacturing Workers Per 1,000 Population
(U. S. average 83 workers)

BELOW U.S. AVERAGE — 7 to 29 / 30 to 82

U. S. AVERAGE AND ABOVE — 83 to 99 / 100 to 168

REGION AVERAGES SHOWN BY ENCIRCLED FIGURES

Source: Census of Manufactures

[15]

1948 was less than that of any other region, though close to that of
the Middle East (102 and 104 per cent — total income payment
chart is not reproduced). The per capita payments of New England
rose roughly as much as those of the Middle East and Pacific Southwest, but much less than in other regions.

2. THE PROBLEM OF DEPENDENCE ON MANUFACTURING

New England's economic eminence, as well as its problems, arise
in no small part from its concentration on manufacturing. Per 1000
population, New England has 137 manufacturing workers, or 65
per cent more than the national average. Even in 1947, its manufacturing employment per 1000 population was more than twice
that of the Southeast, 28 per cent in excess of the Middle Eastern,
and 12 per cent in excess of the East North Central. Chart 5 gives the
picture succinctly.

As a nation advances on the economic front, manufacturing employment tends to become less important. First, technological gains
provide increased output per worker. Thus, the value added by
manufacturers in New England was $756 million in 1899, $23,841
million in 1919, and $74,425 million in 1947. At stable prices, these
are tremendous gains even in the 1919–1947 period. Even from 1919
to 1938, value added increased somewhat. But total employment in
manufacturing declined by 2 per cent from 1919 to 1947 despite
the large gains of output.

Second, in response to technological gains, the public turns more
and more to services. It follows that an area heavily dependent on
manufacturing is likely to suffer from the changed pattern of employment. Industrial areas would have felt the change-over more, had not
war and preparation for war raised the demand for manufacturing
goods.

In the nineteenth century, New England's population doubled
each 50 years; and in the first 50 years of the twentieth century, the
rise was two-thirds. In the great era of manufacturing expansion of
the second half of the nineteenth century, New England's manufacturing employment rose twice as much as its population. In the
years 1900 to 1947, however, its population rose three times as rapidly
as manufacturing employment. It was, however, particularly in the
twenties and thirties when, despite a rise of 4.35 million manufacturing jobs for the country (44 per cent), New England lost 30,000

jobs (2 per cent), that New England felt both the effects of technological gains and the improved competitive position of other areas.
Its population rose by 1 million and the number of manufacturing
jobs actually declined.

That New England's interests were disproportionately in industries which tended to lose ground relatively and in industries which
could easily spring up in other areas, did not help matters. In the
years 1919–1947, our region lost 158,000 jobs (one-third of 1919 employment) in textiles; the rest of the country gained 237,000. In
leather and leather products, the respective figures were a loss of
46,000 and a gain of 30,000. In view of a rise of real national income
of several hundred per cent and the increase of total manufacturing
employment over these years, the large relative losses in these industries are apparent.

Varying industrial structure within New England explains in part
the better record of Connecticut than Massachusetts. The former,
much less dependent on shoes and textiles, increased its jobs in
manufacturing by 21 per cent in these years; the latter lost 11 per
cent of such jobs. These are not the only explanations of the better
economic health of Connecticut. Its proximity to the Middle Atlantic
area is a relevant consideration. An even better long-run record can
be found in New York and New Jersey, the former at least profiting
from a relatively much smaller dependence on manufacturing than
either of the two New England states cited. Although manufacturing
is more important to Connecticut than to Massachusetts, this is more
than offset by her fortunate recourse to growing industries.

3. INTERREGIONAL AND INTERNATIONAL ACCOUNTS

According to the best estimates I could make,[2] New England
exports about $3 billion of manufactured goods (value added), or
more than 20 per cent of the region's income. Like England, New
England must export or die. For the food to feed its population and
the raw materials to keep its people busy, New England pays primarily with exports of manufactured goods.

Of these $3 billion of exports, roughly one-third goes abroad.
Both on the basis of an estimate made for the *Connecticut Full
Employment Commission* and on the assumption that New England's

[2] Exports are assumed equal to output less estimated consumption in New
England.

exports as a percentage of output equals the nation's, the $1 billion estimate seems to be roughly accurate. It is evident that regional trade is much more important than international trade; but the reader should observe that the intensification of competition in interregional trade suggests international trade as a way out. It may well be argued that the quadrupling (in dollars) of United States exports in 1947–1950 over those in late prewar years has been a windfall for New England, offering substitute markets for those lost in intense interregional competition. Ordinarily the nation's export trade is around 5 per cent of the nation's income. New England's trade with foreign countries as a percentage of income is higher, and New England's exports both to other regions and other nations vis-à-vis income are several times the exports of the nation vis-à-vis the nation's income.

From these facts, we draw important conclusions. The first is that New England, greatly dependent on foreign trade, should support free trade more than the region actually does. It is absurd for New England's textile manufacturers to bombard Washington with appeals for protection when their exports greatly exceed imports even on a narrow regional basis. We should, however, keep in mind the point that in reducing tariff barriers Washington should pick the time and industries for diminishing protection according to business conditions and the need of easing the transition for areas with heavy concentration of unemployment. Indeed, New England manufacturers may raise the question of foreign competition in other regions. The answer seems to be that the major competition faced by New England is from domestic, not foreign, producers; that tariffs do not shelter its manufacturers from this competition; and that the gains of export trade for New England's manufactures would more than balance loss of interregional markets associated with free entry for foreign producers.

Another conclusion I draw from these figures is that the interregional, or even interstate, competition is much more intense than international competition. The intensity of this competition explains the great debates over tax burdens, subsidies, social legislation, etc., with industries in each state or region striving to capture the largest part of these vast markets through the reduction of manageable costs.

We draw an even more important conclusion from this material. New England's stake in declining industries is large; and the two most important of these (i.e., textiles and shoes, leather, and leather products) sell outside this region more than 75 per cent of their products. These two industries account for $1500 million of exports, or roughly one-half of all New England's exports, an amount equal to one-quarter of its manufacturing output. Only by continuing exports at a high level can these industries maintain their position. Yet these are just the industries that move with ease, and as they move, New England's markets in outside regions are jeopardized.

The defense against the losses of external markets is the development of new industries which absorb the displaced labor and sell outside New England. Our region is fortunate in one respect, namely, that the area can pay for a large excess of imports with dollars received in profits or interest on past investment made elsewhere, and in part through the sale of services — e.g., insurance, tourist, education. There is also some evidence that New England has been helped in recent years substantially by inward movements of capital — e.g., establishment of branch plants here, inflow of funds via investment trusts. In all these ways, the region obtains dollars which can be used to pay for the raw materials and food required.

Unfortunately, it is not clear that these alternative means of obtaining dollars would suffice to replace the dollars lost as outside markets vanish. The tertiary industries account for about one-half the income of the region. Most of them are purely domestic industries, though to some extent they are tied to manufacturing and to some extent they sell services outside. According to Miss Hartland's study of the New England balance of payments, the service industries provided about one-third of the dollars required to meet the adverse balance in 1939. Yet I estimate these "exports" at only about one-seventh of the total income earned in these occupations. They are, therefore, primarily domestic services. As the tertiary employments expand, however, the purely domestic employment becomes more important, and, therefore, imports of food and raw materials will become a smaller part of the region's income; and, therefore, the maintenance of exports relatively less of a headache.

4. THE BALANCE OF PAYMENTS AND RELATIONS WITH THE FEDERAL GOVERNMENT

Pressure on New England's balance of payments, related in part to competitive losses, appears in a relative reduction of banking reserves and bank deposits in the region and an accompanying pressure on wage rates and prices. (Some banks nevertheless have maintained their relative position in the nation, and particularly the First National Bank of Boston. They have sought business outside the region.) The *relative* loss of exports means more cash payments outside the region and hence loss of deposits and banking reserves; and less money means downward pressure on prices. In the body of this book, we detail the facts in support of this thesis. Here we need note only that in the thirties the deterioration in agricultural areas was even greater than in old manufacturing areas, with the result that New England's balance on commercial account was favorable; any secular decline for New England was more than offset by the catastrophic reduction of income and prices in farm areas. New England also shared in the favorable balance vis-à-vis the outside world. Our gain of gold was not so large as might be expected from a favorable balance of trade and service account of $1824 million for the region in the thirties.

The thirties were a forerunner of even greater drains in the forties as a result of federal activities. In these years, New England lost heavily in bank reserves even though the nation gained. In 1948, the Treasury drain was no less than about $1 billion — a sum equal on a per capita basis to the excess of New England's per capita income over the nation's.

By spending less in New England than it took out, the federal government drained billions out of this area. The total losses are not given merely by a comparison of federal withdrawals and disbursements. New England pays much more than is suggested by the taxes collected in New England. For example, the taxes on tobacco first levied in North Carolina and those on automobiles first levied in Michigan are in fact paid primarily in other parts of the country.

In almost every area of federal spending, New England's share was much smaller than its percentage of the nation's population or income: for outlays on farm support, for RFC loans, for resource development, for relief, etc. The results varied also from state to state. As we said New England was aloof — Connecticut was (in percentage of federal outlays to income) much more aloof than Massachusetts.

These are the facts. What are the inferences? New England's reluctance to accept federal outlays has been costly to the region. The federal government has intervened not merely in relief, but increasingly in resource development, which increases the competitive power of other regions. As a result, the migration of capital from New England has been accelerated, and its transitional problems aggravated.

When New England has tended to ask for help, it has frequently been in the wrong direction: to bail out banking creditors of weak textile firms or to salvage the Waltham Watch Company. Anyone conversant with the history of that company over the last 10 to 20 years knows that it has been one of the more inefficient large corporations in the region. It was in response to unwise soliciting of this kind, to which even the distinguished Massachusetts Senators lent their support, that Senator Fulbright called attention to New England's tendency to exploit poorer areas of the country.

It is important for New England to face up to the presence of the federal government and make *fair* claims on that government. Drains out of New England may continue and may be justified by the underlying poverty of other areas. But in part they result from an ideology held in New England which is surely not appropriate in the fifties.

5. COSTS AND COMPETITIVE POSITION

Most experts in location theory emphasize the importance of labor costs and accessibility to raw materials and markets as the major determinants of the location of industry. As we shall see later, the unavailability of raw materials is a major factor in New England's economic difficulties. This has always been a New England problem but of late it has become an even greater handicap. An analysis of the important industries in which the region's participation has been especially disappointing will show just how important this factor is. Thus, of the 600,000 employees in motor vehicles and equipment, New England's contribution was but 5500, or less than 1 per cent. The significance of this factor has not been adequately realized.

Distance from markets is less of a handicap than is generally supposed. Within 500 miles, about one-third of the country's markets are to be found; and within 1000 miles, about two-thirds. What is more, the 500-mile radius provides almost as large a proportion of the nation's buying power as it did in 1900.

Labor costs are a matter of first-rate significance. In this category, we include wage payments corrected for productivity as well as outlays for executives and managers. Part of the labor costs lie in the fringe benefits collected by labor either from the firm or through the intervention of the government.

One of the most crucial problems of costs is the competition among regions and states to keep costs down as a means of maintaining industries or inducing new industries or firms to enter. By keeping trade unions out, by undercutting in security benefits, by imposing taxes excessively upon consumers and sparing business, by offering subsidies to new firms coming in, by tolerating long hours for women and children and shying away from reasonable minimum wage laws, a state or region can attract industries. This is an important factor in the struggle between the North and the South for industrial supremacy.

Without a doubt, the South's claim for industries is a strong one. In access to raw materials and in availability of large supplies of labor, this area has an advantage over New England and even part of the Middle Eastern region. The South also is close to rich markets. No one can dispute the right of the South to exploit her rich labor resources. Lower wages are a condition for the emergence of the South as a great industrial area. Its wages are low in part because of the vast surpluses migrating from the farms; in part because the South's competitive strength lies in the less advanced and less productive manufacturing areas; and in part because the cost of living is much less.

Lower wages reflecting plentiful supplies of labor constitute a genuine competitive advantage for the South. To this much we agree. But there is also much evidence that the migration of industry to the South at the expense of the North is the result of policies on the part of Southern governmental authorities which cannot be justified on national grounds. Standards of social security are low even when allowance is made for the lower incomes in the South. Factory legislation, wage legislation, and working conditions generally are on sub-national standards. The tax system is geared excessively to burdening the masses and sparing industry. Even the cost of subsidies which help attract industry are passed on substantially to the masses. The struggle against trade unionism, which is a condition for minimum labor standards, has reached drastic proportions, with members of the upper classes inclusive of even doctors and ministers, using the most violent and dubious means of shutting trade unionism out.

Differences in costs arising from low standards of government legislation or lack of it are not healthy reasons for attracting industry. Their effects are to bring about excessive losses to the North, losses not justified by underlying differences in resource availability. The losses would have been even greater had not the South's unwillingness to meet Northern standards resulted in a slowing up of advances in the North. My objection is not to subsidies in the South, for one might argue that, in the absence of tariffs and similar restrictive techniques, no agricultural area could industrialize without artificial aid — for the competition with established industrial regions is unequal. The objection is rather against practices which give the South an unfair advantage by depressing the standard of living of workers through legislation or lack of it. As a result, excessive losses are suffered by the North and the distribution of employment between North and South is moved in the latter's favor. More and more, resources (human, capital, and public services) are wasted in the North; more and more the industry of the nation is carried on at lower standards of living than need be. The same arguments that have been used against cheap Japanese labor may, to some extent, be applied to Southern labor, the only difference being that the argument is germane on grounds of national considerations in the present context and is not in the argument on Japanese standards.

A detailed survey of labor costs shows that wages are still higher in New England than in the South, but the differential has been reduced greatly over the last generation. In general, as noted, New England is no longer a high-wage area. Wage differentials vary according to the regions with which New England is compared and according to the industries and occupations studied. In textiles and shoes, New England wages are still relatively high. In comparison with the Far West and the East North Central, wages in New England in general are low, the explanation in part being the greater concentration in these areas of the highly productive manufacturing industries. Automobiles and airplanes pay much more than textiles and shoes. Pay for skilled workers is often higher in the South where there is still a great shortage of skilled workers than in the North. With a much smaller concentration of white-collar workers, the South pays well in clerical and similar occupations; and New England's pay is low in such occupations. In department stores, for example, wages in New England seem as low as in any area. Whereas low pay in the white-collar occupations, in part related to high educational attainments in the past, gives New England an advantage in the service industries (e.g., insurance), the high pay of skilled workers in the South militates against the growth there of industries requiring large numbers of skilled workers.

Wage differentials are related to the variations in the cost of living. In the South, wages are lower in part because industry is located disproportionately in small towns where the cost of living is low; in part because the cost of living is generally lower in the South than in the North, for the former, new housing and its maintenance, and clothing require relatively small expenditures. In part, of course, the lower wages reflect lower costs associated with low standards of living.

Wages are one problem; wage costs another. The latter depends not only upon wages per hour, per day, or per year, but also upon the productiveness of the worker, the kind of capital used, and managerial efficiency. As far as we can discover, the South has certain advantages in low capital costs which arise from low construction costs, the effectiveness of modern plant which is more plentiful in the South than in New England and which is more easily adapted to changing needs. Low and rigid work loads are a handicap in New England. The general view of experts seems to be that there is little difference between the Northern and Southern worker which cannot be quickly resolved through training; and any advantage of productivity for Northern workers is the function largely of better supervision in the North. On New England management and its deficiencies we shall comment later.

6. TAXATION, FUEL, POWER, AND RIVER DEVELOPMENT

In the controversies over the health of the New England economy, a great deal of the discussion gravitates around the problems listed above. But they are not particularly important cost-wise. The disproportionate time and space allotted to them reflects primarily the fact that these are problems that can be treated, and secondarily the exaggerated views concerning their importance. Unavailability of raw materials, high costs of transportation, high labor costs, inefficient management — these are important competitive factors about which the region seems rather fatalistic. But the government can do something about taxes and power. Who would guess from the allocation of space and time that labor costs are 10 or more times as important as tax costs?

In assessing the burden of taxes on the New England economy, it should be clearly understood that three-quarters of the taxes are federal; that the major taxes are on surpluses, not on costs; that taxes as costs are substantially less than 5 per cent of costs, and differences among the major industrial states are of the order of 1 per cent of per capita income; that the burden of taxes is measured by indirect taxes (sales) as well as direct taxes (pay roll); that the largest differences among regions are in the local, not the state, taxes and these differences can be reduced by choice of low tax communities; that the burden of a tax is measured by who bears the burden, not by who pays it. Should those who proclaim the large contributions of taxes to the loss of industry by New England consider these facts, they would soon realize that taxes are only a small cause of the loss of industry by New England.

This much may be granted. State and local taxes in Massachusetts are somewhat heavier than in the region generally. The tax structure in New England, and particularly in Massachusetts, is oriented more towards taxing business than in other regions. For many, this is a reflection on the region's tax system. But for others, it may well suggest taxation according to capacity to pay, and the Massachusetts tax structure may be accepted as a model for the Southern states and other competitive states to follow (e.g., Illinois). The fault lies largely with the rest of the country rather than with Massachusetts.

The region has its tax problems, however. Being an older region, it is more wedded to the general property tax, the most inequitable and perverse tax of all. That industry deserts with a resultant concentration of the tax on the loyal residents who remain behind further adds to the disabilities of this tax.

Boston has a problem all its own. Suffering from the exodus of population from the central city even more than large cities generally, from the losses of important industries, from poor government over a long period, and, consequently, from a tax rate which results in further losses of activity, Boston passes on part of its tax burden through the Commonwealth to other parts of the state.

It is difficult to see, however, how taxes can be crucial in determining the competitive position of the area, or even of Massachusetts. In the latter, incidentally, state and local taxes as a percentage of income declined from 9.9 per cent in 1936 to 8.8 per cent in 1950. The burden on corporations, to which most of the grumbling is directed, has increased by about $70 million. But in this same period, the corporate profits of Massachusetts corporations increased by 20 times before federal taxes and 10 times after taxes as much as the rise of state corporate taxes. Moreover, these $70 million are in part largely a drain on the federal government; for about two-thirds represent savings on federal taxes.

Fuel and power costs are very high in New England. Average cost per KWH exceeds the national average by 60 per cent, with resultant discouragement of industries in which power is an important cost. Consumption per capita is much less in New England than in the country. Yet we should not exaggerate the importance of this factor. With fuel and power costs but a few per cent of value added in manufacturing, and with power costs rising much less than all costs since 1939, the high costs of fuel and power are not a major factor in New England's competitive problem.

Nevertheless, everything should be done to reduce fuel and power costs. Transportation charges are very high. There have been suggestions from high authority that the public utility companies do not make the most effective use of water transportation. (With returns of 7 per cent on capital virtually guaranteed in practice, the incentive for cost cutting is not too great.) With no federal competition, the public utilities of this area do not experiment with prices as a means of raising sales as much as utilities in other areas; and failure to integrate raises unit costs.

The exploitation of undeveloped hydroelectric power is another weakness of the New England situation. According to the Federal Power Commission about 3 million KW capacity in hydro could be added. New England so far has shown no interest in federal development, though there are 156 such developments in the country. Yet much of the unexploited hydro depends on multipurpose development, which in turn requires federal participation. In connection with federal projects, New England has led in the fight against the St. Lawrence Seaway, which may reduce the traffic of the Boston Port and the New England railroads. These seem inadequate reasons for opposing this project, which clearly will profit the country and in many respects (e.g., more power, cheaper food) will improve New England's economic status.

7. TRANSPORTATION, MARKETS, AND RAW MATERIALS

New England, perched on the northeastern corner of the nation, suffers in high transportation costs for raw materials and finished products. Since its output of raw materials is negligible, the transportation disadvantage is aggravated. Where raw materials are a large part of costs and particularly where transportation charges are large (e.g., where the raw material loses much weight in the process of fabrication), New England suffers special handicaps. It is striking that a region which accounts for about 10 per cent of the nation's factory output produces only 2/5 of 1 per cent (one twenty-fifth of its share of manufacturing) of the nation's minerals. An examination of New England's industrial structure shows that the lack of raw materials, with the resultant high costs, is one of the region's most significant handicaps. Greater reliance on imported raw materials, as domestic sources become relatively less important, tends to reduce this disadvantage.

The case for the New England integrated steel mill rests in part on the region's need for greater access to raw materials. New England's outlying position in periods of scarcity is itself a strong argument for a regional mill; and this case is even strengthened by the rise of iron and steel consuming industries in the area and by the greater dependence on foreign sources of raw materials. (New England's transportation disadvantage is thereby much reduced.) The special claim for a federal subsidy for an iron and steel mill rests in part upon New England's previous, and large, contributions towards helping other areas in distress, upon the crucial need to develop metal industries as substitutes for the declining soft-goods industries, and upon the resultant savings of skilled manpower and public services. It should also be noted that an iron and steel mill will attract fabricating mills to the area.

New England's transportation problem is not the costs charged its businessmen and consumers relative to charges elsewhere. Variations are largely based on cost differentials. Nor is the change-over from basing point and freight absorption to FOB pricing very important, though, since New England is a heavily industrialized area, some losses may result from the decentralizing tendencies associated with higher prices for outlying importers of raw materials and finished goods.

8. SOME ASPECTS OF THE INDUSTRIAL STRUCTURE

In New England, there are industries that are growing more rapidly than in the United States; but they are, of course, a small proportion of the total. These are the stone, clay, and glass products and lumber and lumber products. They employ but a few per cent of the factory workers in the region. Inclusive of transportation equipment, which in the years 1939 to 1947 grew as rapidly in New England as in the nation, these industries account for about 6–7 per cent of New England's manufacturing employment.

The first two industries above and perhaps six-sevenths of the tertiary (e.g., service) industries may be considered domestic industries, that is, New England industries sheltered from foreign (i.e., outside of the region) competition. I assume on the basis of rough estimates that our exports of services (tertiary) are about one-seventh, and that all tertiary industries account for less than one-half of total employment. Actually, there is more interregional competition in the tertiary occupations than is suggested by the New England exports of tertiary occupations. New England may import engineering services, its sons and daughters may choose the growing state universities outside of New England, may use the advertising services of the large New York firms, may lose government contracts to the Southwest. Nevertheless, for the purpose of short-run analysis, we can assume that roughly one-half of our employment is protected from outside competition. All the more important, therefore, is the employment in the volatile manufacturing industries, which account for 45 per cent of the total employment in the region.

Consider, for example, the industries which are losing ground, in the sense that their rate of progress is less than for the region as a whole or for the nation. Eight industries are in this category, the most important of which are textiles, leather and leather products, apparel, paper and paper products, and printing and publishing. In these eight industries, employment dropped from 58.4 per cent of all New England manufacturing employment in 1939 to 46.3 per cent in 1947, or a decline of 20 per cent. In textiles and leather and leather products, the loss of employment was more than 200,000 from 1919, or almost one-seventh of total manufacturing employment in 1947. In relation to economic fluctuations, the decline of 200,000, or one-third of 1919 employment, is equivalent to 400,000. We assume that fluctuations are concentrated in the nonsheltered (largely manufacturing) industries, which account roughly for one-half of employment, or that fluctuations in other occupations are tied to those in manufacturing. We can assume that a decline of 200,000 jobs means a loss of at least 400,000 jobs, since the service industries are in part dependent on a prosperous manufacturing industry. With manufacturing depressed, the region spends less for education, for medicine, for government, for selling, for transportation, for building, etc.

This region also harbors ten industries which are growing more rapidly than all industries in New England, though less rapidly than in the nation. Together with the industries growing more rapidly than in the nation, these industries accounted for 37 per cent of the production workers in manufacturing in 1939 and 47 per cent in 1947, or a rise of more than 20 per cent. Especially important in this group are the metal fabrication, machinery, instruments, chemicals and allied, and miscellaneous. The industrial future of New England undoubtedly depends largely upon the place these industries occupy in the national economy, and upon New England's competitive strength in these industries. The continuance of a war economy obviously will contribute greatly to the demand for workers in these industries. New England will, however, have to show greater aggressiveness in obtaining its share of new plants and government contracts than in the forties.

In textiles and leather and leather products, the decline has been most serious and promises to continue. There is a genuine danger that the South may capture an increasing part of New England's woolen industry, which so far has withstood Southern competition reasonably well. With large supplies of labor, low wages, high work loads, modern capital equipment adjusted to markets of today, with capital and management easily imported, with generous subsidies, with a concentration of efforts directed to attracting the textile industry, the South is bound to gain in textiles. In underdeveloped areas generally, textiles are the first important industry to appear. Southern progress has advanced to a point where the region is more and more encroaching even on the fine counts of textiles.

In shoes, the problem is somewhat different. New England loses to other areas in part because with small capital demands, with small-scale operation and techniques open to all, and with the industry oriented to markets and raw material as well as labor, decentralization is inevitable. The rate of loss, however, may be ascribed, as in textiles, in part to weakness in the New England economy. The developing shoe industry in the Middle Atlantic States and the West, to a much greater degree than textiles in the South, has had to compete with other industries for labor. Nevertheless, the industry has been growing rapidly outside of New England.

An examination of the industrial structure of New England also underlines the great handicaps suffered by New England because of the unavailability of important raw materials. Compare the 10 per cent of national factory employment for New England with 1 per cent in tobacco, 4 per cent in stone, clay, and glass products, 4 per cent in chemicals and transportation equipment, 6 per cent in primary metals and food. These are industries which tend to be established near the source of raw materials.

9. IN SUMMARY

New England is bound to lose relatively in manufacturing as other regions industrialize. The problem of New England is one of adjusting to these relative losses. Fortunately, with continued national gains, in part associated with the high level of public outlays, these losses in the last ten years have been relative, not absolute. But in depressed periods, large absolute losses will certainly occur. Plentiful supplies of labor, low wages, high work loads, and modern capital account for the rapid gains of industrialization in the South and to some extent in other areas. Low power costs, more favorable tax structure, are secondary factors favoring other areas. What is required of New England is more up-to-date management, new plant and equipment, realization by labor of the migratory problems. The unavailability of raw materials and the location of New England are disadvantages which cannot easily be treated. They make it all the more difficult to nurture the new industries which should provide the jobs lost primarily in the soft-goods industries. Remedial action in New England could slow up the losses and stimulate growth of new industries here, thus accelerating adjustments which require less dependence on less advanced (e.g., textiles) industries, more dependence on advanced manufacturing and tertiary industries. An improved relation with the federal government, better exploitation of river resources, and improvement in the tax structure will also help. Of great importance is the advance by less developed areas of working conditions, social legislation, and the like. These regions should not capture industries *merely* by reducing national standards of working conditions. As New England loses its export markets in the United States, the region will have to pay for its indispensable imports by exporting more abroad and by increasing exports of growing industries, both in this country and abroad; and the region will have to become more dependent on domestic industries.

CHAPTER 2

THE OLDER ECONOMIC REGION*

1. CONTRASTS IN GROWTH OF OLDER REGIONS

Regions, like people, age; and in the aging process an economic arteriosclerosis tends to develop. This social disease develops as inhabitants of new industrial regions, full of vigor and enthusiasm seeking a place in industry, confront the older regions with intense competition. These newer areas take industries away from the older ones, for the freedom to manufacture, relatively unfettered by past practices and customs, gives them a decided advantage in the struggle for newer industries. But they offer not only competition; they also provide potential new markets for the older areas. A crucial issue for maturing areas is: Do they gain more from the rising income associated with opening of new economic frontiers than they lose from the competition?

Over the years even the older regions have grown. It is only necessary to point to a rise of New England population from 1.2 million in 1800 to 2.7 million in 1850 and 9.3 million a hundred years later. But, as might be expected, they have lost ground relatively. The opening up of new lands and the industrialization of the South and West necessarily would reduce the relative contribution of the Northeast.

2. WHY OLDER REGIONS LOSE

Why do the older regions lose? Many of their relative losses are inevitable. But in part the results are of their own doing. Those who have arrived are likely to become smug. Similarly with regions.

Management is too often in the hands of the fourth and fifth generation, and these managers often have lost the fire and creativeness of the original builders and seem impervious to new ideas.

* A version of this chapter was published in the *New York Times*, July 29, 1951.

There are, of course, many exceptions. Dennison's is operated by a fifth-generation management and is still a highly successful firm, and field investigators have found much resourcefulness among the family-held and -managed corporations, particularly since many of the weak capitulated in the great depression.

But it is not merely a question of nepotism. Even in the industries largely controlled by newcomers, the older areas are remiss in management. In shoes, for example, New England allowed the West to capture the postwar market for infant and juvenile shoes which anyone with imagination could have forecast from the bulge of births during the war.

This lack of venturesomeness is also evident in the reluctance of bankers to lend. In the recent hearings (summer 1950) on RFC loans, both Senator Douglas and Senator Fulbright spanked the New England business leaders and bankers for their lack of venturesomeness. Said Senator Douglas in discussing a refusal of the Boston banks to lend to Raytheon: [1]

I would like to know just what has happened to the business judgment of the Boston bankers, that they will refuse a loan so that the business has to come running down here to Washington to get government money. The people up in New England are shouting all the time — at least, the leading financiers of New England are shouting all the time — about the horrors of governmental investment; and yet here is a business which is earning $1,500,000 a year on the average for the last six years and whose present orders on hand aggregate $40,000,000, when an investment of $1,000,000 will free it from a rental charge of $324,000 and still the Boston banks will not lend.

(An official of the New England bank involved has written me suggesting some good reasons for not making the loan.)

Nor is it merely management that is to blame. Workers in older areas also become fixed in their working habits. They resist new working conditions, for example, new labor-saving devices which require adjustments in work loads. Thus, a textile engineering firm testified before the *1950 Massachusetts Commission on Textiles* that a completely new 450-loom mill producing combed broadcloth would require, under current labor-management agreements, 158 opera-

[1] Hearings of Senate Subcommittee of the Committee on Banking and Currency on *Study of Reconstruction Finance Corporation* (June–July 1950), p. 293.

tives in the North and 118, or 25 per cent less, in the South. So much for the evidence of economic arteriosclerosis.

Maturity in and of itself raises serious problems. The great New England industrial machine was developed in the second half of the nineteenth century, and was tailored to a market perhaps one-fifth or less the size of the current market. Today, this industrial structure is not nearly so well adapted to a $350 billion national economy as that in newer areas. There, industries can build to fit the vast economy; they can adapt their plants and equipment to the size of markets, and to the advances of technology much more easily than in older areas; for they start fresh.

3. VIGOROUS COMPETITION FROM NEWER INDUSTRIAL REGIONS

The explanation is not merely failure on the part of older regions. It is in large part positive action on the part of the newer regions or the older (e.g., Southeast) regions seeking industrial advances. These regions inherit certain advantages.

First, they profit from almost inexhaustible supplies of labor from the farm. These recruits crowd the city labor markets, depress wages, and, unhampered by old working habits and attracted by what seems to be remarkably high pay, ask no questions about work loads while they display an eagerness to learn and coöperate. The workers are younger and more enthusiastic than those in the mature areas.

Second, and related to the first, wage rates are likely to be lower in newly competing regions. The South's emergence as a great textile center stems primarily from the availability of rich labor supplies and low wages. At the turn of the century the differential in wage rates was about 40 per cent; but, the induced industrialization itself, with its increased demand for labor, had lessened the differential to 10 per cent by the late forties. It widened again in 1950–52, in the textiles at any rate.

Third, the newer industrial areas have the advantage of proximity to rich markets and raw materials. Obviously the Northeast tends to become less and less centrally located. Yet this point can be over-done. The area within a radius of 500 miles, roughly, from the center of Massachusetts, accounted for 74 per cent of the nation's population in 1800 and only 32.3 per cent in 1900. Yet in 1949 it included 31.1 per cent of the total. Relative losses have been very small in the last 50 years, and, in absolute terms, the population rose from 24.5 million in 1900 to 46.4 million in 1949.[2]

Fourth, the attitude of the newer industrial areas towards government is different from that of the older areas. Whereas businessmen in New England are extremely hostile, especially towards federal government, and in New York receptive but not enthusiastic, the people of South and West are more inclined to seek government aid. It is no accident that the great river developments have occurred in the Southeast and Northwest; and that whereas there are 156 federal hydroelectric projects in the nation, there is not a single one in New England. Nor is it an accident that the federal government in one year took out of New England close to $1 billion more than she put in (about 7 per cent of the region's income). Until the emergence of ex-Governor Bowles and Governor Dever, this problem was scarcely recognized except by two or three economists. Significantly, the drain was drastically cut in 1949 and 1950.

Fifth, the citizens of the newer industrial areas arouse their communities and state and local governments in order to benefit their industries. Their tax structures spare business as much as possible and even discriminate in favor of factories pirated from other areas; all sections of the community contribute funds towards providing sites, building, and subsidies for other purposes to attract new industries; institutions of higher learning are used to advance research and technology on behalf of local industries. In New England the great universities, perhaps with some justification, concentrate on national problems, and their neglect of the purely regional problems puts their regional interests at some disadvantage.

To be sure, the great advances made by the South and the West in building up their industries at least in part at the expense of the Northeast, together with near calamities in the Northeast, have sparked a revival of community spirit in the Northeast — note the Manchester Plan and the Nashua Plan, under which community coöperation salvaged these communities from a desperate situation. With losses estimated by the Massachusetts Textile Commission of 90,000 jobs in 25 years as a result of migration of industry from New England in cotton and rayon alone, and with 90 mills with capital of $162 million moved or liquidated, it is no wonder that the North-

[2] Figures from unpublished manuscript of Louis Bean and *Statistical Abstract*.

east has begun to meet community action elsewhere with its own community action. But it still has a long way to go.

Related to the attitude towards government are the problems of working conditions and social legislation, which are more highly developed in mature industrial areas. I heard a leading New England business leader say that a Southern community not only promised 20 years of tax exemption but also that there would be no trade union for 10 years. The Northeast and particularly Massachusetts have been in the van in social legislation. The laws which limit hours of work, fix minimum pay, provide high standards of social security, and give collective bargaining a fair chance are costly when another region sets much lower standards in all these lines. For Massachusetts, the situation has become so serious that the Commonwealth has had to modify restrictions on the three-shift system, and it is becoming increasingly difficult to obtain approval of social security programs — e.g., the defeat of the Sickness Insurance program in 1950.

Testimony before the Tobey Committee of the Senate in 1948 on the closing of the Nashua, New Hampshire mills by Mr. Little of the Textron Corporation can serve as a concrete guide of the problems raised by newer industrial areas.[3] The issue was, of course, the closing of the Textron Mill in Nashua. The hearings made it clear that Mr. Little's conduct was clearly antisocial; but cost problems facing him are disclosed by the following estimates:

1. Take-home pay of Northern workers was 10 per cent more than in the South. Yet Carolina employees produced from 25 to 100 per cent more yards and pounds per hour than many of the Northern workers. Southern mills were producing wide muslin sheetings at the rate of 9.62 pounds per man-hour against Nashua's rate of 5.37.

2. Not only were work-loads much larger in the South but the take-home pay until 15 to 20 years ago had been but one-half as large. In one operation, 61 workers were required in the South and 137 in the North.

3. The illegality of the three-shift system in New England (at least in parts of it) raises costs here, because overhead costs per

[3] Hearings of Senate Subcommittee of Interstate and Foreign Commerce on *Investigation of Closing of Nashua, N. H. Mills and Operation of Textron, Incorp.*, Part I (1948), pp. 27–35.

unit of output are much higher where only one or two shifts prevail.

4. Power costs averaged .71 cent per kilowatt hour in four mills in South and North Carolina; but 1.24 cents in Nashua, New Hampshire, and 1.7 cents in Manville, Rhode Island. If the Southern textile industry had to pay New England rates for power, the power bill, according to Mr. Little, would be increased by $27 million annually.

5. Freight differential for raw cotton favors the South against Nashua by 62 cents per hundred pounds.

6. Property taxes on inventories, plant, buildings, and machinery average 48 cents per spindle in five Carolina plants and $2.53 a spindle in Nashua.

4. ADJUSTMENTS TO ADVANCES IN THE SOUTH AND WEST

The next issue is what happens to maturing economies in the light of better prospects for many industries in the newer areas. One answer is obvious. Capital and management move into the area where other resources are plentiful and cheap. Many of the New England business leaders who are most sensitive to the suggestion that there is a New England problem have underwritten the textile industry in the South and the shoe industry in the West.

This migration is unfortunate only in the sense that it brings severe problems of readjustment for the areas losing plants. I assume, of course, that the developing regions, by virtue of their large and cheap labor supply, power, etc., can produce these commodities — e.g., textiles, shoes, and lumber — more cheaply than the older areas. Our theory of international or interregional trade tells us that the losing areas will soon concentrate on other industries where high labor costs are not a serious deterrent, that is, where high wages are more than offset by high productivity. This explains, for example, the striking growth in metal fabrication and machinery industries in the Northeast, a growth which reflects a rebirth of Yankee ingenuity and leadership.

But unfortunately the adjustment is slow. Workers out of jobs refuse to leave their hometowns and abandon their acquired skills. An interim period of unemployment then depresses wages. Next, industries which can survive only at low wages tend to move in and develop, thus replacing the depressed industries to some extent, e.g., the apparel industry from New York; and service industries (e.g. insurance) profit from the low wages. It is possible, however, for an older region to suffer both from high wages in older industries and low wages in new industries.

There is still another important adjustment that takes place. Since, in response to opportunities for earning a better livelihood, people will move, differences of income tend to be reduced. That capital and management tend to move into regions where labor costs are low further strengthens the approach towards equality of income. With improved direction and better plant, and with increased demand, productivity rises in low-wage areas and wages tend to rise. It does not follow that income equality will follow. First, be-

United States and Regions of United States, Several Variables

	Population Percentage Rise (1929–49)	Net Change in Population in Relation to Natural Increase (1930–48)	Income Payments (1929–48) % Rise	Income Payments Per Capita (1929–48) % Rise
United States	22.13	1.0	149	107
New England	14.37	1.1	102	79
Middle Eastern	17.83	1.2	104	76
East North Central	19.66	1.1	143	106
West North Central	5.88	0.2	164	153
Southeast	19.65	0.5	228	179
West South Central	19.52	0.6	198	153
Intermountain	22.62	0.7	193	146
Pacific Northwest	66.50	3.6	233	108
Pacific Southwest	91.44	4.3	229	77

Source: U. S. Department of Commerce, **Economic Development Atlas**, 1950.

cause of imperfections of knowledge. Second, because of inertia: many will not invest in the South even with higher returns. Third, because other noneconomic considerations may be decisive. The children of old New England families will often prefer to stay in New England rather than desert for better prospects in the West. A final consideration is that differences in resources, climate, etc., despite high mobility, may be reflected in continued higher standards in some areas.

Nevertheless, a tendency towards equalization is at work, as the accompanying table shows. The rise of income payments and especially income per capita was much larger in the South than in New England or in the Middle Eastern States. The rise of per capita income in the Southeast from 1929 to 1948 was 2⅛ times that of the two latter regions. The growth of total income in the Pacific West about equaled that of the Southeast, but large increases in population reduced the per capita gains in the West. Migration from South to North and South to West has been the pattern for many years.

So far we have stressed the fact of relative decline in older regions, the reasons for it, and the adjustments made. Against this general picture of the aging process in an economy, New England may be set as a case study.

CHAPTER 3

THE EMERGENCE OF NEW ENGLAND AS A PROBLEM AREA

1. POPULATION

One index of growth is population. Of course, if unrelated to other factors, population growth is not a revealing index. The large gains of population in India, accompanied by low standards of living and periodic famine, are not symbolic of progress. It is necessary to consider also the continued relation of population to resources available to support the population. It is fair to assume that New England has progressed if, with a given (rising) standard of living, it supports 9.3 million people as it did in 1949 rather than 1.2 million as in 1800.

In the fifty years 1800–1850, the population of New England more than doubled; in the next half century (1851–1900) it doubled again; and in the next fifty years, it increased by two-thirds. In these last fifty years, however, the rise was 3.7 million, an increase exceeding the 2.9 million of the preceding fifty years. This absolute gain hides a relative loss: the percentage of the nation's total population represented by New England has declined by 70 per cent over 150 years, about equal to the relative decline in the Southeast, but three times the relative loss in New York, New Jersey, and Pennsylvania.

In terms of income, the absolute population figures are more relevant, for total income payments must be related to total population. In the last twenty years, New England's net gain in population was substantial; in the thirties there was little change, but from 1940 to 1948 the net increase was 15 per cent of the total inter-regional migration. Accordingly, while total income payments rose by 102 per cent, per capita incomes gained only 79 per cent. This may be compared to increases, for the seven most important industrial states outside of New England, of 130 per cent in total income payments and 99 per cent in per capita income; and to gains, in the five most important industrial Southern states, of 243 and 179 per cent. These high figures, like those in the West North Central and Intermountain areas, reflect the out-migration of population from the region.

2. MANUFACTURING

The New England problem in no small part has stemmed from excessive dependence on manufacturing — in 1949, manufacturing pay rolls accounted for 29.6 per cent of income payments, the highest in the country, and 7.5 percentage points, or one-third, above the national average. As manufacturing offers a declining proportion of jobs, the area excessively tied to manufacturing suffers.

In part the problem has been one of the kind of manufacturing industries in New England. Excessive reliance on textiles and shoes and inadequate stakes in durable goods industries have all been costly to New England. With changed spending patterns, which reveal greater relative outlays on durable goods than in the early part of the century, the areas nurturing durable goods industries (inclusive of investment goods) were bound to advance more rapidly. In 1929, outlays for durable consumer goods amounted to 12 per cent of total consumption expenditure; in 1950, 15½ per cent. In 1929 nonfarm producers' plant and equipment accounted for 9½ per cent of the gross national product; in 1950, for 10 per cent. In 1950, the fantastic achievements of 1929 were again equaled. With high employment incomes for long periods of time, investment goods and consumer durables are likely to play a much greater part in the economy than in the thirties or earlier.

Finally, any area which first develops manufacturing loses ground relatively, and at intervals absolutely, when other areas begin to industrialize. Should the older areas concentrate on industries which are easily localized in other regions (e.g., textiles and shoes), these losses may be substantial. As might be expected, New England's share of manufacturing has declined drastically: from 30 to 9 per cent over 150 years. Yet so long as manufacturing jobs increased rapidly, the proportionate losses were consistent with large absolute gains for New England. The accompanying table suggests the problems involved.

During the second half of the nineteenth century, manufacturing employment in New England increased almost twice as much as did population. From 1900 to 1947, however, manufacturing employment increased only by 22 per cent, while population rose by 63 per cent. In the years 1919–1939 an absolute decline in manufacturing employment took place: there were 338,000 less jobs, equal to 21 per cent of the 1919 figure. By 1947 some of this loss had been regained: total manufacturing employment was only 2 per cent below the 1919 total, although the country as a whole

New England's Population and Manufacturing Employment, 1850–1949

	Rise, Population Millions	Percentage Rise	Rise, Manufacturing Numbers (000's)	Manufacturing Employment Percentage Change
1850–1900	2.86	+105	+507	+190
1900–1947	3.50	+ 63	+160	+ 22
1919–1939	0.99	+ 14	−388	− 26
1940–1949	0.87	+ 10	+353	+ 31

Source: L. Bean, unpublished manuscript and **Handbook of Regional Statistics**.

had gained over 1919 by 44 per cent. The increase in manufacturing employment in New England was only 8 per cent of the rise which took place in the country between 1939 and 1947.

The figures on total employment hide the trends in different industries. The loss of 31,000 manufacturing jobs between 1919 and 1947 includes a loss in nondurable goods of 127,000, offset somewhat by a rise in durable goods employment of 97,000. The major losses were in textiles (156,000, more than one-third the total in that field) and in leather and leather products (46,000 or 30 per cent of the total). The major gains were in machinery (110,000, or 50 per cent over 1919); apparel, paper and paper products, and printing and publicity – a net gain of 52,000.

It is not difficult to explain the trends. Losses in textiles and shoes are related to the decline of *total* jobs available in these industries. (In 1947, despite a large rise of the *nation's* population, textiles and shoes provided only 65,000 additional jobs over 1919.) With large technological improvements in prospect, even at high demand, the employment offered by these industries will tend to decline further. New England's record is much worse than the country's, partly because these are industries which are easily established in other regions, where plentiful labor, low wage rates, and subsidies easily outweigh the experience in older areas. In 1900, New England firms accounted for 80 per cent of all the spindles in cotton textiles; in 1947, for only 17 per cent. While New England lost textile jobs, the *rest* of the country gained 237,000. In leather and leather products, the New England loss was 46,000; the gains for the *rest* of the country of 30,000 jobs.

New England manufacturing advanced in industries where the region retained the advantage of skilled labor and low-wage costs. In apparels, for example, wages were lower than in New York, and New England gained at the expense of the Middle Atlantic States. In the rapidly growing machinery and metal fabrication industries, New England also registered gains though not at the national rates. Wages which were low in comparison with Detroit, Cleveland, and Los Angeles stimulated the growth in these industries and tended to offset unfavorable factors, such as distance from raw materials.

In the years before World War I, New England was a high-wage area. As we shall see later, this is no longer true. In response to relative industrial decline, increased unemployment, and pressure on her balance of payments (associated with an impaired competitive position and with resultant loss of monetary reserves) New England's prices and wages have tended to fall relatively. What was once a high-wage area has become an average, and in some industries a low, wage area. Boston department stores, for example, pay the lowest wages of any large city. In the white-collar occupations, New England's wages are low, and account in part for her advantages in such employments as insurance. Here not only the pressure of unemployment and the resultant reduced supply of money are relevant, but also the large output of high school and college graduates.

Clearly New England's manufacturing position, despite a hopeful comeback in the forties, is precarious. The problem is to find alternative employments for those squeezed out of manufacturing. One possibility is tertiary industries, which have already gained. From 1910 to 1940, the number of gainful workers in secondary industries (manufacturing, construction, etc.) declined from 50 to 41 per cent of all gainful workers, and in primary industries from 10 to 6 per cent. These losses were offset by a rise from 40 to 53 per cent in tertiary industries. But the figures for New England contrast with those for the nation, where a rise of 12 percentage points in tertiary industries compensated for only a slight decline in secondary industry (from 32 to 29 per cent of the total) and for a larger decline in primary industry (from 28 to 19 per cent).

These figures lend themselves to more than one interpretation. An obvious one is that the advance of tertiary industry in New England requires heavy losses in manufacturing because primary employment is relatively small. A second, and more relevant, explanation is that the loss of a strong competitive position in manufacturing permits an increase in tertiary employment which otherwise would not have taken place. What is necessary is that opportunities in tertiary industries should be sufficient to absorb both new workers and those losing employment in primary and secondary industries. Unemployment reflects a failure, on the part of tertiary industries, to accomplish this.

I should like to repeat here what I have said elsewhere: New England's losses are not associated merely with the age of the community. Dr. McLaughlin has compared the growth of 33 manufacturing areas, both old and new, from 1869 to 1935. Manufacturing employment failed to grow as rapidly as population in but five of these areas — Philadelphia, Boston, Providence, Worcester, and Springfield — four of the five were in New England. From 1869 to 1929, the percentage change in numbers of wage earners in manufacturing in the several areas was as follows:

United States	386
33 Industrial Areas	431
New York City	425
Detroit Area	2247
Boston Area	99
Seattle Area	46,879
Birmingham District	80,782

The Boston area had the lowest growth; Worcester next (121); Albany next (128).[1]

The particularity of New England's problems may be emphasized by contrasting it with the much better record of New York.

[1] G. E. McLaughlin, *Growth of American Manufacturing Areas* (1938), pp. 102–103, 120.

One explanation is that New York has a better location with respect to markets. This evades the question of why markets grow so rapidly around New York. The difference in racial stocks may be of some importance. In New York, the immigrants concentrated on industry, finance, and trading, and brought domination in their fields to New York. In Massachusetts (which accounts for one-half the population of New England), the newer immigrants applied their high talents more in politics, possibly through preference, but also, I am sure, because the native stock did not make the best possible use in industry of the great abilities brought in by the new blood. The most illustrative explanation lies in the different structure of the two economies. New York is much less an industrial region than New England, which has concentrated heavily on manufacturing. In an advancing economic society manufacturing loses ground to the service industries: distribution, education, insurance, etc. In short, New York's 32.2 per cent of 1949 income from trade and services and 22.0 per cent from manufacturing must be contrasted with 26.0 per cent of New England income from trade and services, and 28.2 per cent from manufacturing.

Conclusion. New England's problem has not been one of stagnation. Its growth over 150 years has been striking, as is evident in a rise of population 6–7 times. Particularly impressive have been the gains of Southern New England. An area 14,000 square miles, Southern New England squeezes out an income of about $12 billion or $850,000 per square mile. The average for the country is about $75,000 per square mile, or only 9 per cent as much.

Yet New England has its problems. They stem from its great dependence on manufacturing; from the tendency for manufacturing to offer a declining number of jobs; from the dependence on textiles and shoes in its economy; from the losses to other areas, partly associated with growth elsewhere and partly with more aggressive leadership elsewhere. A rise of 4.35 million manufacturing jobs from 1919 to 1947 for the country in contrast with a loss of 30,000 for New England underlines the problem. (In this period, New England's population rose by close to 2 millions, or about 25 per cent.)

As in the human body disease fortifies the defense, so in an area, economic losses tend to bring their cure. Losses from competition, weakening the balance of payments, reduce available reserves and monetary supplies. These repercussions in the monetary field and the pressure of unemployment tend to reduce wages and prices and make the area more competitive. Inward movements of capital and management (and a slower rate of labor growth), and the inflow of cash tend to raise prices and income in the growing areas. Sticky prices in the losing regions, however — e.g., wages — tend to weaken the recuperative process.

The outward loss of cash and the regional competitive problem are much more important factors than has generally been suggested. It is only necessary to compare exports for a state or a region with exports (gross or net) for a nation to realize that trade and competitive position are more important the smaller the unit under consideration. The *excess* of manufactured exports in New England in a recent year was more than one-fifth the region's income; all *net* exports of the United States in a recent year but 2 per cent of the nation's income. Exports and imports are crucial to the state and region. Perhaps this explains in part the great passions aroused by comparative state tax burdens and similar problems.

In periods of decline (e.g., 1919 to 1939), the regions under pressure have to find new industries and in particular to attract them by offering a lower cost structure. The greater relative and, on occasion, absolute losses suffered by New England vis-à-vis New York and New Jersey are associated in part with a failure to attract new industries as older ones weaken. Growth elements have not been adequate.

The advance of the future is likely to be disproportionately in tertiary industries. But if these are to solve the problem of competitive declines, they must include adequate proportions of services salable outside (e.g., insurance or education in contrast to retail services) and must be built on a substantial base of manufacturing, which will provide required goods at home and supplies to be exchanged for goods from outside the region. Otherwise, the growth of tertiary industries will mean only exchange of one service for another, without the required component of basic goods which are the foundation of a high standard of living.

CHAPTER 4

WHAT AILS NEW ENGLAND?

1. THE PRESENT WEAKNESSES LISTED

In the body of this book, I emphasize as handicaps for New England wage rates in some industries, the inflexibility of management and labor (e.g., rigidity of work loads), the dearth of raw materials, the development of large markets elsewhere, the strong community spirit in other areas expressed in large subsidies to tempt new industries, New England's aloofness toward federal aid (reflected, for example, in failure to develop water power), and the structure of taxation. These weaknesses are not of equal importance. Labor costs, lack of enterprise, and scarcities of raw materials are especially significant. Both the literature and public opinion emphasize these and other deficiencies.

Failure to modernize plants is a frequent complaint. An automobile trip through any old textile or shoe town will convince one of the importance of this consideration. Thus Mr. Walter Wheeler, the able Chairman of the New England Council, in one of his maiden speeches, stressed the need of modernization. In World War II, New England had its share of war contracts, but, instead of replacing and renovating plants with government aid, New England disproportionately used up existing plant and equipment. Similarly, labor leaders stress time and again that the trouble with the New England textile industry is ancient plant. In the hearings before the *Massachusetts Textile Commission* (1950), before the Senate Committee on Interstate and Foreign Commerce investigating the *Closing of the Nashua, N. H. Mills and Operations of Textron, Incorporated* (1948), and before the Senate Committee on *Labor-Management Relations in the Southern Textile Manufacturing Industry* (August 1950) labor emphasized the importance of modernization.

This point about modernization has often been coupled with another, namely, the failure of the textile mills to put their capital back into the business.[1] In these hearings quoted, inclusive of an article in *Fortune*, May 1947, the reader will find a detailed statement of the manner in which large loans by Boston and other banks, exploitation of the charitable trust device, and the excess profits tax, enabled Mr. Little to obtain control of several textile companies and then gradually use up their liquid capital.

Unfavorable business climate is another charge made against New England and particularly against the Massachusetts government. Heavy taxes (discussed fully later), social security burdens, and unwillingness to grant reasonable increases in public utility rates are among the examples of unfavorable business climate.[2] In comparison with newer industrial areas, there undoubtedly is less enthusiasm in New England for supporting business and for enticing industries to migrate to New England.

A related problem is the absence of community drives to attract new industries and hold old ones. The difficulties were well revealed when the six governors in 1949 proposed a New England Development Authority, which failed of approval. Indeed, when disaster strikes, New England towns will make heroic efforts, as has been shown in Manchester, New Bedford, Nashua, and other communities. But then it is generally too late. The Boston Federal Reserve Bank has noted the creation of many Community Development Corporations in New England, which purchase sites and in other ways facilitate the entry of new firms. This is a hopeful sign. Yet, despite the dramatic effects of the 1948–49 recession in New England, the corrective measures taken by New England communities did not seem proportionate to their decline.[3]

Taxes are perhaps the most frequent complaint. A typical instance is the statement by the Boston Edison Company that 11.8 per cent of its income is paid in state and local taxes in Massachusetts and only 6.6 per cent in five other large cities.[4] In the last few years, there is evidence of a concerted attack in this vein by New England business, but there is also evidence that its importance is exag-

[1] See, especially, evidence of E. Rieve in *Investigation of Closing of Nashua, N. H. Mills and Operation of Textron, Incorporated*, pp. 58 *et seq.*

[2] See, for example, editorial in the *Boston Herald*, April 14, 1949.

[3] Cf. U. S. Department of Labor, *Community Programs to Combat Unemployment*, editions of November 30, 1949 and March 31, 1950.

[4] *Boston Herald*, December 15, 1948.

gerated (see Chapters 19 and 20). The effects of this campaign may well be to stimulate the outward migration.

Backward management is a frequent complaint, particularly among labor leaders. But more than one business executive voiced similar complaints before the President's Council's Committee on the New England Economy; and scarcely a federal or state investigation touching on New England's economic problem fails to discuss the backsliding of New England's management. For example, the difficulties of the American Woolen Company (prior to present management) and the Cheney Company, according to witnesses before the committee on the New England Economy, stem from too much inbreeding. The Waltham Watch Company is an excellent example of a famous concern which collapsed in no small part because of inept management.

The Waltham Watch Company is an interesting case, especially since, with support and pressure of Massachusetts Congressional leaders, this firm obtained a loan from the RFC; and a member of the RFC staff who contributed towards obtaining the loan subsequently became manager of the company. Here is what the RFC representative, after a careful study, had to say about the management: [5]

A. Direction has been woefully lacking;

B. Knowledge of finances and practices of economy have been absent;

C. Cost methods are antiquated and ineffective;

D. Failure on the part of the Comptroller to know from week to week what obligations are outstanding and what should be done with reference to these obligations has been and is patently evident;

E. No merchandising program has been set in motion calculated to sell the product of this plant;

F. Inspections have been hit or miss with the result that returns have been heavy and prestige required in an organization catering to a nation has been retarded to a very great degree . . .

G. The screening of Swiss importations will not save the Waltham Watch Company . . .

From all of this, we should not draw the conclusion that management is lax on the entire New England front. The fact is that there are hundreds of New England businessmen and firms of which the

[5] Hearings of Subcommittee of Senate Banking and Currency Committee on *Study of Reconstruction Finance Corporation: Loan to Waltham Watch Company,* July 20 and 21, 1950, p. 55.

region may well be proud: e.g., Pratt and Whitney, Pacific Mills, the Dennison Company, J. P. S. Stevens, General Electric (originally a New England firm), Norwich Mills, Gillette Razor. It would be just as wrong to assume that all is well on the management front.

Although Waltham Watch may be an exceptional case of poor management, I am afraid that an interesting and well-written article by Hedley Donovan,[6] for *Fortune*, is misleading in assuming that all is well on the managerial front. Although Donovan starts by listing the handicaps under which New England businessmen operate, and expresses surprise at how well they have done, his attempt to prove that "New England's businessmen are the most dynamic in the country" is going too far. It is well to list outstanding businessmen and firms who deserve much credit — e.g., Putnam of Package Machinery Company, Spang of Gillette Razor Company, Winslow of United Shoe Machinery Company (although this company may be blamed for some New England losses in the shoe industry), Blackall, Jr. of Woonsocket Precision Tool, Dewey of Dewey and Almy, Sperry of Scoville Manufacturing Company, Edwards of Saco-Lowell, Wheeler of Pitney-Bowles, Axelrod of various textiles mills, and others. But to leave out of account the many second-rate businessmen whose lack of enterprise, whose failure to keep up on new techniques of production and selling and labor management, whose sell-out to outside interests on the first occasion in order to obtain security — these omissions give a misleading impression of the status of management in New England today.

The reader will find much better balanced statements of New England's managerial talent in two articles by C. Hartley Gratton in recent issues of *Harper's*[7] and by A. H. Raskin in the *New York Times* (May 30, 1950).

Within the confines of a brief article in the *Times*, Mr. Raskin lists most of the problems, including wage costs, taxes, research, new industries, old plants, and managerial weaknesses. He describes the situation as a challenge and notes the potential solutions, involving a resurgence of business leadership and the development of new industries in metals, plastics, and services.

---

[6] "Watch the Yankees," *Fortune*, March 1950.
[7] "What Makes New England Go?", *Harper's* (August 1949); and "Where is New England Going?", *Harper's* (September 1949).

Yankee businessmen, long accused of having let the competitive spirit run out of their hardened arteries, are teaming up with state and municipal authorities from Maine to Connecticut in projects intended to finance industrial expansion and attract new enterprises.

Left at the post in what is fast becoming a "war between the states" for a bigger share of the nation's post-war industrial progress, New England has sought to make up for its slow start . . .

. . . . .

This pessimistic view is reinforced by doubt that many of the fourth and fifth generation controllers of New England wealth are not concerned enough about the situation to let any sunlight into their time-fogged notion of how a business should be run or how their funds should be invested.

In his second article, Mr. Gratton also assessed the situation with candor and objectivity.

. . . Of themselves the facts do not *compel* one either to pessimism or optimism about the future. But they do make it perfectly clear, I think, that the New England region is challenged today by adverse national developments of a most pretentious kind . . .

. . . Uncritical boosterism is, under current conditions, largely a form of defeatism, since it leads logically either to inaction or to pleas to others to join the New Englanders in the "soup" in which they currently wallow . . .[8]

Relevant to the problem of management is the complaint by several witnesses before the Committee on the New England Economy that the melting pot process had not advanced as well in New England as elsewhere, with a failure to make the most effective use of all racial stocks. It was even said that in many textile communities only Anglo-Saxons could rise to supervisory or executive posts, one result being a greatly narrowed reservoir of talent for executive posts.

A frequent complaint is instability, but since this problem was treated at length in the report of the Committee appointed by the President's Council, a few words will suffice here. It is difficult to assess the degree of instability of New England industries vis-à-vis the nation's. An industrial area is likely to suffer large fluctuations; but in the twenties and thirties New England's decline and rise were of smaller proportions than the nation's. As New England extends

[8] *Harper's* (September 1949), pp. 94, 98.

its interest in durable goods industries, instability will increase. The large decline in 1948–49 relative to the nation is undoubtedly associated in part with the long-run decline in textiles and shoes and in part with the special circumstance which encouraged the closing of numerous mills.

Security against military attack is a problem which may greatly affect New England's industrial future. With large concentration of industry, any deliberate decentralization to avoid susceptibility to bombing would be costly to New England. So far, this has been a small factor in the loss of plants to inland areas, but its importance may increase. For example, in late 1950, the government announced that South Carolina was to be the situs of a $260 million hydrogen bomb plant. The amount involved was one-half the value of all plants established and planned in the state since 1945. Aside from vulnerability, New England might have been as desirable a location as the South, although access to cheap labor and power were, also relevant.[9]

Again, a Mississippi advertisement in *Fortune* entitled "Industry's Release Against Modern War" says:

Mississippi offers not only protection in the event of an all-out war, but will provide tax-free plant sites and buildings for industries . . .
Here is a typical example: On January 15, 1951, citizens of Greenville, Miss. voted 2306 to 31 in favor of issuing $4,750,000 in bonds for a site and building for the Alexander Smith and Sons Carpet Company, of Yonkers, New York, nationally known manufacturers.[10]

Finally, there is the issue of political ineptitude. One is struck by the relative ineffectiveness of some New England congressmen in achieving legislation more beneficial to this area. The explanation may be (1) the attitude of the people towards federal government; (2) the great influence of Southern congressmen reëlected year after year, and serving as chairmen of important committees. Certainly many New England congressmen, and especially senators, are men of ability. Nor is New England underrepresented, although obviously its influence has declined with the opening of the country:

[9] *Christian Science Monitor*, December 11, 1950.
[10] A similar advertisement by the Erie Railroad says: "The medium-sized town with its better living conditions has always been a good choice for a new plant. The present international situation with the trend to decentralization has made it even more so."

in 1790, New England's 29 members in the House were 27 per cent of the 106; in 1940, its 28 representatives were but 6 per cent of the 435 total.[11] In one respect, New England is overrepresented: the region had 6.4 per cent of the population in 1940 and 12.5 per cent of the Senate seats.

In the last year or two, high officials in New England have at last become interested in relations with the federal government. This is evident in Governor Dever's vigorous efforts (in contrast to Connecticut's) to obtain a fair share of federal aid. The increased interest in these problems derived much support from a statement of Mr. Erickson, the able President of the Boston Federal Reserve Bank, before a congressional group.[12] In this address, Mr. Erickson stressed the drains of cash out of New England resulting from federal activities, the support given to competing areas, the unfavorable effect upon New England of tariffs and agricultural policy which raise the prices of raw materials and food for new England. But the distinguished President did not go so far as to suggest that New England might seek federal aid. This is a problem which we discuss fully later. More recently, Senator Benton has shown a keen awareness of the problem of improved relations with the federal government.

It is not our intention to suggest that New England suffers all kinds of handicaps and has no advantages. The fact is that New England has an excellent climate for all-year production, primacy in industry, highly skilled workers, more than its share of the educated, low transportation rates to foreign countries, unusual research facilities, a location within 500 miles of one-third of the purchasing power of the nation, and 1000 miles from two-thirds of the nation's purchasing power, large advantages in tourist trade, insurance, education, medicine, and other services.[13]

In a series of interesting articles in the *Christian Science Monitor* (July 1950), Mr. Everett M. Smith elaborates on some of the great advances made by New England industries. (Also see Lawrence Dame in the *Boston Herald* in August–September, 1951.) For ex-

[11] Cf. G. B. Galloway, *Congress at the Crossroads*, p. 347, and U. S. *Statistical Abstract* (1948), p. 314.

[12] *The New England Economy — 1950 Model*, May 2, 1950.

[13] Cf. C. D. Hyson and A. C. Neal, "New England's Economic Prospects," *Harvard Business Review* (March 1948).

ample, New England is the home of the world's largest manufacturing plant devoted exclusively to the production of hand-measuring and precision instruments — the L. S. Starrett Company, of Athol, Massachusetts. Again, New England has been the center of the clock-making industry since 1773, when Thomas Harland, a European clockmaker, arrived in Connecticut. The Sessions Clock Company, of Forestville, Connecticut, now boasts of a fifth generation of clockmakers in its management. In 1912, Mr. Warren started the advances which culminated in the electric clocks now manufactured in six Telechron plants. The American Falcon Company, of Chelsea, has been turning out rulers for 147 years — boot, wooden, rulers in pica and agate measures for newspapers, and other specialized products. Age does not necessarily mean decay.

CHAPTER 5

THE LONGER HISTORICAL VIEW: EARLIER COMMENTS AND DIAGNOSES

It is instructive to compare the complaints, vocal and frequent, about the failings of New England in 1950, with those which have been made during the past hundred years.

1. PESSIMISM

Pessimism about New England's future is an old disease. Professor Oscar Handlin reminds us that William Ellery Channing of Boston said in 1836:

> We are a city too much given to croaking. I have been told that we were on the brink of ruin ever since I knew the place. Those whose duty it is to carry forward society despair of it. They despair of the body of people, despair of our institutions, despair of liberty through the world. I lament our want of faith in human improvement.

In 1790, the Governor of Massachusetts doubted that its free institutions would last out the decade. Even earlier, Cotton Mather was pessimistic; and in the 1650's Bradford bemoaned "the coming of the mixed multitudes who had adulterated the primal purity of the New Cannan." [1]

H. Keyserling wrote in the *Atlantic Monthly:*

> New England's great and very original charm is, also, that of a dying culture. There is little likelihood that it will survive even for a century, all the less so as it represents an artificial civilization from the point of view of the earth . . . In centuries to come, America will probably see New England's main, because more lasting achievement, in the fact that its sons are chiefly responsible for the colonization of the South and Middle West. [2]

[1] Oscar Handlin, "The Withering of New England: The Prophets of Gloom," *The Atlantic Monthly*, 1950, p. 49.
[2] *The Atlantic Monthly*, 1929, p. 304.

Again, Henry Adams, writing in the latter part of the nineteenth century, described New England in 1800 as backward, with farmhouses no better than in Charlemagne's time, antiquated equipment, and population increases smaller than any other colony. Despite a century and a half of industry, intelligent labor and pinching economy, Boston was still poor. Indeed,

the extraordinary prosperity caused by the French wars opened to Boston a new career . . . The new epoch of American history (1815) began by the sudden decline of Massachusetts to the lowest point of relative prosperity and influence she had ever known, and by an equally sudden stimulus to the South and West.

While Boston was the Bristol of America, New York was the Liverpool and Philadelphia the London.[3]

With the gradual loss of commerce and with the aid of the tariff, New England opened up a new economic era for itself, particularly in the second half of the nineteenth century, by developing its manufacturing. The problem of paying for its imports, which we discuss fully later, is an old problem for New England, not blessed with significant staples. The rapid industrialization provided not only the means of paying for the required food and raw materials, but also a surplus which was exported in the form of capital.

As early as 1860, a writer estimated a balance of payments between North and South as well as the sales of shoes from New England to the South; and he commented on the North's greater dependence on the South, for the latter had the required raw materials and food and could develop into a great manufacturing area. According to this writer, the balance of payments was as follows (even at this early date, the South was a debtor area — note item 5 below): [4]

$ Million

Sent North		*Sent South*	
1. Bills and raw materials	263	3. Domestic goods	240
2. Other produce	200	4. Imported goods	106
	463	5. Interest, brokerage, etc.	63
		6. Southern travelers	53
			463

[3] H. Adams, *History of the United States of America*, I, 16–25, 103.
[4] T. P. Kettell, *Southern Wealth and Northern Profits* (1860), p. 75.

With the building of the Erie Canal, New England began to lose ground as a center of commerce; and the opening of the rich agricultural lands further weakened its economic position as an agricultural area and later as a lumber area. Equally unfortunate was its failure to develop railroad ties with the West, as did other ports on the Atlantic Coast. Adams, in 1879, commented on the failure of New England leaders to envisage the possibilities.[5]

" . . . for nearly one hundred years the people [of New England] struggled along seemingly unable to discover that the greater part of the land was thoroughly unfit for agriculture and during all this time crops of glacial boulders alternated with harvests of trouble." [6]

Handlin puts the situation well: [7]

The arduous nature of the contest against the unfriendly elements of the environment can be traced in the familiar story of the New England economy of the early nineteenth century. Back-breaking farming, commerce pursued under the competitive disadvantage of absence of a fertile back country and of inadequate transportation links to the interior, industry that operated without ready access to raw materials and with quickly antiquated sources of power — these were then the dominant characteristics of the region's system of production. Yet despite these adverse conditions, there were brilliant attempts to resolve them — Merino sheep, the China trade, the clipper ships, the Lowell mills . . .

The complaints of degeneration since 1870 have been no different from those heard in the land in the two centuries previous. New England's troubles are the same; what is different is the failure to cope with them. In transportation, in commerce, in industry, a succession of missed opportunities marks the course of these seven decades. Against obstacles there might have been a thriving trunk line railroad to the west, the Cunarders might have continued to come to Boston, an automobile center might have developed in Duryea's Springfield.

From this, Dr. Handlin contends that conditions which previously goaded into action now accounted for a withdrawal: as is evident in excessive interest in family trees, a failure to merge with the newer immigrants, an unwillingness to take risks (of estates of $25,000 or over probated in the four eastern counties of Massachusetts, 70 per cent in value were tied up in trusts which discouraged risk-taking); the reluctance to share schooling with the newer stock.

[5] This failure has been frequently stressed.
[6] J. H. Redway quoted in H. W. Odum and H. E. Moore, *American Regionalism* (1938), p. 348.
[7] "The Withering of New England," pp. 49–50.

Writing in 1933, James Truslow Adams commented on New England's difficulties in a vein somewhat similar to Handlin's.

"In New England, balked by soil, topography, climate, and the comparatively stationary population, the people had to turn to other means for the accumulation of capital. Work and thrift were not only virtues but economic necessities . . . "[8]

In accounting for sectional individuality, Adams also commented on the absence of immigration in the first two centuries of New England's history, the in-training of its leaders, the dependence on outside imports, and hence the need of Yankee ingenuity and shrewdness in selling and the need of being as self-sufficient as possible, the shortage of labor reflected, for example, in the "slavers" who brought back factory workers to the mills in the first half of the nineteenth century, the failure to connect with the West through vigorous railroad development. In Adams' view, the training, character, and ideals of New England would appear to be better adapted to quality than quantity production.[9]

In *New England's Prospect*, Edward Filene dwells on New England character and stresses an unwillingness to breed new ideas, and an excessively contented attitude. His prescription, as opposed to Adams', is quantity production, for unless New England captures industries producing in vast quantities, the area is bound to lose ground.[10] The absence of mass production in New England and its spread elsewhere accounts in no small part for New England's difficulties.

Over the years, the doubters and pessimists about New England's future were numerous and vocal. Even in the ascendancy of New England's manufacturing, the humanitarians, for example, Thoreau, Emerson, Channing, Mann, etc., protested the growth of the factory town, the changed relation of capital and labor, the shift of power to the industrialists.[11]

The factory-towns, Haverhill, Lawrence, and Lowell, were spewing smoke, wealth and desolation. Thousands of immigrant working-people . . . slaves of the lords of the loom who had lured them hither, were

[8] *New England's Prospects: 1933,* ed. by J. K. Wright, American Geographical Society (New York), pp. 5–6.

[9] *New England's Prospect,* pp. 7–12.

[10] *New England's Prospect,* pp. 65–72.

[11] F. T. Carlton, *Economic Influence upon Educational Progress in the United States, 1820–1850* (1908), pp. 36–42, and *Indian Summer.*

slowly transforming the landscape. More and more as the factories spread, the owners abandoned the region loving it less the less they laboured for it, and ruled their slaves from Boston through the whips of agents.[12]

Although in the minority, there have been optimists also; [13] for example this writer of 1911.

The friction of "the decadence of New England," which has for many years been a favorite topic of critics of this region, and has been too much considered by our own people, may be dismissed with a few words of explanation. It has never had standing with well-informed people, and it could never be substantiated by those who dwelt upon it with the greatest unction. It is a fact — a creditable and glorious fact — that New England has contributed many thousands of its virile youth to the newer sections of the country, and has itself lost their services and been deprived of their constructive work.

"With great pleasure have I heard of the grain fields of the West, of the far Pacific coast land that flows with milk and honey, of the iron and coal of Pennsylvania. As I have heard the story of how upon the South nature has poured with a lavish hand every blessing of climate and soil and timber and mineral wealth I have marveled at its potentialities. Then, as I have thought of my own state, I have contrasted the barrenness of its natural resources with the wealth of which you have boasted, and I have been forced to say that of these heaven-given advantages Massachusetts has none. We boast of no natural resources. We can only boast of what we have been able to do through the utilization of the brains and energy of our people. Instead of grain fields at home, we draw our foodstuffs from the West. Instead of cotton plantations at home, we feed the spindles of our mills with the product of the South, and even sent unto faraway Egypt for some of the cotton for our finer products. Instead of iron mines and coal mines at home, we look to Alabama and Pennsylvania for iron and steel, and to the Virginias and Maryland for the coal which runs the machinery of our factories. Gathering from the world these materials, we have touched them with the magic wand of energy, of trained brain and hand, and they have poured out for us a flood of gold and given us an industrial development which has made Massachusetts one of the wonders of the business world."

When we remember that on this little bit of rock-bound soil, using the materials drawn from other sections and other lands, Massachusetts has built a business structure so solid, so vast and all-comprehensive that with 3,000,000 population it is turning out manufactured products equal to 60 per cent as much as the 14 southern states, and that its working people have out of their accumulated earnings put in the savings banks of Boston and neighboring cities over $700,000,000, or only about $200,000,-

[12] *New England Indian Summer*, pp. 50–51.
[13] G. French, *New England* (1911), pp. 15, 362–363.

000 less than the total national banking capital of the United States, we may well ask ourselves if the delegate from Massachusetts was not justified in boasting of the power of brains and energy.

2. THE PROBLEM OF MIGRATION

Earlier writers seem to have voiced many of today's complaints, including the competitive threat from new areas and the decline in brilliant leadership. Both these circumstances could be explained by migration, the characteristic feature of New England life.

Except for the urban centers of the Coast, New England's physical geography, therefore, had fostered the growth of a simple, thrifty, inventive folk who struggled bravely with the inhospitable hills and the region's climate, grew strong in experience, increased in numbers beyond the capacity of the arable lands to sustain them under the conditions of the time, and spread leaders and Yankee ideas over the West.[14]

Almost from the very beginning, New England lost more by out-migration than it gained from inmigration. From 1790 to 1820, 800,-000 New Englanders migrated. By 1850, the population of the area was 2¼ millions, but in the absence of migration it would have been 4½ millions. The decade of the nineteen forties was unique — there was a large net inmigration. Over 200 years, the region lost its most adventurous and frequently its most able.

" . . . The very process of sifting by which other sections called away the youthful, the less satisfied, the more optimistic and adventurous, tended, it is true, to leave in a stronger position, the most conservative in those regions of New England which were the most affected." [15]

New England was not pleased with the migration of its best brains. The fear of competition with newer areas was reflected, for example, in the views expressed at the Hartford Convention on the

[14] F. J. Turner, *New England, 1830–1850, Huntington Library Bulletin* (May 1931), p. 155. Cf. G. French (ed.), *New England: What It Is and What It Is To Be* (1911), p. 6.

[15] F. J. Turner, *New England, 1830–1850*, pp. 157–158, 173. For discussion of causes of migration, also see L. K. Mathews, *The Expansion of New England* (1909), pp. 259–272; H. G. Pearson, *An American Railroad Builder, John Murray Forbes* (1911), pp. 101–103; and P. W. Bidwell, "Rural Economy in New England at the Beginning of the 19th Century," *Transactions of the Connecticut Academy of Arts and Sciences* (New Haven, 1916), pp. 350–351.

entry of new states and later in opposition to the entry of Texas.[16] Very early it was realized that New England capital was developing the South and West, competitive areas, and from the West came early protests at the exploitation by New England.[17]

In the 1896 Democratic Convention, Senator Tillman of South Carolina said: " . . . we were mere heavers of wood and drawers of water, tied in bondage, and all our substance being eaten out . . . Massachusetts, Pennsylvania and New York are almost as wealthy as all the other states put together, with less territory and comparatively more population . . . " [18]

Both the movement to the cities and the migration to the West are well expressed by Van Wyck Brooks:

> The old farmers were dying out . . . the men whose hoeing was a sleight-of-hand, who made their own ox-yokes and axe-helves, chopped their three cords of wood a day, knew every medicinal herb that grew in the field or stream. These tamers of the wilderness were vanishing from the land. They were hewing their way to the West, along the Great Lakes, while the young men were turning to the cities.[19]
>
> The young men were scattering in all directions. Their imagination was caught by the West, and scores who might have been writers were seeking their fortunes in railroads, mines, and oil wells.[20]

3. EARLIER DIAGNOSES

Along with the writers and historians who noted the changes which were taking place, New England has had its share of economic surveys. In general, the causes of distress and the suggested cures have resembled those of recent years, although earlier analyses were often superficial.

As long ago as 1923 the textile industry was receiving special attention in Massachusetts, and the advantages of the South were described in familiar terms; lower wages, longer hours of operation,

[16] A. B. Hart and C. Channing, eds. American History Leaflets, *Report of the Hartford Convention*, by P. O. Simmons (1906), pp. 2–27.

[17] P. W. Bidwell, "Rural Economy in New England," p. 245.

[18] J. S. Ogilvie, Ed., *Life and Speeches of William J. Bryan* (New York, 1896), pp. 32–36. Also see *Selections from the Diaries of William Appleton, 1786–1862* (1922), p. 24.

[19] Van Wyck Brooks, *The Flowering of New England, 1815–1865* (1936), p. 409.

[20] Van Wyck Brooks, *New England: Indian Summer, 1865–1915* (1940), p. 184.

a lower cost of living, and newer plants.[21] In the same year unemployment was investigated, and the committee recommended establishing depression reserves and planning public works to be used in depression.[22] Little analysis was given to underlying causes. In 1930, general business depression was the problem, and in public hearings held by the Massachusetts Industrial Commission in Lowell almost every conceivable diagnosis and therapy were suggested.[23] Among the interesting points made was an insistence on a nation-wide work limit of 48 hours to diminish overproduction, and direct selling of textiles to expand sales at lower prices. At this time and later, the emphasis was on federal legislation to set minimum wages and control production. Some witnesses stressed also inefficient management and suggested tax refunds to manufacturing establishments.

A third report for 1935 (private) showed that the major difficulty lay in manufacturing; that three-quarters of the employment in Massachusetts manufacturing was in declining industries, and that the service industries were not likely to absorb the unemployed.[24] Replacement by service industries is a problem today.

In 1939, the Commonwealth once more paid attention to the migration of industrial establishments, with a careful analysis of periods of decline and the long-term trends in industries.[25] Again the emphasis was on lower costs and inducements to move to the South, and weak management in Massachusetts. While the report concluded that taxes were not high, further advances in social legislation were not recommended. The conclusions in this report were

[21] Massachusetts Department of Labor and Industries, *Report of Special Investigation into Conditions in the Textile Industry in Massachusetts and Southern States Submitted to the Governor and Council, August, 1923.*

[22] Massachusetts House Document No. 1325, *Report of the Special Commission on Unemployment, Unemployment Compensation and the Minimum Wage,* 1923.

[23] *Public Hearings held by the Massachusetts Industrial Commission,* Lowell, Mass., March 3, 1930, in order to *Secure Suggestions for Improvements of Business. . .*

[24] *Unemployment and Prospects for Reemployment in Massachusetts with Particular Reference to Manufacturing Industries,* by D. H. Davenport and others, Harvard Graduate School of Business Administration, Research Study No. 15, 1936.

[25] House Report No. 2045, *House Preliminary Report to the General Court of the Commission on Interstate Cooperation Concerning the Migration of Industrial Establishments from Massachusetts,* January 1939.

not unlike those of the 1950 Textile Commission, where management, work-loads, social security, and legislation concerning working conditions were especially stressed. The authors of the 1949 Sickness Report insisted, however, that social security was not a significant factor in Massachusetts' losses.[26]

A 1931 report dealt with the problem of unemployment. The causes of industrial migration were held to be heavy taxes, inclusive of special inducements offered by outside states, the raw materials, lower wage rates, and favorable labor laws in the South, and New England's aging plants and equipment. The Commonwealth's responsibility was limited, it was held, to studying the problem and providing work.[27]

In a private report for the Massachusetts Industrial Commission, Freeland, Bates and Lawrence, in 1931, brought attention to the unwillingness of established firms to tolerate new firms which might compete for labor. Its main recommendation was the repeal of legislation that put the Commonwealth at a disadvantage in relation to other states.[28]

A Rhode Island report of 1935 also stressed high wages and taxes and urged restriction of output under NRA codes.[29] In 1935, an unofficial report for the Pennsylvania Manufacturers Association held that less hostile legislation plus diversification had led to more favorable developments in Pennsylvania than in Massachusetts.[30]

In 1947, the Commonwealth tried to meet criticism by stressing the gains of social security and the rise of wage rates in competing states as well as the favorable record on labor relations in this Commonwealth.[31]

[26] *Report of the Special Commission and Study Relative to the Establishment and Administration of Cash Sickness Compensation,* May 1, 1950.

[27] Massachusetts House Document No. 1298, *Special Report of the Department of Labor and Industries of an Investigation of the Causes of Existing Unemployment and Remedies Thereof,* 1931.

[28] *A Brief Study of Industrial Massachusetts Made for the Massachusetts Industrial Commission by Freeland, Bates and Lawrence, Inc.,* Boston, Mass., 1931.

[29] Rhode Island, *Report of Commission to Investigate Problems of the Cotton Textile Industry,* 1935.

[30] *The Flight of Capital and Industry from Massachusetts: A Study Made for the Pennsylvania Manufacturers Association,* by Warren F. Doane, Philadelphia, Pa., 1935.

[31] Massachusetts Development and Industrial Commission, *The Facts Concerning Industrial Advantages in Massachusetts,* 1947.

An excellent list of actions that might be taken was presented as a result of a survey of the New England Council and the Federal Reserve Bank of Boston, followed by a meeting in November 1949.[32]

4. CONCLUSION

The historical survey of the economic diseases of New England in the last two chapters is revealing in several respects. The old diseases come up again and again: the dearth of raw materials, the managerial deficiencies, related to some extent to the development of the New England character, the building up of competitive regions with New England talent and capital, the shortage of labor (Miss Martineau, in her travels, comments on the lack of labor as a disadvantage for New England manufacturing but with true vision anticipates the large contributions of female labor), the continued losses of New England as a trading center, first with the opening of the Erie Canal, then with the failure to tie up with transcontinental railroads and throughout with the great advances of the New York and other ports. Points made throughout the nineteenth century are still being raised in the 1950's. One important factor — the dearth of raw materials — receives less attention today than it should.

Pessimism about New England's future is an old condition. The limited natural resources for the large population account in part for the pessimism and also for the migrations which contributed so much to the development of the West and South, as well as increased markets and intensified competition for New England. When confronted with crisis in the nineteenth century, New England rebounded — e.g., the development of manufacturing when the region began to lose its preëminent position in commerce. It remains to be seen whether or not New England in the next generation will meet the challenge of the South (and West) with improved management, wiser financial policies, nurturing of new industries. The facts are known. What is required now is action.

[32] U. S. Department of Labor, *Community Programs to Combat Unemployment*, November 30, 1949, p. 1.

CHAPTER 6

STATE AND LOCAL DIFFERENCES

So far in this study we have spoken of the problems of New England. But as Professor John Black shows in his distinguished new book, *The Rural Economy of New England,* there are diverse parts to this region.[1] Agriculture is most important to Vermont and Maine; industry to the other states, although no state is without significant farming areas. Connecticut, drawn both by the Middle Atlantic and the other New England states, resembles both New York and Massachusetts. In this chapter some of the important variations in the New England problem, by states and localities, will be discussed. Generally speaking, the state and local breakdowns highlight the regional difficulties: the relative decline in manufacturing traceable to losses in the textile and leather industry, relative cost differences, variations in plant and equipment, and relations with the federal government.

1. GROWTH

From 1800 to 1950, growth trends varied greatly from state to state. Thus, from 1800 to 1950, the population of Southern New England increased by 9 times, of Northern New England by 2⅔ times. In this same period, the population of Vermont increased but 1 2/5 times (from 154,000 to 368,000), whereas that of Massachusetts increased by 10 times (from 423,000 to 4,691,000).[2] Northern New England grew more rapidly in the first half of the nineteenth century, when agricultural development was important. Southern New England gained in later years, with the advance of manufacturing and trading.

In the years 1940 to 1950, New England gained 787,000 from natural increase and 96,000 from inmigration. But this total gain includes a 17.4 per cent increase in Connecticut; 11 per cent in

[1] John D. Black, *The Rural Economy of New England* (Cambridge: Harvard University Press, 1950).

[2] Figures from U. S. Census.

Massachusetts; and less than 10 per cent in the other states. The migration gain was concentrated in Connecticut, where inmigration equaled the natural increase. Maine actually lost 26,000 from migration (natural increase was 93,000), as did New Hampshire and Vermont, where a natural increase of 38,000 was almost nullified by outmigration of 20,000.[3]

In its more rapid growth than the rest of New England, Connecticut is also like New York, New Jersey, and Pennsylvania. Its income rise from 1929 to 1948 was one-half more than that of Massachusetts and its population growth 80 per cent greater. Even on a per capita basis, the gains exceeded those of Massachusetts by one-quarter.

2. VARIATIONS IN GROWTH AND INDUSTRY STRUCTURE

We can explain Connecticut's gains by its concentration on manufacturing, particularly the high-paying and fast-growing durable goods industries, where employment increased markedly. This per-

New England States: Income and Related Variables, 1929–1948

	Income Percentage Payments, Rise, 1929–48	Per Capita Income Payments, Percentage Rise, 1929–48	Percentage of Employment in Manufacturing, 1948	Percentage Rise of Employment in Manufacturing, 1929 to 1947
United States	194	107	22.4	48.0
New England	102	79	31.9	19.1
Maine	144	115	26.5	30.5
New Hampshire	118	93	31.5	4.9
Vermont	106	104	22.2	14.2
Massachusetts	85	68	30.2	12.3
Rhode Island	101	84	35.7	4.8
Connecticut	132	85	37.1	39.0

Source: Economic Development Atlas, Handbook of Regional Statistics, and Report of Committee on the New England Economy.

formance must be contrasted with Rhode Island and Massachusetts, as in the accompanying tables. Notable also are the large gains for Maine and Vermont, associated with improved agriculture and substantial advances in manufacturing.

Durables account for 62 per cent of manufacturing employment in Connecticut, but only 40 and 24 per cent respectively in Mas-

[3] *Distribution of Counties According to Percentage Change of Population. . .* , Preliminary Release, U. S. Census, 1951.

sachusetts and Rhode Island; textiles and leather and leather products account for 11 per cent of Connecticut manufacturing employment, and 26 and 42 per cent in Massachusetts and Rhode Island. These figures alone can largely explain Rhode Island's record in recent years — the least satisfactory of any New England state.

Major Sources of Income Payments in the New England States, 1948 (Selected components as percentage of total income)

Area	Agricultural Income	Government Income Payments	Manufacturing Pay Rolls	Trade and Service Income	All Other Income
Continental United States	10.2	13.9	22.4	27.0	26.5
New England	3.2	13.5	31.9	25.6	25.8
Connecticut	3.0	9.9	37.1	22.9	27.1
Maine	10.2	15.2	26.5	24.5	23.6
Massachusetts	1.6	14.7	30.2	27.3	26.2
New Hampshire	4.9	13.4	31.5	25.4	24.8
Rhode Island	.9	15.2	35.7	24.6	23.6
Vermont	15.4	12.8	22.2	24.9	24.7

Source: **U. S. Department of Commerce, Office of Business Economics.**

These data reveal marked differences in employment in the various states: Massachusetts the largest "loser" and Connecticut the largest "gainer."

The reader should consult Table 10 (page 22) of the *New England Economy: A Report to the President* (1951) for more details on changes in the industrial structure of individual states. The net loss of 30,000 jobs in New England manufacturing includes a gain in Connecticut of 69,000 while Massachusetts lost 89,000, some losses in New Hampshire and Rhode Island and appreciable gains in Maine and Vermont. In textiles and leather and leather products, Massachusetts lost 158,000 jobs and Connecticut, only 16,000. In durables, the latter gained 76,000 and the former, only 21,000. These figures suggest the importance of the industrial structure. They also point to a tendency for industry to migrate to the rural areas (Northern New England), where wages are lower, labor less militant, and rents and power less costly. The gains of both Connecticut and the agricultural states of New England are evident in the table on page 69, showing the rise of manufacturing employment, 1919 to 1947 (1919 = 100).

Changes in Monthly Averages of Numbers of Workers Employed: 1947 Compared with 1919 (In thousands)

	United States	New England	Maine	New Hampshire	Vermont	Massachusetts	Rhode Island	Connecticut
All manufacturing	+4,353.1	−30.2	+8.8	−13.9	+2.6	−89.0	−7.4	+68.7
Durable goods	+2,507.4	+97.2	−.4	−2.4	+1.7	+21.0	+.9	+76.4
Electrical machinery	+497.4	+52.1	...	+.5	+.5	+28.5	+3.1	+19.5
Machinery, except electrical	+728.3	+57.8	+2.5	+2.2	+2.0	+16.3	...	+34.8
Nondurable goods	+1,845.7	−127.3	+9.2	−11.5	+1.0	−110.0	−8.3	−7.7
Textiles	+81.1	−156.5	+1.7	−15.4	−.9	−106.3	−20.2	−15.4
Leather and leather products	−16.6	−46.3	+4.0	+2.2	+.2	−51.8	−.2	−.7

Source: Report of the Council's Committee on the New England Economy, p. xxiii.

(1919 = 100)

United States	144
New England	98
Connecticut	121
Maine	110
Vermont	108
Rhode Island	95
Massachusetts	89
New Hampshire	84

Source: **Report on the New England Economy,** p. 23.

3. MORE DETAILS ON COSTS

A report submitted to the research staff of the Connecticut Full Employment Committee claims that in that state the plant and equipment are more modern and industrial relations are better than elsewhere in the region; and some Connecticut businessmen even seem to resent the association of their state with New England's economic problems.

But let us consider some costs. Power costs vary greatly and Connecticut labors under a disadvantage, ranking 42nd in industrial power costs. The three Northern states average 25th.

Pay-roll taxes are another burden on industry. But here Connecticut's costs are low vis-à-vis Southern New England and about equal to those of Northern New England. Its percentage of unemployment in May 1949 was 8.6; that of Massachusetts, 10.5; and of Rhode Island, 23.8. The 1949 cost of unemployment insurance for Connecticut was 3.1 per cent of payrolls; for Massachusetts, 3.6; for Rhode Island, 6.3.

Taxes have always been a source of annoyance to businessmen. Connecticut's particular gripe is the large personal property taxes paid by business, but the absence of an income tax attracts many from New York and Massachusetts. The taxpayer in Massachusetts bewails the corporation taxes; but while local taxes are heavy, state taxes are less heavy relatively. What seems to vex businessmen is not the total taxes levied (actually they stand up well against rival industrial states), but the fact that more taxes are levied on business, and less on consumption.

4. CAPITAL INVESTMENT

How much capital is being invested is a barometer of business enterprise, of business profitability and costs of producing. The plant with modern plant and machinery has a distinct advantage.

We find little comfort in the recent census figures on outlays for new plant and equipment; New England's expenditures are much less than might be suggested by the percentage of its manufacturing employment and by the need for modernization. Yet there are two important offsets.

The first — areas adding many new workers require much more investment per worker. Obviously other areas, where manufacturing is increasing faster than in New England, will require more investment.

The second — areas more dependent on durable goods industries will invest more than others; for these industries require more investment per worker. This is another reason for expecting smaller net investment in New England.

But what of state differences? In 1947, New Hampshire made a remarkable record: the state increased its investment by 627 per cent over 1939, as compared with 381 for the United States and 310 for New England. Connecticut, oddly enough, added but 265 per cent of the 1939 amount — next to last among New England States. Possibly the explanation here may be that expanding old industries requires less new capital than new industries. Incidentally, New Hampshire alone of the United States spent more per textile worker ($403) in 1947 than the average of five Southern states ($341).

The textile study reveals outlays of 18 per cent less per worker in 1947 for New England than for five Southern states. Here we have to allow, however, for the larger proportion of new workers in the South; and (on the other side) the lower costs of construction in the South.

5. OTHER DIFFERENCES

Industrial states in New England contain a large proportion of workers relative to population. Massachusetts and Rhode Island, with a heavy concentration of textiles and related industries, have an unusually large proportion of female workers. The industrial states of New England also have fewer very young and very old members than nonindustrial states.

States also vary in the export of commodities and services. While a large part of New England manufacturing is exported, it is concentrated in certain industries. Where these industries are important — textiles (in most states), shoes (in Massachusetts and New Hampshire), machinery (especially in Massachusetts), and fabricated metal products (in Connecticut) — exports are large. Connecticut and Massachusetts are also large exporters of insurance services, the latter of finance services, and all New England except Rhode Island of large tourist services.

In their relations with the federal government, the states reflect different attitudes. Northern New England uses federal services relatively more; and Connecticut is especially distinguished by much larger payments to the Federal Treasury than withdrawals.

Finally, there is the problem of instability. Both the largest decline and the best recovery were made by Connecticut from 1929 to 1939. The disappointing recovery of Massachusetts and Rhode Island may be associated with their industrial structure. In the upsurge of 1940–1948, Maine topped the others, with Massachusetts last (139 per cent increase in income payments for Maine and 97 for Massachusetts). Finally, in the 1948–49 recession the maximum decline in manufacturing employment occurred in Connecticut and Rhode Island and the minimum in the three Northern states; in nonagricultural employment, the maximum decline was in Maine and the minimum in Vermont. In general, Connecticut seems to be the most unstable state, though in 1919–1939 Vermont was equally unstable.[4]

Connecticut seems the healthiest economic community of New England, though a widespread drop in employment would probably have the greatest effect in that state. It is no wonder, in view of its great relative progress, that Connecticut's manufacturers are much more optimistic about the future than those of other New England states. Rhode Island is least optimistic.[5]

6. LOCAL VARIATIONS

Localities vary greatly in the rate of their economic ups and downs. Communities largely dependent on textiles, for example, will lose ground, while those with more diversified or durable goods industries gain ground relatively. In the *Report on the New England Economy* (1951), it was shown, for example, that both in 1937–38 and in 1948–49 private nonagricultural employment declined sub-

---

[4] For further details, see *Report of the Committee on the New England Economy*, Tables 19–21, pp. 36–37.

[5] Cf. Table 18 of *Report of Committee on the New England Economy*, p. 34.

stantially more in Bridgeport than in Waterbury, and about four times as much in Bridgeport as in the average of Hartford, New Haven, and the state as a whole. The explanation of these facts lies in the much greater concentration of manufacturing and especially metallic manufacturing in Bridgeport and Waterbury.[6] The towns harboring metallic manufacturing grow more; but they are also more vulnerable to depression conditions.

On the basis of a study of 89 municipalities by Wells and Perkins and a study by Professor Morris Lambie,[7] we find that of 89 munici-

Number of Wage Earners in Manufacturing, Value of Manufacturing Product, Proportionate Gain of Value Product to State Gains, and Retail Sales, 1939 (1919 = 100)

	Number of Wage Earners in Manufacturing 1939	Value of Manufacturing Product 1939	Value Gain of Product Relative to State Gains 1939	Retail Sales (1929 = 100)
Milton (1)	123	312	200	81
Revere (3)	231	180	300	112
Canton (7)	115	119	194	85
Worcester (31)	59	74	121	85
Boston (38)	60	67	109	72
Fall River (60)	64	45	73	88
New Bedford (78)	50	35	56	79
Brockton (82)	41	30	49	90
Danvers (89)	40	16	24	98

Source: Wells and Perkins, Compilers, **New England Community Statistical Abstracts** (1942).

palities in Massachusetts, 16 were producing more in 1939 than in 1919 and 73 were producing less. In this twenty-year period, as reflected in increased direct taxes per capita, rise of school expenditures, and decline of relief expenditures, the suburban towns and resort towns improved their position most.

From the Wells and Perkins study, I have listed above a number of communities. The large variations in the development of industry and incomes (as suggested by retail sales) will be evident at once.

The figures in parentheses give the ranking of each community in terms of the *change* in value of manufacturing products. In 1939, the range of variation in value of product was from 312 per cent of

[6] *Committee on the New England Economy,* pp. 46–49.
[7] Wells and Perkins, Compilers, *New England Community Statistical Abstracts,* 3rd ed., 1942; and Morris B. Lambie, *Experiments in Methods of Municipal Analysis* (1941).

1919 (Milton) to 16 per cent of 1919 (Danvers). Boston had lost 40 per cent of its manufacturing jobs and 33 per cent of its product. It is interesting that the variations in retail sales do not correspond closely to those for manufacturing value. The large textile and shoe towns ranked low in the change of manufacturing product (from 1919 to 1939). In addition to the towns listed above, the ranking for Lawrence was 47; for Lowell, 59; and for Haverhill, 84.

From 1906 to 1940, 224 municipalities decreased their average property valuations and 127 increased them. In these same years 303 raised their tax rates and 46 reduced them. As might be expected, there were large relative movements. Thus, in direct taxes per capita Fall River fell from the 9th decile in 1920 to the 3rd decile in 1940 — here we note the effect of losses of industries and *higher* per capita rates for those staying behind. Also note Gardner from 7th to 3rd; Taunton, 6th to 3rd (1906 to 1939); New Bedford and Lowell, 9th to 7th (1906 to 1940); Clinton, 7th to 3rd (1906 to 1940). The resort towns improved their positions (less taxes) — e.g., Dennis, 5th to 10th; Chatham 3rd to 10th, Truro, 4th to 9th.[8]

According to a 1951 study of markets made by Messrs. Larson and Poteat for the Department of Commerce, *Selling the United States Market*, 14 cities in the 164 largest metropolitan areas experienced a decline in population from 1940 to 1950. The losses were largely concentrated on New England textile and shoe towns and Pennsylvania coal towns. But there were also substantial gains registered by many New England towns.

7. CONCLUSION

In summary, New England is a region composed of six states and hundreds of communities. Advances and declines are far from uniform. Over the long period since 1800, manufacturing areas have gained more than the others. But in the last 30 years, the manufacturing states and communities have encountered serious problems of adjustment. Connecticut, with its close relations with the Middle Atlantic States and its concentration on thriving industries in the last generation, is a manufacturing state with a much better record than the rest of the region. Even among manufacturing towns, records over the last 20 to 30 years have varied greatly. It is only

[8] Figures from M. B. Lambie, *Experiments in Methods of Municipal Analysis*.

necessary to compare a community with diversified manufacturing or one favored by a large metal-fabricating plant (e.g., Pittsfield) with a town relying heavily on a soft industry (textiles or shoes) — e.g., Brockton, New Bedford, Haverhill, or Lawrence, to perceive the extent of variation.

CHAPTER 7

NORTH VERSUS SOUTH

1. THE ISSUES

In the body of this book, I have commented at various points on Southern competition, which has won a large part of the textile industry, threatens to wean away even more, and is capturing part of the shoe and paper industries. With abundant labor supplies, low labor costs, cheap power, and a tax structure favoring industries, the South offers keen competition to New England. It would be a mistake, however, to consider the problem merely from the viewpoint of New England. It is in part a problem of North versus South. Losses of the Middle West and Middle Atlantic States to the South are also relevant to our study.

Since 1940 the South has made even greater progress in metals and machinery, in paper and paper products, and in chemicals than in textiles. In fact, textiles in 1947 accounted for but 27.4 per cent of all Southern production workers in manufacturing as compared with 35.3 per cent in 1939. (The absolute rise for textiles was from 476,000 to 554,000 production workers.[1])

According to an analysis by Southern leaders, in the years 1939–1950 the South had gained 18,000 industries (plants?) and a million new jobs. Pointing to an increase of 14 million cotton spindles in 50 years, establishment of 16 rayon plants, large growth in paper and pulp, production of 38 per cent of the nation's aluminum pig in 1949, and one-third of the nation's furniture, Southern leaders also stressed a rise of banking facilities since 1932 at double the national rate — suggesting large inflows of liquid capital as well as growth.[2]

[1] C. B. Hoover and B. A. Ratchford, *Economic Resources and Policies of the South* (1951), p. 126. This volume is the most comprehensive available on the Southern economy.

[2] *New York Times,* July 5, 1950.

2. THE GAINS OF THE SOUTH

Thirty years ago, Gilbert and Pogue, in *Power Resources*, summarized the claims of the South as follows (concentration of industry is greater than anticipated in this statement): [3]

Coming into action late the industrialization of the South, unhampered by tradition and unencumbered by obsolescent power establishments, took over the practices best suited to its needs. Thus while the Northeastern states form an illustration of centralized industry . . . , the South displays a regional development of industry nowhere intensely focused but spread, on the contrary, in diluted form over a large area. The contrast is suggestive; for permanence, for well being, for the common good, it would appear that a balanced economic use in which each section manufactures in a large measure its own products, is preferable to a highly intensified manufacturing area setting up its own interests in opposition to more extensive producing areas.

Messrs. Odum and Moore, in their book *American Regionalism* (1938), on page 361, expressed the South's interest in industrialization as follows: There is an "enormous waste incurred in extraregional processing of materials produced and consumed in a region unless the region has such a great comparative cost advantage as to outweigh this factor."

In the later discussion, I emphasize especially the cost structure and particularly labor costs. But markets and availability of raw materials are also of great importance. In an excellent study of migration of industry, Messrs. McLaughlin and Robock [4] concluded that of 88 new plants located in the South in recent years, 45 per cent were primarily oriented to the market, 30 per cent to materials, and 25 per cent to labor.[5] The inference to be drawn from these conclusions is that the large cheap labor force in the South is not so important as is generally assumed. These conclusions should not, however, be applied to textiles. In this survey of reasons for plant location, availability of power, water, and fair tax treatment were occasionally given as the decisive factors.

An examination of reasons for several locational decisions further clarifies these problems.

---

[3] Quoted in Rupert Bayless Vance, *All These People* (1945), p. 280.

[4] *Why Industry Moves South* (1949).

[5] *Why Industry Moves South*, p. 26.

They are as follows:

Assembly Plants. When a market becomes large enough, General Motors and Ford establish assembly plants near these markets. They have recently done so in the South.

Batteries. Battery companies have built several plants in the South recently, the main reason being proximity to markets in the South and East Coast. The cost of the raw materials required is roughly equal in the South and Middle West. Proximity to markets is important because the weight of batteries relative to value is high.

Candy. The Curtiss Candy Company built a large plant in Dallas, Texas. Nearness to market is important to give customers both better service and fresher products.

Machinery-Farm Equipment. The International Harvester Company opened two plants in the South. Analysis revealed that savings in transport were involved in moving compact materials into the South and moving the final product shorter distances.

Rubber Products — Tires and Tubes. Crude rubber is imported, and carbon black, tire fabrics, and synthetic rubber can be supplied from the South. A tire factory in the South therefore saves cross hauling. Conditions for selection of a site were adequate power and fuel, a large supply of cold ground water for cooling, and good rail and highway transportation. In choosing the Miami, Oklahoma Plant, B. F. Goodrich started with 90 possible locations. Unavailability of adequate water supplies cut the list to 26; inadequacy of fuel and power further reduced the list to 12; and transportation deficiencies cut the list to three.

While these are instances of consumer goods plants oriented to the market, McLaughlin and Robock also describe many plants oriented to industrial markets. One of the most important examples is synthetic fibers, which serve the important textile industries in the South. Thus in the last few years the Celanese Corporation has built a $40 million plant in Rock Hill, South Carolina; American Enka, a new plant near Morristown, Tennessee; a nylon plant at Chattanooga, Tennessee; an orlon plant at Camden, South Carolina. The South is expanding facilities in electrical equipment, forest products, iron and steel, and the products of paper.

Material-oriented plants originate in the high cost of transporting required materials. Thus, the manufacture of phosphorus requires

10 to 15 tons of phosphate rock for one ton of the finished product. In the manufacture of pulp and paper about 2½ tons of pulpwood are required per ton of final product. The advantage of proximity to the source of raw material is obvious, and in 1945 32 per cent (value) of the nation's minerals were obtained in the South.[6] (Less than ½ per cent came from New England.) Agricultural products, forest products, mineral products, natural gas and petroleum, power — these are abundant in the South, encouraging the growth of industries which locate near their source. An example was the establishment of an $8 million non-ferrous tube plant in Decatur, Alabama, by the Calumet and Hecla Consolidated Copper Company. Despite the fact that the raw materials come from the parent company in Michigan and the finished product is shipped primarily to North Central and Northeast, the low cost of TVA power was decisive.

In establishing a paperboard plant in Georgia, a continuing supply of pulpwood was the primary factor. Other conditions included "a large water supply, waste disposal facilities, transportation facilities for receiving raw materials and shipping finished products, labor supply, attractiveness of the community as a place to live, and the receptiveness of the local population."

Labor-oriented plants are most frequently mentioned in connection with the migration of the textile industry out of New England. But the new plants in the South based on favorable labor conditions also include apparel, machinery, and shoes. Apparel companies move into small towns where wage rates are low. Much progress has been made in the machinery industry. Thus, the Monroe Calculating Company decided to build a new plant in the South rather than expand its East Orange, New Jersey plant any further. Transport costs are a small item, for the price of the product is high in relation to transport charges. What the company wanted was plenty of labor in a moderate-sized town. From a list of 50 possible locations in eight states (four in the North), the company finally chose Bristol, Virginia-Tennessee.

In shoes, the advance has been from St. Louis southward. Since only 400 to 600 workers, half female, are required for a factory, the

---

[6] Report of the Joint Committee on the Economic Report on *The Impact of Federal Policies on the Economy of the South* (1949), pp. 8–9.

choice is generally a small town. Subsidies from the towns and low wage rates are decisive.

The reader should also consider what is said in Chapter 17 on relative wage advantages in the South over New England. Over the years, however, any advantage of the South has steadily declined. In textiles, however, the differential increased in 1951–52.

Where the South's wages were relatively high, they are generally explained by higher productivity: the type of industry, more skilled labor used, or better equipment and higher valued product. For example, in the postwar, Southern pulp and paper mills paid much higher wages to skilled labor than did New England mills. The Labor Department explains this advantage for the Southern worker

Annual Wages — South as a Percentage of the United States

	All Covered Industries	Manufacturing	Mining	Transportation, Communication, etc.	Construction	Services
1939	74.7	69.3	97.4	75.4	67.8	70.3
1944	78.1	74.4	93.6	83.1	86.4	73.1

Source: U. S. Department of Labor, Labor in the South (1947), p. 44.

by the more recent development in the South and hence greater use of modern, wider and higher-speed machines. "In the former [New England] region only about one-seventh were tending machines with screens over 150 inches in width and/or operating more than 700 feet per minute, while in the latter two regions [Southeast and Southwest] over two-thirds were tending machines of this type." Again, the wage differential between North and South before the war was 12 per cent or less for steel works and rolling mills, chemical production of rayon, and petroleum refining. In these highly productive industries, technological processes tend to be standardized. But in cotton-woven goods the wage differential was 19 per cent and for cotton yarn 26 per cent.

Over a long period, Professor Lester found that the trends varied greatly with industries. Thus, Southern cotton textile wages were 60 per cent of Northern in 1890 and 83 per cent in 1944; but in these same years Southern farm wages declined from 78 to 63 per cent of Northern, and wages in the building trades from 95 to 88 per cent (in 1942).[7] That the continued industrialization in the South tends to raise wages relatively in the South is also suggested by another official study (*Labor in the South*).

In Chapter 15, I discuss some aspects of relative productivity in New England and the South. From their examination of the facts, McLaughlin and Robock conclude that productivity of labor in the South is as high as in the North. In fact, they quote several companies which insist that labor productivity is higher in the South: "Southern workers right out of the mountains were producing 25 per cent more on highly precise work than employees in the company's Northern plant."[8] The Norge Division of the Borg-Warner Corporation established a plant for refrigerator compressors in Chattanooga, Tennessee. The compressors require accuracies of 1/10,000th of an inch and greater. Yet the firm seems satisfied with its 300 employees on high precision work.

3. INCOME AND MIGRATION

Differentials in labor supply and wages reflect differentials in per capita income. What troubles the South is its low average income. Even in 1949, per capita income in the Southeast was only $882, in the Southwest, $1166, or in the region as a whole about 25 per cent less than the national average of $1330. (The Far West and the Middle East averaged $1610 and $1565 respectively.) Differences in real income, that is, in purchasing power, were somewhat less. From 1929 to 1949, the South had made progress in narrowing the gap. The rise of income payments was 213 per cent, as compared with 139 per cent for the nation.[9]

Many explanations are offered for the low per capita income in the South. In 1937, Professor Spengler pointed out that the large proportion of workers in agriculture and the small amount of capital per worker in industry were relevant considerations.[10]

In contending that regional income differences were related primarily to variations in the size of community and that incomes were roughly similar in communities of equal size in North and South,

[7] R. A. Lester, "Trends in Southern Wage Differentials Since 1890," *The Southern Economic Journal* (1945), pp. 339–340.

[8] *Why Industry Moves South*, pp. 73–75.

[9] *Survey of Current Business* (August 1950), pp. 18, 20.

[10] J. J. Spengler, "Population Problems in the South," *Southern Economic Journal* (October 1937), pp. 138–141.

Mr. Klarman's conclusions became a target for those who contended that the occupational structure and the proportion of non-white population were relevant. Klarman seems to have obtained his conclusions in part by comparing whites only.[11]

The importance of occupational distribution is suggested by the following: [12]

	South	Non-South
1. Per cent income from agriculture, 1947	17.2	7.8
Per cent income from manufacturing, 1947	14.8	23.9

2. The majority of industrial production workers in the South were in low-paying industries — e.g., 27.4 per cent in textiles; 14.8 per cent in lumber and products; 10 per cent in food and products; and 6.4 per cent in apparel.

The Department of Labor well summarizes the problem:

> The low-wage level of the South is accounted for in large measure by the predominance of agriculture and the relatively large supply of unskilled labor competing for jobs in comparatively few industries. Other important factors include large population relative to employment opportunities, decentralization of industry, comparative lack of unionization, and limited degree of protective-labor legislation by the States.[13]

In response to the higher incomes to be obtained elsewhere, people have been moving out of the South in large numbers. As early as 1850 several states were losing population in this way, and since 1880 all Southern states except Louisiana and Florida have lost.[14] Yet despite large importations of capital the movements have not been adequate to equalize incomes.[15] In part differences persist because migration is not sufficient to offset the great natural increase. Both because the South is substantially rural and because of the large non-white population, birth rates are high. With only about 27 per cent of the nation's population, the South accounted for 59 per cent of the natural increase in the years 1940–1947. Southern families have 1.5 children under 18 years of age as against 1 or less

---

[11] H. E. Klarman, National Bureau of Economic Research, *Studies in Income and Wealth*, VI (1943), 207–231. Cf. H. M. Oliver, "Income, Region, Community Size and Color," *Quarterly Journal of Economics* (August 1946), pp. 588–598.

[12] *Economy of the South*, p. 19; Hoover and Ratchford, *Economic Resources and Policies of the South*, p. 126.

[13] *Labor in the South*, B.L.S. Bulletin No. 898 (1947), p. 69.

[14] Vance, *All These People*, pp. 110–111.

[15] *Economy of the South*, p. 27, and *Why Industry Moves South*, pp. 96–97.

in other regions.[16] The excess of births furnishes large numbers of migrants and is partly responsible for the cheap labor made available to factories.

Some aspects of Southern vital statistics follow: [17]

1. Population increases varied greatly among Southern states, with Texas and Florida accounting for the largest rises from 1940 to 1948, and these two states and Oklahoma from the years 1900 to 1940. Oklahoma, Arkansas, and Mississippi actually lost population in 1940–1948, whereas Florida, Texas, and Virginia gained 28.1, 14.9, and 13.9 per cent, respectively.

2. The Northeastern, Border, East North Central, and Pacific states have been the main beneficiaries of the Southern migration. On the basis of population statistics, the net migration was from New England to the South: in 1940, 64,360 born in the South lived in New England and 81,258 born in New England lived in the South. This is an interesting commentary on New England's contribution to Southern development.

3. In 1940, there were 4.72 millions born in the South (12 per cent of its population) living elsewhere and 2.08 millions from elsewhere living in the South — a net loss of 2.64 millions.

4. From 1930 to 1948, the South's net migration was especially large. The Southeast lost 3.3 millions, or about one-half of the natural increase. The West South Central lost 1.5 millions, or about two-fifths of the natural increase. The Pacific area, with net inward migration of 5 millions, was the major beneficiary — their gains roughly equaled the South's losses.

Writing in 1937, Professor Spengler, concerned over low standards of living and the large rural population, estimated a need for 860,000 additional manufacturing jobs in the South by 1950. He could scarcely have envisaged the gains actually made. From 1939 to 1947 the increase in manufacturing production workers alone was more than 700,000. (See footnote 10.)

4. THE SIGNIFICANCE OF SOUTHERN COMPETITION

In general, students of Southern industrialization view it as beneficial both to the South and the nation, and few would dissent from

[16] Odum and Jocher, ed., *The University of North Carolina Sesquicentennial Publications* (1945), p. 124.

[17] See the able discussions in Hoover and Ratchford, *Economic Resources and Policies of the South*, esp. chap. 2; and *Economy of the South*, p. 4.

this conclusion. McLaughlin and Robock conclude that the growth of local markets and the availability of resources account largely for the advance of the South; that of 88 new plants only 2–3 might have been established in New England; that the net effect of Southern development is a larger national output; and that even when New England suffered, as in textiles and shoes, the gains of the South allowed New England to expand in more productive industries.[18] Along with Hoover, Ratchford, and Van Sickle, Mc-Laughlin and Robock expect industrialization to raise the average income in the South, and to yield a more diversified economy.[19] They understress, however, the adjustment problem raised for the North.

The extent to which the rate of advance is accelerated by subsidies is, however, relevant to these conclusions. There seems to be some difference of opinion concerning the amount of help received by firms moving into the South. Many companies insist that they are not interested in subsidies, for communities offering aid restrict their freedom. That New England is greatly disturbed by tax and other concessions, is evident from the following statement of the Connecticut Development Commission in 1940:

The prime object of these state promotional efforts has been to attract new manufacturing enterprises, to stimulate travel trade, to induce new residence, and to enlarge demand for agricultural products. In a number of cases, well organized state planning programs have been incorporated with development activities. The net effect of these multiple promotional campaigns was to bring to bear upon the economic resources of Connecticut a series of competitive forces of most serious implication to the welfare of the people of this state.

It would be difficult to overstate the degree and intensity of this interstate economic struggle. Connecticut was absolutely defenseless against heavily financed and well organized state governmental agencies aggressively engaged not only in attempting to deflect from Connecticut the natural flow of new manufacturing enterprises but deliberately seeking to induce long established Connecticut concerns to relocate their operations in other states . . . "[20]

[18] *Why Industry Moves South*, pp. 122–124.
[19] Hoover and Ratchford, *Economic Resources*, pp. 366–367, and J. V. Van Sickle, *Planning for the South*, chap. iv.
[20] A. Lepawsky, *State Planning and Economic Development of the South* (1949), pp. 64–76, 145–146.

In the *Boston Globe* of June 11, 1951, Mr. John Harriman, its able financial writer, comments on a deal made by Textron with the city of Elizabethtown, Tennessee. The company is to receive a completely equipped plant, to employ 1000 workers, for an average outlay over 50 years of $187,500 in rentals. The taxes alone would amount to $390,000 in Massachusetts.

A problem similar to that raised by Southern industrialization can be seen in exaggerated form in Puerto Rico. Into this island, offering substantial subsidies and wages much lower than the South, there has been a movement of industry from the States. The Textron case publicized the unusual conditions in Puerto Rico, with free movement of capital and techniques out of the States and no tariff impediments. Why not produce at low wages in Puerto Rico and sell in the United States market? Favored by large subsidies, no local income tax for ten years or more, no United States tax on profits made there, favored also by a large reservoir of cheap labor (a minimum wage of 25 cents per hour in textiles, about one-quarter of the New England wage, and 15 cents for hand sewing), the Textron Company planned five new plants in Puerto Rico.[21]

The head of the Textile Workers of America commented thus on the Puerto Rican situation: "After the government stupidly in my opinion, buys the mills for them [Textron], builds them for them, exempts them from taxes, it will permit these products to come into this country and compete with our people." [22]

I have raised some questions about the rate of Southern industrialization. It may well be that the industrialization is taking place too rapidly from the national viewpoint and *a fortiori*, from New England's interest. Low costs in the South (and even more in Puerto Rico) reflect not only plentiful supplies of labor but also a depression of national standards of working conditions, social security, trade unionism, etc.

In the writer's view, it would be well not to accelerate the industrial advance of the South (or of Puerto Rico). One approach is to assure minimum working standards through federal legislation. Pres-

---

[21] Senate Hearings of Subcommittee of Committee on Interstate and Foreign Commerce, *Investigation of Closing of Nashua, N. H. Mills and Operations of Textron, Incorporated* (1948), II, 755–777.

[22] Hearings on *Textron*, I, 68.

sure from the South tends to slow up the great social advances of the Northeast and other regions. A recent tendency to set minimum wage standards through federal legislation is a step in the right direction. Yet, Professor Van Sickle is highly critical of this legislation on the grounds that the effect is to slow up the exodus of Southern workers from low-paying agricultural occupations into the more productive industrial occupations. Messrs. Hoover and Ratchford maintain, however, that setting wages under the Fair Labor Standards Act has not significantly interfered with employment in the South.[23]

Apparently, Professor Van Sickle would not object to minimum wages if they reflected regional differences in the cost of living. Actually, the differences in labor costs between South and North greatly exceed variations in the cost of living: in part, because of the larger supplies of labor in the South; in part, because of concentration in industries producing low-valued product; and, in part, because of the special privileges given industry by legislation or lack of it. There surely can be no objection to regional differences based on variations in the cost of living (but not on differences in the *standard* of living) or on the basis of productivity. Differences in labor costs associated with low standards of working conditions and social security are another matter.[24]

5. CONCLUSION

The South has every reason to industrialize, with its growing markets, availability of raw materials, and cheap labor. Other areas gain from the important advances of the South, as rich neighbors mean greater demands for output. But the South may be industrializing too rapidly. In so far as the advance springs from low standards of living and legislation, and *excessive* subsidies related to governmental policy, the South tends to capture an inordinate part of the nation's output and tends to stop social progress elsewhere. As migration continues and differences of income tend to disappear, the South's attraction as an industrial magnet will be reduced. But

---

[23] J. V. Van Sickle, *Planning for the South*, pp. 188–190; Hoover and Ratchford, *Economic Resources*, pp. 415–417.

[24] On social security, Hoover and Ratchford are wrong when they attribute smaller social security taxes in the South *only* to the lesser degree of industrialization, *Economic Resources*, p. 197.

the time of equality of incomes and the end of inward migration of capital and management and outward migration of people is still far off. New England's relations to the South are especially important; and despite the McLaughlin conclusions, the advantages of low labor costs for the South are especially important for New England's future; and the South's advances especially affect New England.

EXTERNAL RELATIONS OF THE NEW ENGLAND ECONOMY

INTRODUCTION

In Chapters 8–11 (Part II), we concentrate on the external relations of New England. We are especially interested in the manner of paying for the heavy imports of food and raw materials, in part reflected in an adverse trade balance, a perennial problem for the region; in the stake of New England in international trade; and in the relations of this area to the federal government. The problems are a little technical but should interest the lay reader and the economist.

One of the crucial problems of the New England economy is its great dependence on exports to other regions and countries. About one-half of the output of factory products is exported, especially textiles and shoes. The dependence on outside markets for 75 per cent or more of their output is one of the weaknesses of these industries. This intense competition at home strengthens the interest of New England in foreign markets. Professor Vining, in a pioneering study of regional economies, estimated that the typical state's primary or active (i.e., export) employment would be about 30 per cent.[1] Obviously for a region the typical figure would be smaller, since the region is more self-sufficient than the state. New England's exports, approximately 25–30 per cent of total output, seem to exceed those of the typical region.

Perhaps the most interesting aspect of New England's balance of payments is the relation of the region to the Treasury. That New England has suffered pressure on its balance of payments, as a result of an impaired competitive position, is suggested by the downward *relative* trend of deposits, bank reserves, wages, and prices. The tendency of the Treasury to take out of New England more than it puts in further weakens New England's interregional position. That, despite these drains, this region actually gained gold reserves over the last twenty years is associated with the large inflows into the country.

In general, New England's balance of payments raises questions concerning its competitive position, its attitude towards federal government, and its position on trade and tariff policies.

[1] R. Vining, "Location of Industry and Regional Patterns of Business-Cycle Behavior," *Econometrica* (January 1946), pp. 49–50.

CHAPTER 8

NEW ENGLAND'S BALANCING OF ACCOUNTS

1. THE BALANCING OF ACCOUNTS

A region, like a nation, exports and imports. Its exports consist of commodities as well as services. New England, for example, sells insurance services, education, recreational facilities (for example, summer hotel services), to residents from other regions and countries. For its sale of commodities and services, it receives dollars; in return on past investments outside of New England, it also receives interest payments and dividends in the form of dollars.

These are the major items in the current balance of payments. If current dollar receipts are less than current dollar disbursements, New England may balance its accounts by exporting gold or its equivalent (in its account with the Gold Settlement Fund in Washington), or (and) it may import capital, inclusive of repayment of capital previously invested outside. In recent years, New England has paid for an excess of commodity imports with net earnings on services, inclusive of earnings on capital, and imports of capital. Its adverse balance on current account has been aggravated by outward transfers on Treasury account. This area pays more into the Treasury than the Treasury disburses in this area. Over the last thirty years, however, the New England region has gained gold despite adverse balance on commodity and Treasury account, partly because of the enormous inward flow of gold into the country as a whole. The pressure on New England's balance of payments is reflected not in losses of gold but in a failure to attract as much gold as have other regions. In the forties, however, there were actual losses of gold from New England.

These interregional relations are of primary importance. A region must pay its bills. In comparison with international trade, interregional trade is of much greater importance. Whereas international trade is of the order of 1/20 of the income of the nation, trade between New England and other regions amounts to about one-quarter of its income.

While, over the short run, an adverse balance may be met by releasing monetary reserves, each area tries to maintain its competitive position by keeping relative costs and prices down and by introducing new products and services. The increasing tendency to determine wage rates and prices on a national basis deprives the region of one of its strongest defenses, reduction of costs. (One may well imagine the difficulties that would confront Great Britain, if, for example, her wage rates were determined by international decision.) The region is under an additional handicap, namely, that it cannot resort to *all* the protectionist devices open to a nation when confronted with an adverse balance of payments: exchange depreciation, exchange control, tariffs, quotas. A region cannot so neatly turn off its adverse conditions which come in the form of reduced demand and increased unemployment.

On one score, the region is at an advantage. The United States Treasury may step in and redress unfavorable balances. Intervention by the federal government is, however, likely to take place only when a major disaster has occurred — e.g., the agriculture debacle of the early thirties. Continued help is offered to the low-income and debtor areas, but is not usually available to older regions suffering from economic arteriosclerosis.

In this connection, the reader should consult the Hearings on the RFC.[1] In the course of these hearings, which were concerned largely with loans made by the RFC to business concerns, Senator Fulbright was eloquent on the favorable economic conditions in New England and the weakness of their claims on the Treasury. In fact he went further, to stress the fact that New England had exploited the rest of the country. Inquiring where the accumulation of New England's capital came from, the Senator said:

> . . . Over the years, there has been a vast accumulation of capital much greater than taken out. There are few natural resources in New England. Most of the benefit of the oil and bauxite and the wood and everything

[1] Hearings of Subcommittee of the Committee on Banking and Currency of the United States Senate on the *Study of the Reconstruction Finance Corporation.*

else of the South until very recently — I agree with you until very recently — has accrued to the benefit of New England, New York, and Philadelphia.[2]

. . . . .

. . . But the statistics will show that the per capita income of Massachusetts and Connecticut is far above the national average. As a matter of fact, Connecticut's per capita income is more than twice what it is in Arkansas.

Because the wealthiest area happens to have a slight recession, I do not know that this is an excuse for pouring money in . . .

. . . . .

That is the richest part of the United States. There are worlds of capital in Boston . . .

. . . . .

New England has been exploiting the Southwest of this country for 150 years. They have practically drawn all the capital from these areas into Boston. I see no public interest to help pouring it all back, if we are going to be frank about it. It is not a distressed area compared to Arkansas and Alabama and Mississippi today. I do not think that is a good reason . . .

. . . . .

But it is hard for me to believe that Connecticut and Massachusetts are in such terrible condition up there. They may not have quite the same control of the rest of the country that they had years ago when they had it by the neck; that is true. There has been a slight loosening of the throttle hold they had. But I don't think it is the RFC's duty to try to perpetuate that.[3]

2. SYMPTOMS OF DETERIORATION

A highly productive region with a good market for its products and in a strong bargaining position will tend to accumulate increasing shares of the country's bank deposits (cash); and its regional central bank will tend to attract increasing proportions of gold reserves. A decline in the region's share of deposits and gold, on the contrary, suggests a relative deterioration.

In 1914, the bank deposits of the six New England states accounted for 9.1 per cent of the country's deposits; in 1929, for 7.8

[2] Hearings, *Study of the Reconstruction Corporation*, p. 328.
[3] Hearings, pp. 321–322.

per cent; in 1941, for only 6.7 per cent. Over the period 1920 to 1941, reserves of the twelve reserve banks in the country rose by 8 times; those of the Federal Reserve Bank of Boston, which serves most of New England, rose by only 4½ times.[4] Of course, these results have also been affected to some extent by Federal Reserve open-market operations, but the net over-all movement of deposits from 1914 to 1941 is unmistakable, and it points to a relative decline for New England.

An examination of the figures on deposits in reporting banks and in reserve banks (largely reserves of member banks) for the forties reveals a continued downward trend in the relative importance of the New England area; for its share on several indices is from 4 to 5 per cent of the nation's total. A striking fact is that from 1941 to November 1950 the gold held by all Federal Reserve banks rose by about $850 million, or 3 per cent, but Boston's (New England's) gold holdings declined by $350 million, its share of the total falling from 5⅔ per cent to less than 4 per cent.[5] According to the October, 1951 *Monthly Review* of the Boston Reserve Bank, the region lost $162 million additional in the first 8 months of 1951.

As pressure on the balance of payments is felt, the resulting loss of cash and deposits is reflected in relative declines in prices. The pressure on the New England economy is illustrated by the fact that from 1935–1939 to October 1946 the cost of food at retail rose by 110.2 per cent in three Southern cities and 91.8 per cent in Boston.

3. TERMS OF TRADE

An area's interregional position depends in part on relative selling and buying prices just as a businessman's position is related to a comparison of his buying and selling prices. That is why we now turn to the terms of trade, or the ratio of a region's export and import prices. That relationship in a base year, obtained by comparing these prices, properly weighted, is designated by 100.

What is the significance of this relationship? It gives the exchange rates of a region's exports for its imports. Should the terms of trade,

[4] The last slightly overstates New England's relative decline, since Fairfield County, Connecticut (with 16 banks) was taken from the Boston Federal Reserve District in 1916.

[5] All figures from Federal Reserve, *Banking and Monetary Statistics* (1943), and *Federal Reserve Bulletin*.

that is, import prices divided by export prices, decline from 100 to 50, that would suggest New England was receiving twice as much as in the base year for a given quantity of exports. Or should this ratio rise to 200, this would mean that New England had to export twice as much to pay for a given quantity of imports. A 100 per cent increase in import prices would cost about $1 billion a year, or 7 per cent of the region's income. A change in the terms of trade can have many causes.

For example, a decline in export prices may result from oversupply or saturated markets for one of New England's major industries — e.g., textiles; or it may be a federal policy — e.g., farm — which raises the prices of New England imports; or a rise of productivity in some New England industries which is reflected in lower prices. The first two may be considered adverse factors; the last, favorable.

4. RECENT HISTORY OF THE TERMS OF TRADE

In the depression period, New England's terms of trade improved substantially. This is to be explained largely by the relative decline in the prices of raw materials and food. Thus, Dr. Hartland finds an improvement from 100 in 1929 (import prices divided by export prices) to 92.7 in 1931 and 86.2 in 1933. It is important to emphasize the fact that much depends on the prices of farm products. The net adverse balance of New England with the rest of the country in 1939 was $985 million. Of this amount, $758 million was paid for agricultural products and $187 million for products of mines and forests.[6] The decline of import prices relative to exports was indeed a windfall for New England in the thirties.

We can estimate the terms of trade roughly for later periods by observing the movement of farmers' parity (*Ratio of Prices Received to Prices Paid — 1910–14 = 100*):

1929	92
1932	58
1939	77
1946	113
1950	100
Dec. 1950	108

Source: Economic Report of the President, January 1951, p. 195.

[6] P. C. Hartland, *Balance of Interregional Payments of New England* (1950), pp. 9, 37.

A deterioration in New England's terms of trade is suggested by the increased ratio of prices received over prices paid by farmers. The former very *roughly* corresponds to what New England buys and the latter to what it sells. The rise from 58 in 1932 to 77 in 1939 and 113 in 1946 reflects the large price increases in raw materials and food. Primarily these are the result of recovery and war; but government policy undoubtedly was important. Although the rise in parity was very costly to New England, 1932 farm prices were at record low levels and the *industrial* areas could not expect such good fortune permanently.

It is not easy to estimate the cost of higher relative import prices, in part because interregional trade figures are only roughly accurate. Yet the cost of adverse movements of the terms of trade (from trough to peak) may well be a billion dollars or more yearly, or as much as 7–10 per cent of the income of the region on the following assumptions:

1. That the prices of what the farmers buy and sell are a rough index of New England export and import prices.

2. That the adverse trade balance of New England in the forties is given by Dr. Hartland's estimate of the adverse balance in 1939 corrected by price changes.

3. That exports of New England are primarily manufactured goods and amount to a minimum of $3 billion – as estimated later in the text.

4. That exports and imports of manufactures are roughly in balance as they seem to have been in the thirties.

On these premises, an adverse balance of roughly $2 billion (almost exclusively agricultural) would cost the region about $1.5 billion more than this excess would have cost in 1932. (Prices received by farmers in late 1950 were four times as high as in 1932.) This estimate does not include an allowance for a quantity rise of imports.

In fact the actual cost is probably nearer $1 billion than $1.5 billion, since terms of trade do not seem to fluctuate as widely as prices received and paid by farmers. (Processed food and raw materials rise less than the unprocessed.)

5. GENERAL PRICE INDICES AND THE TERMS OF TRADE

Price movements are also suggestive of the changes in the terms of trade.

A. Consumer Prices, 1929, 1939, 1948 (1935–39 = 100)

	All Items	Food	Apparel	House Furnish-ings	Rent	Fuel, etc.	Miscel-laneous
1929	122.5	132.5	115.3	111.7	141.4	112.5	104.6
1939	99.4	95.2	100.5	101.3	104.3	99.0	100.7
1948	171.2	210.2	198.0	195.8	117.4	133.9	149.9

Source: Bureau of Labor Statistics

1. In food — largely an import item — the rise has been substantial.

2. In apparel and house furnishings there has also been a substantial rise. The major items included are exported by New England, which points to favorable terms of trade.

3. Fuel is almost exclusively an import item — and here the region gains because the price rise was only moderate.

4. Rents (a decline in prices) is a local commodity, which does not affect the terms of trade.

5. Miscellaneous is also largely local, including numerous services.

In general, this breakdown does not suggest serious deterioration in the terms of trade; but since the index is for finished goods and services, the high prices for raw materials are frequently concealed. A comparison of prices for raw material and finished goods points to a much greater deterioration for New England than does the table above. Furthermore, as noted earlier, the significant fact is the rise in prices of raw materials and food, since the adverse balance is largely in these items.

At wholesale levels the rise of food prices stands out, and there is no evidence of a decline in prices of hides, leather and leather products (or in shoes), and of textile products. These have risen about as much as *all* wholesale prices from 1929 to 1949. At least a relative reduction of sales has not been accompanied by a deterioration in selling prices. One may suggest, of course, that the high price level has jeopardized sales. In cotton textiles, the price rise has been 200 per cent from 1939 to 1947, as compared with a rise of less than 100 per cent for all commodities. But prices of woolens and worsteds may well reflect declining demand, for their prices rose by but 60 per cent from 1939 to 1947.

CHAPTER 9

THE BALANCE OF PAYMENTS OF NEW ENGLAND, PREWAR AND POSTWAR

1. PREWAR

Here we rely largely on Dr. Hartland's study, which covers the period 1929–1939.

The reader will note the following:

1. In each year considered, the adverse balance on trade account, i.e., the excess of New England imports from other regions and abroad over New England exports was more than $1 billion. In 1939, the figure was $1306 million (inclusive of freight and shipping); the six-year average for alternate years from 1929 to 1939 was $1230 million.

2. How was this adverse balance met? The major factors may be suggested by the plus or credit items in the 1939 column. (These are all net, that is, the excess of receipts over disbursements.)

		$ Million
a.	Gross capital account and residual	685
b.	Interest, dividends, net rents, and royalties	502
c.	Insurance	297
d.	Recreation and travel	93
e.	Gold outflow due to government account	80
		1,657

According to this study, the adverse balance is met primarily by an inflow of capital (inclusive of repayment of past loans), and earnings on past investments.

The total of the plus items greatly exceeds the $1306 million adverse balance on trade account. The importance of insurance, travel, and recreation, and the unimportance of education as an export service, despite New England's eminence in education, are worthy of note.

444819

Balance of Interregional Payments of New England ª (Millions of dollars)

	1929	1931	1933	1935	1937	1939
Current Account						
Commodity trade	−1,032.1	−909.9	−871.3	−1,121.1	−1,329.8	−1,122.2
Freight and shipping	−217.1	−164.8	−130.2	−141.9	−166.8	−184.4
Total Balance of Trade	−1,249.2	−1,074.7	−1,001.5	−1,263.0	−1,496.6	−1,306.6
Recreation	+136.2	+52.4	−11.0	+60.7	+135.7	+95.8
Passenger transportation	−4.8	−3.5	−2.0	−1.6	−2.3	−2.5
Total Travel Account	+131.4	+48.9	−13.0	+59.1	+143.9	+93.3
Insurance	+196.1	+160.8	+75.4	+260.1	+310.0	+297.1
Education	+13.6	+11.8	+10.4	+9.9	+10.5	+9.9
Interest, dividends, net rents and royalties	+239.0	+609.0	+482.0	+493.0	+555.0	+502.0
Current account excluding balance of trade	+580.1	+830.5	+554.8	+822.1	+1,008.9	+902.3
Net current account	−669.1	−244.2	−446.7	−440.9	−487.7	−404.3
Gold and currency						
Federal Reserve notes	+14.0	+13.9	+16.4	+11.5	+14.1	+12.0
Gold inflow due to commercial & financial transactions	−95.2	−145.7	−182.6	−193.0	−177.9	−292.6
Gross gold movement	−81.2	−131.8	−166.2	−181.5	−163.8	−280.6
Gold outflow due to Government account	+49.7	+129.2	+171.3	+85.5	+214.0	+80.0
Net gold movement	−31.5	−2.6	+5.1	−96.0	+50.2	−200.6
Capital Account and Residual						
Interbank deposits	+18.1	−46.2	−14.2	−36.1	−2.1	−15.0
Federal Reserve Foreign Acct.	−0.1	+4.7	−1.3	+0.7	+5.3	+14.9
Treasury transfers	−49.7	−129.2	−171.3	−85.5	−214.0	−80.0
Gross capital movement and residual	+732.3	+417.5	+628.4	+657.8	+648.3	+685.0
Net Capital Account and Residual	+700.6	+246.8	+441.6	+536.9	+437.5	+604.9

ª A plus sign indicates a net import; a minus sign a net export. To avoid confusion, it should be stressed that a plus or minus sign indicates the direction of the flow of funds resulting from any given transaction. Thus, a plus sign indicates that funds are moving into New England (as a result of transactions in insurance, for example, or as a result of capital movements); a minus sign that funds are moving out of the region (for imports of commodities, in general also to pay for imports of gold). Thus, an "import" of capital (borrowing, say, to a greater extent than

3. An item of substantial importance is the inflow of gold due to commercial and financial transactions. Since the region has to pay for this gold, this item ($281 million) is an offset to credit items. Imports of gold have to be paid for just as imports of commodities have to be paid for.

4. The balance may be summarized as follows: Against an adverse balance on trade account of $1306 million, there were credit items on investment and rental income and services of $902 million. The remainder was covered by an inflow of capital, the latter also offsetting a large inflow of gold.

A reading of Dr. Hartland's book will suggest the difficulties of obtaining a regional balance of payments and will also underline the ingenious use of material made by Dr. Hartland. Nevertheless, as Dr. Hartland would readily agree, the figures are subject to a large measure of error. In this connection, it should be noted that the inflow of capital is obtained by the residual method, and is accurate only in so far as errors (not offset by errors in the opposite direction) in other items do not persist.

One may be particularly puzzled by the substantial inflow of capital in these years. For an area which in the past developed the South and West and which even today exports capital to build up competitive areas, the inflow is of surprising magnitude. The importation of funds by investment trusts, in turn in part invested here, the development of branch plants of large corporations domiciled elsewhere, the growth of new industries at the expense of the Middle Atlantic States, the purchase of summer homes in this area, and the import of capital from abroad — all of these are undoubtedly relevant.

2. POSTWAR

On the basis of crude estimates, we can draw up the main items in New England's balance of payments for 1949.

First, there was the adverse trade balance of $1306 million in 1939. Since the excess of imports over exports is primarily in farm products and foods, the $1306 million may be inflated by the average rise, of 142 per cent, in wholesale prices of farm products and foods from 1939 to 1949. The adverse balance then becomes $3160 million for 1949. Actually, since New England's income rose little more than 130 per cent, this is a generous estimate.

Exports (and hence imports) of manufactured products may be estimated at around $2850 millon in 1947. Total imports would then be about $6 billion, or more than 40 per cent of the region's income. This figure seems rather high, though many small countries with more diversification than New England have imports equal to 25 per cent of their national income. The manner of obtaining the estimate of exports is as follows:

1. In 1947 New England accounted for 6.82 per cent of the national income, and we assume that her consumption was 7 per cent of the nation's total.

2. When New England's *value added in manufacturing* exceeds 7 per cent of the nation's, the difference is assumed to be exported to other areas.

3. The estimated exports (value added by manufacture) from New England in 1947 was then $2850 million:

The Major Items	*$ Million*
Textiles	860
Leather and Leather Products	350
Machinery (except Electrical)	400
Miscellaneous Manufactures	300
Electrical Machinery	180
Fabricated Metal Products	170
Rubber Products	130

Second, the problem is how was the adverse balance of payments of $3160 in 1949 met?

	$ Million
1. Interest, dividends, net rents, and royalties	900
2. Insurance	525
3. Recreation and transportation	285
4. Capital inflow	2,000
	3,710

These figures are the 1939 estimates blown up: the rise of interest, dividends, net rents, and royalties is suggested by the growth of these incomes in the nation and in New England.

The insurance total is based upon New England's net insurance income from outside blown up by the percentage rise of life insurance income for the nation from 1939 to 1949.

Recreation outlays in the nation trebled from 1939 to 1949. A corresponding multiple is applied to net income of New England from recreation and transportation.

From 1939 to 1949, gross national investment rose from 10 to 33 billion dollars; and by 1950 to $48.5 billion. Since the inflow of capital into New England in 1939 was in part foreign capital, I have not increased the 1939 figures by the full rise of gross private investment.

Of course, these are the crudest of estimates. In so far as the 1939 figures are off, these for 1949 are erroneous. In addition, we assume that the net flow of income into New England from outside closely follows the national increase in rents, interest, dividends, insurance income, and outlays on recreation. The association of the increase in net inward movement of capital with the rise of total investment is also subject to error.

The excess of credits (despite a tendency to lose gold in the forties) over debits may be associated in part with government transactions which are discussed in the next chapter.[1]

[1] Income and recreation figures are from the Annual Income Number of the *Survey of Current Business*; New England figures on income and categories of income from the August issues of *Survey of Current Business*; insurance figures from *Life Insurance Fact Book* (1949); gross investment from the *Economic Report of the President* (January 1951).

The reader should also compare more refined estimates of New England exports of manufactured goods on p. 102.

CHAPTER 10

TREASURY DRAINS

1. THE INCREASED IMPORTANCE OF TREASURY DRAINS OUT OF NEW ENGLAND

One of the most controversial problems confronting New England leaders is the relation of this region to the federal government. As federal activities have extended and spending grown, cash transfers from one region to another have tended to rise. Since the early thirties, these activities have resulted in a flow of funds from industrial to agricultural areas; from the Northeast to the South and West; from the rich to the poor. This flow is revealed in the account of each region with the Treasury, fiscal agent for the federal government.

The Treasury obtains its cash from taxation and borrowing. Federal taxes contributed 44 per cent of all governmental receipts in 1939, 80 per cent in 1945, and 70 per cent in 1949. These funds have been obtained increasingly from taxes on income, private and business, and the result is to increase the burden on richer areas. Thus, whereas personal tax and nontax receipts and corporate taxes accounted for 25 per cent of all governmental receipts in 1939, they accounted for 60 per cent in 1945 and 52 per cent in 1949.[1]

Twenty years ago these drains from the richer areas were not matters of great importance. Thus, in 1929, per capita income in New England exceeded the nation's by $158, or 23 per cent; and direct net Treasury transfers were but $9 per capita, or 6 per cent of the excess of per capita income in New England over the nation's. By 1948, per capita income in New England was only $91 above the national average, and Treasury transfers amounted to $83, or 91 per cent of the excess. The net effect of these transfers has been to bring New England's per capita income down virtually to the national average.

[1] *Survey of Current Business*, July 1947 and July 1950 (calculated).

It is not surprising, then, that a clash occurs between those who insist the proper policy of New England is to spurn federal "handouts" and fight the encroachments of federal government and those who insist that an area which faces serious problems of adjustment should seek a fair share of the disbursements of the Treasury — e.g., why, when the federal government pumps cash into the Southeast for hydroelectric power, thus reducing costs for an area that is growing in part at New England's expense, should New England refuse such aid?

That net Treasury transfers from New England dropped from $760 million (6 per cent of the area's income) in 1948 to $239 million in 1949 reflects, I believe, an increased disposition to seek federal aid, particularly by the Commonwealth of Massachusetts. Preliminary figures for 1950 yield a net *inflow* of $62 million and a small inflow for the first eight months of 1951, a changeover related in part to New England's depression and Governor Dever's aggressive search for federal funds.

2. PAYMENTS AND RECEIPTS ON TREASURY ACCOUNT: NET TRANSFERS ANALYZED

The Boston Federal Reserve Bank, in an elaborate and valuable survey, has summarized the transfer of funds out of New England as a result of federal government activities as follows:

Transfers of Funds from New England as a Result of Activities of the Federal Government, 1929, 1940, 1948 ($Million)

	1948	1940	1929
(1) Net Treasury Transfers from Treasury General Account to Other F. R. Districts	760.0	170.0	49.7
Excess of Federal Taxes Shifted to N. E. Taxpayers over Federal Taxes in N. E. Shifted to Other Districts	216.7	53.2	34.5
	976.7	223.2	84.2
(2) Adjustments of Transfers — Interest Paid in N. Y. for Account of Various N. E. Interests, Redemption of Securities in N. Y.	100.0	33.0	7.3
	876.7	190.2	76.9
(3) Percentage of New England Income	6.9	3.1	1.1

Source: (1) and (2) Boston Federal Reserve Bank.
      (3) Calculated from (2) and **Survey of Current Business** (August 1949).

In 1948, total receipts of the federal government in New England were $2621 million, of which *taxes* accounted for $2477 million, or 18 per cent of the region's income. In 1929, the corresponding figure was only $236 million, or 3½ per cent of the region's income.

In 1948, New England received back $1785 million, or two-thirds of all *federal receipts (adjusted)* in the area. The remainder, $779 million, measures the net loss of the region on account of federal transactions. In 1929, total expenditures in the region by the federal government were $228 million, or 75 per cent of adjusted receipts.

The direct drains on a region resulting from Treasury transfers do not measure the entire cost of federal operations, for some taxes levied in one area are ultimately paid in others. For example, the heavy excise taxes on automobiles are largely levied on manufacturers in the Middle West but paid by consumers elsewhere.

The following table illustrates the problem: its data indicate that New England's tax payments are much less than its consumption, which is roughly 6.68 per cent of the national total. But this is because the table shows only payments made, for the most part, by producers, and relatively few are located in New England. The real burden includes tax payments which consumers in New England have made on behalf of producers elsewhere.

Per Cent of Taxes Paid by New England, Fiscal Year 1949

Alcohol taxes	2.26
Tobacco taxes	.09
Stamp taxes	3.80
Manufacturers' excise tax	3.28
Sugar tax	3.74
Transportation of property	3.73

Sources: U. S. Treasury Department, **Annual Report of the Commissioner of Internal Revenue, Fiscal 1949,** pp. 64–111; Survey of Current Business (August 1949), p. 9.

Any estimate of the additional burden is necessarily rough. Some taxes are not passed on to consumers, and it is not easy to calculate the incidence of taxes on pay rolls and corporation incomes. The classical theory holds that pay-roll taxes fall on the worker, in which case New England labor pays New England's pay-roll taxes. If the tax is shifted to consumers to any extent,[2] then New England, with relatively heavy pay-roll taxes, passes on part of its burden to

[2] See Part III of my *Economics of Social Security*, where I discuss this problem at length.

other regions. Corporation income taxes may be shifted when business is not charging what the traffic will bear. In an economy of large-scale enterprise and particularly in very prosperous times, an increase in corporation income taxes often results in higher prices.

In view of the difficulties raised by the application of the theory of tax incidence, the Federal Reserve estimate of the net burden in New England, that is, the excess of taxes shifted to New England over taxes shifted to other areas, can be accepted only with substantial reservations. The first table of this chapter shows this item at $34 millions in 1929, $53 millions in 1940, and $217 millions in 1948.

I have used another approach to this problem by adjusting per capita income for various taxes paid:

1. In a year in the forties, the three Southern New England states, which account for about 85 per cent of the region's income, paid federal income taxes equal to 13.2 per cent of the per capita income; the corresponding percentage for the United States was 10.6 per cent and for Northern New England, 7.8 per cent. It is clear that federal income taxes were much heavier on part of New England than on the nation generally.[3]

2. A similar analysis for the reduction of per capita income resulting from federal taxes, exclusive of the corporate tax, yields heavier inroads on New England's income. Thus the average for Southern New England was close to 20 per cent; for the United States, 17 per cent.

For all federal taxes, the results for a year in the forties were:

Percentage Reduction of State Per Capita Income Resulting from Federal Taxes (Two Alternative Estimates)

	U. S. Average	3 Southern New England States	3 Northern New England States
1.	25.3	29.3	22.9
2.	25.3	33.0	24.2

On the basis of an average of Rows 1 and 2, the cost of federal taxes to Southern New England (at present incomes) was about $100 per capita more than for the country generally and for North-

[3] This material is based on a Report of the Treasury Committee on *Intergovernmental Fiscal Relations*.

ern New England about 20–25 dollars less. For all of New England, the cost of federal taxes exceeds the national average by about $75 per capita, or close to the excess of New England's per capita income over the nation's.

Next, payments to the federal government must be analyzed in terms of investment, for transfers result not only from tax payments but also from the net increase in government securities held within the region. Total transit clearings reflect the current balance of payments, and a net transfer to a region's account reflects an excess of (1) exports, exported services, and capital inflow over (2) imports, imported services, and capital outflow. Included in the outflow of capital is New England's investment in securities, both private and public.

By adding the gold flow, the inter-reserve bank transfers (reflecting transfers to Treasury account), and Federal Reserve Note Clearings, we obtain the total transit clearings, which in the thirties amounted to $1874 million:

	$ Million
Inter-Reserve Bank Transfers	1,223
Inflow of Gold	505
Redemption of Federal Reserve Notes (net)	146
	1,874

Gold flows into the country during this period were large, and New England was able to transfer large sums via the Treasury and yet increase holdings of government securities. The increase in bank-held government securities during the period was $1236 million, an amount roughly equal to the losses on Treasury account.

From that angle the cost of Treasury transfers does not seem to have been serious. But we would have to know the net amount of purchases of government securities by all New Englanders (not merely by banks) to estimate the relationship of outward drains on Treasury account to the purchases of government securities. Had total purchases during these years been equivalent to the ratio of New England's income to national income, then New England would have increased its holdings of government securities by roughly $1800 million. Actually, because government securities were heavily bought by trust funds and other financial institutions in New York, New England's share might have been somewhat less than this sum.

Treasury transfers are, primarily, equalizing accounts, strengthening the low-income areas or those suffering from adverse payments balances. If funds are drained out of one area, the banks find their reserves reduced, and they sell securities in order to recoup them. Hence, the Treasury transfers may reflect favorable balance of payments or they may induce sales of government securities.

The data given above may be interpreted to mean that the adverse balance on Treasury account during the thirties resulted from heavy purchases of government securities — that is, from increases in investment rather than from drains by taxation. Investment certainly increased also during the war years (Treasury transfers averaged, annually, $1765 million from 1942 to 1945). But also during the forties New England lost gold, in the amount of $350 million, while gold reserves elsewhere in the country were increasing. This reversal of the gold inflow of the thirties ($505 million was gained, net) certainly reflects a burden on New England's balance of payments from transfers to Treasury, rather than increased investment. Finally, increased investment cannot be the whole explanation for the years 1946–1948, when the national debt declined by $25 billion. And our analysis, in previous pages, of New England's tax burden leads us to conclude that the enormous increase of Treasury transfers (from 3 per cent of the region's income in 1940 to almost 7 per cent in 1948) represents a substantial drain, not merely increased investment. Had Treasury receipts in New England been pumped back into the area, the size of the Treasury transfers would surely have been smaller.

3. PAYMENTS OF FEDERAL GOVERNMENT

General Remarks. New England states do not receive as much from federal government disbursements as might be suggested by income relative to total United States income. They do not benefit even in proportion to their relative population.

This broad generalization applies to grants of the federal government, to federal assistance generally, to outlays on public works, to defense expenditures, to disbursements of lending agencies, to civilian pay rolls, and even to benefit payments of the Veterans Administration. Perhaps the only important exceptions are the federal payments for Old Age and Survivor's Insurance and administration of unemployment compensation. It might be expected that social security benefits would be disproportionately high in the industrial states where coverage is *relatively high.* Since these outlays on social security are tied to the pay roll taxes collected in the beneficiary states, the relatively favorable position of New England states in this area of disbursements is not particularly significant because transfers are not involved.

In some classes of outlays, Northern New England fares better than Southern New England. This is particularly true in outlays for public works, resource development, hospital construction, agricultural supports, and the like. The lower density of population, the greater recourse to agriculture, and the lower per capita income largely explain the more favorable record of Northern New England. But since the three Southern states account for 85 per cent of the income and 80 per cent of the population (but only 22 per cent of the area), the greater benefits realized by Northern New England offset the relative "discrimination" suffered by Southern New England only in small part.

A statistical summary of this position is shown in the accompanying table.

This table points up several conclusions, several of which have already been suggested.

1. Federal disbursements in New England are relatively small as compared with the percentage of New England's population and income to the nation's total. Note especially the important columns (3), (4), (5), (6).

2. New England's participation is especially small in ascending order:

	%
Commodity Credit Corporation, Disbursements	(0.80)
Public Works Disbursements	(1.05)
Reconstruction Finance Corporation, Loans	(1.52)
Civilian Pay Rolls	(5.03)

Compare these with New England percentage of income payments (6.68) and population (6.26).

New England and Individual States in New England — Percentage of Incomes, Population, and Various Disbursements by Federal Government and Amount of Disbursements, 1948, 1949, or 1950

	(1) Per Cent U.S. Income Payments 1948	(2) Per Cent U.S. Population 1948	(3) Federal Income Payments 1948	(4) All Aid Payments Individuals 1949	(5) Federal Budget Expenditures for Veterans and Benefits, V.A.	(6) Civilian Pay Rolls 1949	(7) Grants 1949	(8) Public Works 1950	(9) Loans R.F.C. 1949	(10) Disbursements C.C.C. 1948	(11) Old Age and Survivor's Insurance 1949
Total Federal Outlay $ Million			15,923	3,639	6,195	6,042	1,817	1,719	611	2,169	624
New England States % of Total	6.68	6.26	5.90	5.75	6.31	5.03	5.76	1.05	1.52	0.80	10.19
Southern											
Connecticut	1.64	1.36	0.97	1.02	1.08	0.59	0.83	0.22	...	Neg.	2.25
Massachusetts	3.40	3.17	3.25	2.98	3.53	2.88	2.96	0.36	...	Neg.	5.31
Rhode Island	0.57	0.51	0.62	0.60	0.59	0.58	0.49	0.03	...	Neg.	0.93
Northern											
Maine	0.53	0.61	0.58	0.52	0.55	0.66	0.61	0.08	...	0.78	0.86
New Hampshire	0.32	0.36	0.28	0.34	0.31	0.16	0.38	0.29	...	Neg.	0.56
Vermont	0.22	0.25	0.19	0.28	0.25	0.16	0.49	0.08	...	Neg.	0.29

Sources: Survey of Current Business (August 1949), p. 9; Annual Report of the Commissioner of Internal Revenue, Fiscal Year 1949 p. 110; U. S. Bureau of the Budget, Division of Fiscal Analysis, Memorandum of February 23, 1950, Federal Grants-in-Aid and Shared Revenues, Fiscal Years 1949 and 1950; ibid., February 24, 1950. Expenditures for Direct Public Works, Civil and Defense, By States or Other Area and Function, Fiscal Years 1949 and 1950; ibid., Estimated Expenditures from Major Trust Accounts, Fiscal Years, 1949 and 1950; ibid., Estimated Budget Expenditures for Veterans Services and Benefits, By States, Fiscal Year 1949; ibid., June 1, 1950, Estimated Expenditures for Payrolls of Civilian Employees Serving the New England States, Period 1949; Department of Commerce, Enclosure 183436 (1950).

3. Northern New England fares somewhat better than Southern New England in obtaining federal funds.

4. Especially striking is the poor record of Connecticut. Compare Massachusetts and Connecticut:

Massachusetts and Connecticut: Percentage of Income Payments and Percentage of Federal Disbursements, 1948, 1949, or 1950

	% Income Payments	% of Federal Income Payments	% Col. (2) of Col. (1)	% of Federal All Aid Payments	% Col. (4) of Col. (1)	Veterans Admin. Payments	% Col. (6) of Col. (1)	Civilian Pay Rolls	% Col. (8) to Col. (1)
	(1)	(2)	(3)	(4)	(5)	(6)	(7)	(8)	(9)
Conn.	1.64	0.97	58	1.02	62	1.08	65	0.59	36
Mass.	3.40	3.25	96	2.98	88	3.53	104	2.88	85

Source: Based on preceding table.

The reader will observe that in these important areas of federal disbursements, Massachusetts receives relatively from about ½ to 1⅓ times more relative to the state's income payments than Connecticut. Connecticut's receipts for federal public assistance are also much less than is reflected by her related income or population. In Massachusetts, assistance payments exceed the Connecticut level relative to population and income.

	(1) Grants-in-Aid to States $ Million	(2) Total Federal Revenues Collected in State $ Million	(3) Ratio of Grants to U.S. Revenue
Vermont	6.9	37.1	19
Maine	14.0	105.9	13
New Hampshire	7.3	68.8	11
Massachusetts	63.3	1,127.6	7
Rhode Island	9.7	183.8	5
Connecticut	20.0	592.9	3
All New England States	121.2	2,116.1	6

Source: Senate Committee on Expenditures.

In a report for the fiscal year ending June 30, 1950 (*New York Times*, February 26, 1951), the Senate Expenditures Committee published grants made by the United States Government as a percentage of federal revenues collected in the state. For reasons already suggested, the latter, of course, does not measure accurately the burden of the federal taxes on each state. Yet the results are interesting.

The ratio of grants-in-aid to states to federal taxes collected varies from 38 per cent in Mississippi to 1 per cent in Delaware. In general, the agricultural states receive much larger grants relative to collections than the industrial states. The figures for the New England states are presented on page 112.

4. CONCLUSION

The receipts of the Treasury in New England exceed its payments, with the result that per capita incomes are roughly equalized as between New England and the country. This conclusion may, however, be misleading in so far as federal receipts represent investments by New England in federal securities rather than tax payments. At any rate, an examination of the net outward movement on Treasury account in the last twenty years indicates unmistakably that these transactions are now far more significant for the New England economy than in the twenties. In 1949, however, the Treasury drain declined greatly, and in 1950 there may have been an inflow.

The total net drain includes not merely the excess of Treasury receipts over payments in New England, but also the excess of taxes actually *paid* by New England over those *collected* in New England. When allowance is made for this tax burden (in contrast with the distribution of initial payments of these taxes), then a further drain out of New England is revealed. As mentioned earlier, however, the results are subject to a large margin of error.

It is clear that more goes out than comes in on Treasury account. How does New England pay its treasury accounts net? In part by paying out gold. In the forties, this factor seems to have been important. In part by exchanging claims on the large inward flows of gold from abroad. Hence in the years 1933–1939 large inflows of gold were compatible with substantial net payments to the Treasury, for New England could exchange part of the gold that otherwise could have been credited to her account. In part the financial institutions met the bill by selling government securities and thus obtaining dollars. Actually, over the last twenty years, New England has increased its investments in government securities and added to its gold supplies (except for gold losses in the forties) despite drains on Treasury account. Its net balance on transit account (the *excess* of exports, export services, and capital inflow *over* imports, import services and capital outflow inclusive of purchase of government securities) was adequate to finance large Treasury drains and pay for substantial gold inflows.

These drains on Treasury account raise fundamental issues. Should New England agitate against increasing federal government activities in order to save its dollars? Or should New England demand a fair share of the dollars spent? Since problems of adjustment are serious, New England might, for example, demand more federal outlays for social security programs — e.g., subsidies for federal unemployment insurance and liberalization of old-age insurance. New England might also be more receptive to outlays on multiple-purpose river development.

Whatever its interests, it is clear that New England's receipts from federal programs have been disproportionately low. Even in the advances of the RFC, on which it might be expected that a "distress" area might have had special claims, and despite the large publicity given to RFC loans in New England, the region's receipts were much below its share of income and, *a fortiori*, of manufacturing income. The benefits obtained from federal disbursements also varied from state to state: Northern New England, with large areas and relatively low incomes, profited more than Southern New England; and Connecticut, too proud to tap a federal government and particularly a Democratic administration, accepted relatively little from the federal government. Massachusetts was much more receptive.

CHAPTER 11

NEW ENGLAND'S STAKE IN INTERNATIONAL TRADE

1. THE MAGNITUDE OF THE PROBLEM

Exports of 10 to 15 billion dollars per year are an important factor in the American economy. Even though exports are subsidized through foreign grants and loans (e.g., foreigners pay with dollars provided by our government) and pushed through direct subsidies (e.g., sales of cotton below costs), they were only about 5 per cent of the gross national product in the years 1947–1950 as compared with 8–9 per cent in the twenties.

Yet New England has a large stake in this trade. First, because this region is a manufacturing area, and manufactured goods play an increasing part in the exports of the United States — thus from 1851–1860 to 1926–1930, exports of semimanufactured and manufactured goods rose by 71 and 74 times, respectively, whereas exports of crude materials and crude foodstuffs rose by only 8 and 20 times, respectively.[1] From 1936–1938 (annual average) to 1949, the export of finished manufactures rose from $358 million to $1641 million, or from 49 to 55 per cent of all exports.[2]

New England needs markets not only to pay for its imports of raw materials and food but also to pay for its large imports of manufactured goods. Furthermore, in so far as she penetrates foreign markets, the loss of interregional competitive power is offset.

Unfortunately we do not know the contribution of New England to the nation's export trade. In 1928, replies to a questionnaire suggested that New England's exports were $200 million, or 3 per cent of the region's income. Since the exports of the nation were then 9 per cent of the national income, the 3 per cent estimate seems too low.

[1] S. E. Harris, *Foreign Aid and Our Economy* (1950), p. 59.
[2] *The Economic Report of the President* (January 1951), p. 213.

The fact is that a questionnaire directed to New England's businessmen could not elicit correct answers, for they do not have the required information. It is necessary to adjust exports from New England for imports of raw and processed materials which are embodied in New England's exports; and, of course, to add to New England's exports its contribution to the exports of other areas — e.g., through the machine tools exported to the automobile industry of the Middle West, the textile machinery to the Southern textile industry, the instruments to the West Coast aviation industry, the cloth to the Middle Atlantic apparel industry. We surely need more studies of these cross-currents.

But let us note that if New England's exports were as large relative to income as the nation's in 1949, then its exports would have been $756 million (5.7 per cent of the $13.3 billion of income). (Note that these are merely exports abroad, not to other regions as in the previous chapter.) With manufactured products of *all* kinds about 75 per cent of total exports, and with manufacturing pay rolls in New England exceeding the national average by one-third, an estimate of $1 billion of exports from the region is probably not far out of the way. In 1949, New England accounted for one-tenth of the total employment in manufacturing, and manufactured exports of all kinds were roughly $10 billion. Again, by applying ratios, New England's exports seem to be around $1 billion. Exports for the nation were one-sixth of manufacturing output. A similar proportion for New England yields $1 billion of exports.

The reader should note that with exports of manufactured goods at $1 billion, New England's exports abroad are about one-third of its total exports (international and interregional); they account for about 7 per cent of its total income and perhaps one-sixth of total manufacturing output. All exports, to foreign countries and to other regions in the United States, may well account for more than one-half of its output of manufactured goods.

2. ISSUES OF POLICY

In the last twenty years New England has undoubtedly suffered from federal policies which have tended to reduce the prices of manufactured goods and to raise those of agricultural commodities. Antitrust and particularly tariff policy have tended to depress prices of manufactured goods, or at least to moderate their rise. Since 1930, duties on *dutiable* commodities have been reduced from 52.8 to 15.3 per cent; on *all* commodities, the average duty has fallen from 17.7 to 6.0 per cent.

This policy of freer trade tends, of course, to increase the competition confronting New England manufacturers in domestic markets. In so far as increased imports lead to expanded exports, there may be no net loss; but in recent years the relation of exports and imports has not been too close.

On national grounds, there is a great deal to be said for the policies of freer trade. Tariffs should be reduced and trade should increase. Unfortunately, the long-run requirement to solve the problem of dollar shortage is not an increase of imports and a corresponding rise of exports, the objectives under the reciprocal trade agreements, but rather a rise of imports not countered by an increase of United States exports. Only in this manner can the outside world obtain its needed supply of dollars. As the war threat deepens, the case for additional imports becomes even stronger.

What should the attitude of New England businessmen be to the policy of encouraging imports? Surely not to take the protectionist line as New England has for generations.

The crude protectionist should note that the exports of textiles and most important manufactured goods exceed the import value. It is difficult to understand why the representatives of the cotton textile manufacturers should testify, before the Committee on Reciprocity (1950), that the way out of the dollar dilemma is to abandon foreign aid and cut exports. In most items of interest to New England, exports exceeded imports. Thus, in 1946, exports of cotton yarn were 17 million pounds; imports, ½ million pounds. Exports of cotton cloth were 775 million yards in 1946, imports 44 million yards; exports of metal-working machinery $160 million, imports $1 million. We gain more from exports than we are damaged by imports.

Nevertheless, an examination of the hearings on any tariff bill will reveal pressures on the part of New Engand manufacturers for higher tariffs, quotas, or opposition to concessions under reciprocal trade agreements. Thus, in 1947, the watch-manufacturing industry was especially vocal. Difficulties of the Waltham Watch Company largely inspired the opposition to importing Swiss watches. The case for import quotas did not seem strong, for the difficulties of

the Waltham Company were in no small part the result of inefficiency. Yet the heavy dependence on this industry by the workers
in Waltham suggested the need of temporary relief. Spokesmen for
the hat industry, where imports greatly exceeded exports, had a
stronger case. In one late prewar year, 65 per cent of the wage
earners in Danbury and 51 per cent in Norwalk were employed in
the manufacture of hats. In the face of heavy imports and the losses
resulting from change of fashions, a case might be made for tariff
relief to ease the exodus of workers from the industry. In woolens
the case was less strong, though here again there was concern over
a decline in employment because the industry faced increased wage
differentials in relation to foreign countries. Certainly the authorities
might move slowly in reducing barriers. The fisheries industry, confronted with increased imports from Canada, also was insistent on
strong protectionist measures; but here natural causes and monopolistic wage and price policies also seem to be relevant. The fishing
industry demanded too much.[3]

I believe that the correct position for New England to take would
be a support of the freer trade principle; but with the following
reservations:

1. Concessions should be made slowly in industries upon which
New England is greatly dependent and which are suffering from
over-all curtailment of demand or from migration out of New England. Particularly is this point relevant for commodities produced
in one-industry communities — e.g., wool in Lawrence. In other
words, the government should ease the transition by spreading
over long periods of time tariff reductions affecting depressed industries or areas; by concentrating reductions in periods of prosperity
rather than in depression; by reducing tariffs further in growing
industries; and by supplementing fiscal policy with positive actions
(1) to introduce new industries into areas affected adversely by
these policies and (2) to stimulate the outward movement of labor
from these areas.

2. Any reduction of tariffs on manufactured goods should, in so
far as possible, be offset by concessions on imports of raw materials.
Tariff reductions in recent years on raw materials have been help-

[3] See Hearings, House Ways and Means, *Reciprocal Trade Agreement Program,* pp. 405–406, 543, *et seq.,* 627–629, 931–933, 938–945, 945, *et seq.,*
1728, *et seq.*

ful: hard fiber cordage, jute, burlap, raw wool, softwood lumber, zinc, bauxite, copper, manganese, pig iron, and steel ingots are examples.

3. A major problem in which New England has a great interest is the manner of solving the problem of dollar shortage. This country has put much emphasis on a rise in imports. This policy concentrates the burden of adjustments on particular industries, which have to face the new competition. What is written under No. 1 above is relevant here.

A second approach is a reduction in United States exports. Countries confronted with dollar shortages have tended to emphasize this solution. By discriminating against United States exports, by devaluing currencies, Europe and Asia have improved their competitive position in third markets and have also raised barriers against United States exports.

In 1948–49 a defender of New England's interests might well have contended that United States policy tended excessively to capturing the markets of New England industries, both at home and abroad. He might well have insisted on a more gradual adjustment, through continued grants and loans. In this way, the cut of United States exports and (or) the rise of imports, the condition for equilibrium in the dollar market, could have been spread over a longer period of time. Current cold-war mobilization puts a somewhat different light on our problem. With shortages of labor and facilities in prospect, the appropriate policy for years, both for New England and the country, may well be to reduce exports and increase imports.

One can well understand the angry protests of Lawrence wool manufacturers in 1948 and 1949 when they pointed to the burden of ERP on the taxpayer, the improved productivity and increased competitive power of British manufacturers resulting from ERP aid in machinery and technology, and the loss of markets by Lawrence manufacturers to countries profiting from ERP. The woolen manufacturer could not understand why he should pay the bill both in taxes and loss of markets. Indeed, he was the victim of a policy easy to defend on national but not on regional grounds.

4. The final remedy should be help to the region to offset the damage done by policies supportable on national lines. On this score, the failure of New England industries to share equally in the exports under ERP is relevant. Thus, from April 1, 1948 to Decem-

ber 31, 1949, exports of machinery and vehicles were 30 per cent of all exports; but only 16 per cent of ECA exports; of paper and paper products, 11 and ½ per cent, respectively.[4]

3. CONCLUSION

New England may well sell a billion dollars' worth of goods abroad annually. Although its foreign sales are much less important than sales to other parts of the country (just as its imports from abroad are much less important), they nevertheless are of vital significance to the region. Any gains of competitive power will be reflected in exports both at home and abroad. That the large relative (and to some degree absolute) losses are especially striking in *interregional* competition underlines even more the importance of international trade for New England. What is lost in sales to the South may be made up by increased sales to Latin America.

It is not appropriate for New England to support the protectionist position, when the world economic and political situation demands easing of trade restrictions. New England may rightly insist, however, that its special problems be considered. The timing of relaxations in trade barriers, the choice of industries to be affected by increased competition from abroad, the degree of dependence on foreign aid (and hence maintenance of exports) against loss of domestic and foreign markets, the offsets to injury done to New England by freer trade policies — in these and other matters, the government should consider the peculiar plights of New England.

---

[4] Observe, however, that the exports under private account (e.g., for machinery) may rise because the ECA makes dollars available for other purposes.

PART III

LABOR AND RELATED COSTS

INTRODUCTION

I have devoted Chapters 12–18 (Part III) to a consideration of labor costs: hourly straight-time earnings, wage rates for identical operations, wage rates corrected by productivity and types of industries, the significance of the varying cost of living, social security payments, and unionization. Here we review the disadvantages in labor costs suffered by New England vis-à-vis the South, the advantages vis-à-vis other areas in the most advanced types of industries and in white-collar jobs, and the gradual narrowing of the gap between North and South. Productivity depends on the intelligence of the worker, and the work loads, management, and capital equipment with which labor operates. Despite some important exceptions, New England's productivity generally suffers from inflexible work loads, unsatisfactory management, and antiquated plant and equipment.

In Chapter 4, I discussed briefly managerial weakness. The reader will find further discussion in this part and more extended comments on both management and capital in Chapter 7 of the *Report on New England Economy* to the President.

As New England loses industries to other areas, it might be expected that the displaced workers would find employment in other industries. But if demand is deficient, labor relatively immobile, and wages and work loads rigid, the effect may well be unemployment. In the generation before World War II, the expected adjustments were not forthcoming. In the forties, artificially expanded demand allowed some displaced workers to be absorbed despite immobility and the various rigidities. Indeed, the general demand conditions and federal policies are of vital importance for an area intent on adjustment.

CHAPTER 12

THE SIGNIFICANCE OF COSTS

1. COSTS AND THE COMPETITIVE POSITION OF A REGION

A region, like a nation, seeks to keep its costs at a minimum. Failure to maintain a competitive position in relation to other areas means loss of markets, of employment, and a reduced standard of living. A region is rich in proportion to its capacity to sell commodities and services wanted by other regions and nations. Competitive position is of special importance to a region like New England, with an area of but 63,000 square miles or 2 per cent of the nation's total, which is far from self-sufficient in raw materials, food, and even manufactured goods, to a maturing region which has to sell outside not only in order to pay for its "imports," but also in order to produce at high levels of output which allow the maximum economies of scale, that is, minimum costs.

The competition which a small region faces is primarily competition within the country, a fact which is evidenced in the large interregional trade vis-à-vis international trade. (Cf. Chapter 8.)

A region will not sprout grass in its major cities merely because costs rise more rapidly than elsewhere or fall less. According to the theory of international trade, an area adversely affected by a relative deterioration in its competitive position will lose cash to others as it sells less and buys more. The discussion in Part II showed the importance of transfers in the balance of payments. Under the pressure of reduced supplies of money, following payment for the excess of imports, employers in the injured area will tend to cut down output. If, in response to the threat of unemployment, workers accept cuts in wage rates or increased work-loads, the region's competitive position will be reëstablished. But if wages and work loads are rigidly fixed, then the result will be unemployment. The result of declining competitive power may be obscured in a period when there are more jobs than workers to fill them — e.g., 1950. But we may be certain that the region's standard of living will suffer as incomes fall and prices of "imported" goods and services remain relatively unchanged and, therefore, as the purchasing power of wages declines — that is, unless the deterioration is met by an appropriate rise of productivity.

In practice, particular industries first feel the impact of the worsened condition. In New England, textiles and shoes have been the harbingers of general setbacks. International trade theory suggests that in these circumstances textiles and shoes will cease to be export industries or their position on the scale of export industries will be lowered and their contributions to exports lessened. Labor and capital will move out of these industries and seek employment in other occupations which have not been damaged to an equal extent.

As textiles and shoes provide less exports to pay for the region's imports, either other industries must increase exports, more dollars must be received in other ways (e.g., reducing the diversion to other regions via the United States Treasury, enlarging imports of capital),[1] or New England must become more self-sufficient.

Our experience with depressed industries suggests that unemployment accompanies the deterioration. The Galenson Report reveals a surprising lack of mobility of Massachusetts workers, particularly those in the depressed textile towns.[2] The inference to be drawn is that the economy accepts its losses partly in the form of unemployment or in disguised unemployment, that is, greater recourse to less productive jobs (e.g., farm work or improvised government work). This failure to move is the usual response of the stranded worker. British experience in the generation before the war confirms the unwillingness of workers to move. Capital ultimately comes in; but only after some time, when it no longer pays to use whatever capital is left.

Yet there is also evidence, as we shall see, of growth in new industries, e.g., nonferrous metals, machinery, and apparel. But the growth is not often in the depressed areas, and the labor represents new workers, rather than the displaced older workers. The substantial expansion of tertiary industries in New England, which are

[1] Cf. Chapter 8.
[2] The Commonwealth of Massachusetts, *A Report on Unemployment Compensation Benefit Costs in Massachusetts* (1950), pp. 27–28.

largely nonexportable, shows that major export industries have declined without adequate replacement by new export industries.

2. THE STRUCTURE OF COSTS

Relative costs are important not only to the loss of competitive power in older industries, but to the new industries which develop. When a firm or industry or region scans the cost of doing business, it pays most attention to the costs which account for a high proportion of total costs.

a. *Labor.* Labor costs are the most important single cost. In 1947, wages accounted for 40.6 per cent of the value added in manufacturing in the United States; and for 44.8 per cent in New England. Wages and salaries are about two-thirds of the national income. The greater proportion of wages and salaries to national income than of wages to value added in manufacturing is explained by the large amount of wages derived from the service industries, inclusive of management pay in national income figures, and the hidden wages and salaries in other manufacturing costs included as part of value added, e.g., power and transportation. But whether the appropriate percentage is 45 or 65, labor is the crucial factor in costs.

Labor costs depend not only upon the wage rates paid but also upon the output per dollar of wages. High wage rates do not necessarily disadvantage an area: the high rates may be offset by correspondingly higher productivity. The fact is that comparisons of wage rates as symbolic of labor costs have to be used with great caution. For example, wage rates per hour are lower in the South than in the North. The difference is related to the kinds of industries in the South — primarily less productive, as textiles, and requiring less capital than the more productive durable goods industries,[3] the kinds of commodities produced in particular industries — e.g., low-count, cheap textiles in the South; the output of identical commodities per hour of work — e.g., does the Southern worker produce less than the Northern? It is necessary, then, to correct for productivity as evidenced in the kinds of goods and in the quantity produced. Furthermore, the amount and quality of management and capital

[3] For the importance of the pattern of industries as the explanation of low average wage rates in the South, see J. W. Markham, "Some Comments upon the North–South Wage Differential," *The Southern Economic Journal* (January 1950), pp. 279–283.

are relevant. A greater output per hour of work in the North may reflect more capital per worker. The increased costs of capital are relevant.

In the current dispute over the competitive position of New England vis-à-vis the South, much has been made of the larger work loads in the South and of the unwillingness of the New England worker to adjust his load to new working conditions. It is said that he will not tend 80 looms instead of 40 even though, as a result of technological advances, the energy output for tending the larger number is less than that involved in tending 40 old machines. It is indeed difficult to weight work loads under comparable conditions. Yet there is a tendency for a given work load to be embedded in the older industrial communities, and workers become rather fixed in their attitudes toward work loads.

b. *Management.* Management is another important element of cost. To some extent management is paid in profits rather than salaries; and it is presumed that profits are a payment out of surplus, not a cost. But executive salaries are a significant item. Here again, however, the test is productivity — what management contributes as well as what it is paid. It has often been said that New England executives are paid not too much, but too little; and it has also been said that the executives in New England are unenterprising and frequently inefficient. It is important that New England businessmen should receive rewards adequate to entice men of outstanding ability and adequate to preclude large migrations of ability to the South and West. *It is important that management share in profits so that the cost structure be affected as little as possible by rewards to management.* New England could gain substantially by tethering the rewards of management increasingly to profits rather than to the cost element, namely, salaries.

c. *Capital.* A third cost element of considerable importance is capital. First, there is the cost of obtaining capital. One of New England's early advantages was the availability of capital to be used in business enterprise. In a period when capital moved with difficulty this was an important asset for the region. With time, however, this advantage has been lost. Capital is much more fluid than it used to be, moving with little friction to the areas where it can earn the most. As the money market has expanded from a regional to a national one, particularly in response to the operations of the

Federal Reserve System, and as communications have improved, the advantage of both *availability* and lower costs of capital has become less and less important. The South and the West prosper in part because capital from New England moves South and West in response to higher prospective earnings; and the entrepreneur, often the New England businessman, can obtain capital for use in these regions on terms almost as favorable as New England. That taxes are frequently less in the South and West further impairs New England's advantages as a producer of capital.

The cost of capital consists not merely in the interest paid on the original investment. A relevant problem is the amount of money required to keep the plant up, that is, the costs reckoned in depreciation and obsolescence accounts. On this score an older region profits from having written off a substantial part of its capital and thus from incurring smaller capital charges related to the original investment than newer regions. Newer regions have also to construct new plants, and present or recent construction costs are high. It probably is no exaggeration to say that the construction cost of a new plant in the South will be at least four times as much as the original cost of the average textile plant of similar capacity already operating in New England. For a given capacity, the South will then have to invest four times as much capital and incur much heavier annual charges for interest and write-off. (If both regions construct new plants, however, the South has an advantage in lower construction costs.)

It is not clear that a firm advantage lies with the Northeast, even on the assumption that the plant in the North is already built and has yet to be built in the South. Against the increased capital cost, the South gains in much more effective plant: large savings in heat, in movement of materials and men, and much higher labor productivity associated with better working conditions. That these advantages are genuine is suggested by the popularity of the new one-story type of plant not only in the South but among enterprising firms in New England.

In still another aspect the newly built plant is more efficient per dollar invested than the plant constructed in 1850–1900. A new operator takes into account the market that is appropriate for a $300 billion economy, and in a world vulnerable to bombing attack. His output and location are adapted to conditions of today, not to those of 1900. In textiles, it is much easier to adapt to new fibers by building new plants.

In the discussions of business enterprise, much has been said of the need of generous allowances for tax deductions for modernization and obsolescence. These not only provide employment in the capital goods industries but they also keep costs down. These issues have a special relevance for New England, an area with relatively old plant. Generous allowance for depreciation and obsolescence would favor such an area more than other regions. The tax incentive would stimulate scrapping ancient plant and equipment. Unfortunately, it also requires financial sacrifices to build a new plant: current withdrawals of cash have to be reduced. Even when profits were large, as in the forties, New England textile firms modernized inadequately and either increased their withdrawals of profits excessively or used liquid funds primarily to expand elsewhere.

One other aspect of the problem of capital requires attention. We note with interest an increased tendency in New England to provide capital through community efforts or (and) public subsidies. These efforts are in response to depression conditions in some communities, to the efforts of competing areas to wean away plants and industries from New England by making tax concessions, offering free sites, plants at no rent or cheap rent, etc. But they are often more than that. They reflect an awareness of the importance for the community of maintaining morale of workers, of saving large investment in plant and community services, and of reducing the costs of unemployment. They also reflect to some extent the difficulties confronting new entrants who have ideas, initiative, and general ability and some working capital, but who need additional capital. Often it will pay to provide capital through community efforts.

It is clear that these community efforts are on the increase, and, for example in Maine, with the blessing of state authorities. It is important that they should not be the means of bringing about uneconomic uses of capital, either by transfers within New England or interregionally. They may be justified as policies which stop uneconomic transfers out of New England; and in defining uneconomic transfers, we consider the costs of stranded communities. A memorandum of the Connecticut Full Employment Committee reveals a hostility towards tax concessions to attract new plants but a willingness to use tax concessions to discourage migrations.

Perhaps we should comment on the size of the business enterprise here; for clearly this is relevant to economies of capital and costs. In general, the size of the business is larger in New England than in the country; but recent developments have tended to lessen the difference. The table below reveals that, though the average number of employees per establishment is still larger in New England than in the United States, the increase over the past fifty years was almost twice as great in the nation and in the Southeast, and more than three times as great in the Central States, as in New England. In part the explanation is the growth of vast enterprises, generally in the durable goods industries, outside of New England and especially in the Central States; and in part the rapid industrialization of the South. New England is no longer the outstanding area of large-scale enterprise that it was at the turn of the century.

Number of Workers per Manufacturing Establishment, 1899 and 1947, U. S. A. and Regions, and Percentage Rise

	United States	New England	Central States	Southeast
Number, 1899	24	40	21	22
Number, 1947	59	73	78	57
Percentage rise, 1899 to 1947	146	82	271	159

Source: Calculated from **Handbook of Regional Statistics** (1950), p. 18.

d. *Other Costs.* So far we have discussed briefly the major elements of costs. Labor costs will receive particular attention later. Power, fuel costs, and taxes, also to be treated later, require brief mention here. Percentagewise, they are not as significant as the elements discussed so far, but they are costs which can be significantly influenced by public policy. On the other hand, the major taxes are federal, over which states and regions have little control. Moreover, a large part of taxes are on surpluses (e.g., income and corporation taxes) and hence are not part of the cost structure. Another part (e.g., pay-roll taxes) are assumed by most economists to be passed back in the form of lower wages, and hence do not affect the competitive position.

Transportation costs are vital to a region perched in one corner of the nation. As the country grows to the South and West, this isolation means higher transportation costs, and therefore, competitive losses unless sellers in New England are prepared to absorb part of the increase.

CHAPTER 13

LABOR SUPPLY

Labor costs depend on the supply of labor, which affects both wages and productivity, and, before we turn to the problem of wages, we discuss briefly the related problem of labor supply. An area that can draw on large reservoirs of labor clearly is in a favorable position, for not only are wages likely to be lower but in these circumstances labor is likely to be more attentive to proposals for adjustments to changing technology. There are marked differences between New England and the South in this respect.

In the years before World War I, one of the great advantages of the New England States lay in the large inflow of immigrants and, to a lesser degree, the exodus from the farms. By 1940, the foreign-born in New England were 1.5 million out of a native white population of 6.8 million, or about 22 per cent, a proportion exceeding the national average of 12 per cent. Immigration and the farms as sources of labor for New England's factories are of small importance now.[1]

In 1940, New England's urban population was 6.4 million; her rural population, 2.0 million, or about 24 per cent of the total. For the country the percentage of rural population was 43.5 per cent in 1940 and 41.0 per cent in 1947. The Northeastern States' rural population actually rose from 23.4 per cent of the total in 1940 to 25.1 per cent in 1947, whereas in the South the proportion declined from 63.3 to 57.0 per cent. Or compare the figures for the New England states and a few strong competitors:

Percentage of Rural Population, 1940

Massachusetts	10.6
Rhode Island	8.4
Connecticut	32.2
North Carolina	72.7
South Carolina	75.5
All Southeast	67.9

Source: Handbook of Regional Statistics, pp. 6, 38, 209.

[1] *Statistical Abstract* (1950).

These large reservoirs of manpower in the Southern States contribute to the industrial strength of the South. Wages are low on
the farms, and especially in the South. Families are large. Attracted
to the factories, where pay is particularly high as compared to the
farms, and living conditions are much superior, the new labor, in
contrast to New England's labor, is beset by few inhibitions relative
to methods of work, work loads, and the like. As the demand for
Southern manufactures rises, the steady migration from farm to
factory keeps wages from rising in proportion to the increase of
demand. Low wages and an unusual willingness to coöperate on the
part of labor improve the South's competitive position.

An official comment is relevant here:

> . . . Because of the absence of work traditions in the South, manage-
> ment of new mills have found little or no opposition to work assignments
> greater than in similar occupations in the North. It was pointed out also
> that this variance in worker attitudes had, in the past, made easier the
> introduction of the new and more efficient machinery in established mills
> in the South, which in turn further improved the competitive advantage
> of manufacturers in that area.[2]

That the incentive to move from the farms is great is evidenced
in various ways. The average net income per person engaged in
agriculture and in industry was:

	Agriculture	Industry
1933	290	950
1939	507	1278
1949	1735	2900

Source: BAE, Agricultural Outlook Charts (1951), p. 32.

It is clear that there are still large differentials in favor of industrial earnings; but it is also clear that an advantage of more than
200 per cent in 1933 has been reduced to one of little more than
50 per cent by 1949. The large relative gains of farmers in the war
period is even more strikingly shown in a rise of hourly earnings
of 173 per cent for farm workers from January 1941 to October 1945
and of but 44 per cent for factory workers.[3]

One should not conclude too quickly from these figures that
migrations from farms to cities will not continue to bestow indus-

[2] The Commonwealth of Massachusetts, *Report of the Special Commission
Relative to the Textile Industry* (May 12, 1950), p. 29.

[3] BAE, *Agricultural Wage Stabilization in World War II* (1950), p. 74.

trial advantages on the South. But clearly the incentives are less than they were in the thirties, and with continued mobilization farm wages are likely to continue to gain vis-à-vis factory wages.

The industrialization of the South (and the West) is part of the patterns of the times. Everywhere rural areas want to industrialize. Analysts find a high positive correlation between percentage employed in the factories and average per capita income. In a comparison of state income and percentage of *labor force* in agriculture, Massachusetts, Connecticut, and Rhode Island, with 2.7, 4.0, and 2.1 per cent of their population in agriculture (record low figures except for New Jersey, with 3.2 per cent), were in 1939 near the top in per capita income — only exceeded by four or five states. Mississippi, Arkansas, South Carolina, Alabama, Kentucky, Tennessee, and Georgia, all with 30 per cent or more of their workers in agriculture, were also the states with incomes below $300 per capita.[4]

Where jobs are to be had, the migration to the cities continues. In the thirties the farm population remained virtually unchanged (net) with a substantial rise in the bad years of the depression and a decline in the later thirties. From 1939 to 1949, the farm population declined from 30.5 million to 27.8 million, or close to 10 per cent. From 1929 to 1949, with a total population rise of 27.4 million, the farm population declined by 2.5 million. By 1975, it is expected that the farm population will fall by 4 million additional. At that time the farm population would be 13 per cent of the middle estimate of total population, as compared with 24 per cent in 1929. This exodus is the result partly of the higher incomes available in the city and (related) the rise of productivity on the farms which, in the face of inelastic demand for many farm products, tends to displace farm workers more than factory workers.[5] By 1948, *gross* production per farm worker had risen 42 per cent above the 1935–1939 level in comparison with a rise of but 21 per cent in manufacturing and mining.[6]

[4] L. Bean, *International Industrialization of Per Capita Income*, Studies of Income and Wealth, vol. 8, 1946 (NBER), pp. 128–129. Also see J. L. Fulmer, "Factors Influencing State Per Capita Income Differentials," *The Southern Economic Journal* (January 1950), pp. 63–69, 279–280.

[5] *Agricultural Outlook Charts* (1951), pp. 14–15.

[6] BAE, *Farm Production Practices, Costs and Returns*, Statistical Bulletin No. 83 (October 1949), p. 63.

In short, the *new* industrial areas are likely to continue to profit from in-migration from the farms, with attendant relative advantages for New England's rivals. Despite smaller financial incentives, it is anticipated that the gains per year in the next 25 years will even exceed those of the last 20 years and even those of the forties. Actually, the gains of the city at the expense of the farm greatly exceed the figure suggested by the decline of the farm population, for excess of births over deaths is much larger on the farms.

CHAPTER 14

LABOR COSTS

1. THE IMPORTANCE OF LABOR COSTS

In our discussion of labor costs, the most important element in New England's cost structure, we are of course concentrating on manufacturing, with which the region is most concerned. Furthermore, New England excels in industries where labor is important.

In the 1947 Census, the ratio of wages and salaries to value added by manufacturing was 40.6 per cent for the country as a whole. The average for New England was 44.8 per cent. In the most important industries, the ratio was as follows: [1]

Industry	Wages ($ million)	% to Value Added
1. Textiles	610	49.0
2. Machinery (except electrical)	464	49.8
3. Fabricated metal products	237	46.9
4. Leather and leather products	207	45.5
5. Electrical machinery	182	40.8

Source: U. S. Census of Manufactures, 1947.

2. THE COSTS OF MANAGEMENT

We leave out of account the salaries paid to executives. Witnesses before the Committee on the New England Economy commented on the low salaries paid to executives in New England. To many this may seem an advantage. Though this means lower costs for business executives, the cost in terms of less skillful management and reduced output is probably even greater. The net effect is probably higher costs in New England. The low pay and slow rate of promotion in New England result in weaning away much of New England's executive leadership. We cannot leave this issue without pointing out that New England may be the area of opportunity for ambitious business

[1] Cf. National Resources Planning Board, *Industrial Location and National Resources,* p. 69.

executives. The average age of business leadership is high here, whereas the new industrial areas are being sated with young executives. The ambitious will have to wait long before these leaders in the newer industrial areas retire or die.

3. THE LEVEL OF INCOME AND WAGES

Before we discuss labor costs in detail, we should be clear on the meaning of wage and income levels. There was a time when New England was clearly a high-income and high-wage area. But the differential has been gradually whittled away. Whereas in 1929 average income in New England exceeded the national average by 23 per cent, in 1950 the excess was only 8½ per cent.

A high-cost area that is confronted with increased competition from growing areas begins to lose markets. In prosperous times, the losses are only relative; in depressed times, they are absolute. The resulting pressure of unemployed resources brings about reduction in wages, and the decline is consistent with the ensuing loss of purchasing power. Thus, the losses suffered by the textile industry in the twenties brought about excess capacity, surplus labor, and active searching for jobs. The pressure of unemployment brought down wages. One result was that the apparel industry began to move from New York into New Bedford, among other places. Other low wage industries followed. Fortunately, in July 1938, the Massachusetts Department of Labor and Industries set a minimum wage of $14 for a 40-hour week. And, fortunately, New England has been making important advances in the high-paying metal fabrication and machinery industries.

That New England is no longer a high-wage area is revealed by a study (1945–46) of the Department of Labor, which compares straight-time hourly earnings for comparable work for 22 cities. Boston ranks fourteenth, with wages lower only in six Southern cities, Indianapolis, and Minneapolis, the last two being much smaller cities than Boston, which may explain the lower wages. Average hourly earnings in Boston were more than 20 per cent less than in New York City, almost 20 per cent less than in Detroit, and 13 per cent less than in Los Angeles, Pittsburgh, Seattle, San Francisco, and Portland, Oregon. Here we have the one corrective to outward migration of industries, and an encouragement to an inward flow.

4. HOURLY EARNINGS

The difficulties in measuring labor costs have already been mentioned: the level of wages, hours worked, type of industrial structure, job performed, productivity, and the cost of living have all to be taken into consideration, and these will be discussed in detail. A comparison of hourly earnings, by regions, gives a *first* approximation of relative labor costs in manufacturing.

The following table shows hourly earnings in a prewar year. New England industries were already paying less than the national average, and 16 per cent less than the West; but earnings in the South averaged 19 per cent less than in New England.

Hourly Earnings, 1937 (Cents)

United States	64.8	New England = 58.8
		Middle Atlantic = 66.3
North	69.1	East North Central = 75.6
		West North Central = 61.8
South	47.8	
West	69.7	

Source: Beal and Hinrichs, "Geographical Differences in Hours and Wages, 1935 and 1937," **Monthly Labor Review** (May 1940).

Second, hourly earnings in 27 industries are available for the early postwar years. This series has an advantage over the first in that differences in wages associated with a greater concentration of industries producing high value products are eliminated. (The area with metal-fabricating industries will pay higher wages than that with the apparel industry.) Differences associated with the kind of products turned out by a *particular* industry still remain.

In this study New England ranks fourth, with the Pacific, Middle Atlantic, and Great Lakes areas ranked 1, 2, and 3, respectively, and the Southeast last, that is, 8. Hourly earnings in New England were higher than the national average in 19 industries and lower in 8. The differentials (above national average) were especially prominent in textiles and shoes, two declining industries; but hourly earnings were below the national average notably in metal fabrication, an industry growing in the area.[2]

An examination of certain individual industries in which New England is especially interested reveals that hourly earnings are

[2] U. S. Department of Labor, *Labor in the South*, BLS Bulletin No. 898 (1947), pp. 58–62 and table in appendix.

relatively high compared with the South and relatively low compared with the West and frequently even with neighboring states in the Middle Atlantic group.

In many instances (leather goods, dyeing and finishing, wood and household furniture) Southern earnings per hour are from 25 to 35 per cent below those in New England; in others (knitted underwear, boots and shoes, woolens and worsteds), the differential is from 10 to 20 per cent. *The relatively high wage level in New England vis-à-vis the South helps, of course, to explain New England's industrial decline.* The following table gives more detailed material on this point.

Hourly Earnings, by Industries and Jobs, 1945–46 (U. S. Average = 100)

	New England	Southeast
Metal-working	97 (7 items)	76 (6 items)
Paper and allied products	97 (3 items)	80 (5 items)
Apparel	95 (6 items)	85 (5 items)
Textiles (cotton)	108 (3 items)	91 (3 items)
Footwear	107 (1 item)	101 (1 item)
Hosiery	102 (6 items)	94 (2 items)
Nonmanufacturing	99 (6 items)	81 (6 items)

Source: Based on **Labor in the South**, p. 58.

It should be observed that there are important industries in which the South's advantage is even greater than for textiles and several for which its advantages are less.

It is possible to relate hourly wages to value added and thus obtain the average value added by manufacturing per dollar of wages. This gives a *very rough* index of labor costs because differences may be ascribed to varying combinations of labor, capital, and management. The North might have a higher index merely because it uses more capital. The table below reveals that *on this basis* New England labor costs were the highest in the country and the South and West had important advantages.

Indexes of Value Added per Dollar of Wage Costs in Manufacturing in Various Areas (Northern Area = 100)

West	= 118	New England	= 97
North	= 110	Middle Atlantic	= 100
South	= 100	South Atlantic	= 109
		Southwest	= 115

Source: National Resources Planning Board, **Industrial Location and National Resources** (1942), p. 224.

5. WAGES FOR COMPARABLE OR IDENTICAL WORK

A better index of labor costs is one based on identical operations. Thus it is possible to compare the wages of loom tenders, card grinders, loom fixers, janitors, etc. But here again we warn the reader that workers receiving the same pay for identical operations do not necessarily turn out the same output.

A study of 31 urban areas in the spring and summer of 1943 revealed that Boston ranked 23rd in manufacturing wage rates and 17th in nonmanufacturing; for Providence the respective figures were 20th and 14th, respectively. New England was well on its way to becoming a low-wage area. Taking manufacturing wage rates in the median city as 100, Detroit, Toledo, and Portland, Oregon had indexes of 131, 127, and 117, whereas Boston's index was but 86.[3]

In 1945–46, Boston's average hourly earnings for *comparable* work was 95 (median = 100). Of 22 cities listed, wages were lower only in the South and two relatively small cities in the Midwest.

6. DIFFERENCES BY INDUSTRIES

In the last few years the Bureau of Labor Statistics has released many regional comparisons of wage rates for identical operations. These studies reveal that conditions vary greatly from industry to industry.

In some textiles, the difference between Northern and Southern wages is relatively small. Thus in rayon and silk textile mills, the span of wage rates for weavers was:

New England	$1.26–$1.33
Philadelphia area	$1.20–$1.40
South	$1.24–$1.33

In the unskilled tasks, however, the differences remain large; and in part because of wage legislation in the North.

It should not be assumed, however, that large differentials still do not prevail in some textiles. In cotton textiles, wages in the three New England regions are the three highest of eight regions (Connecticut and Rhode Island, first; Fall River and New Bedford, sec-

[3] U. S. Department of Labor, *Intercity Variations in Wage Levels*, BLS Bulletin No. 793 (1944), p. 6.

ond; and Northern New England, third). In woolen and worsted textiles, still another study for 1949 reveals the following order:

Men's occupations — 1 = Philadelphia and Rhode Island; 3 = Lawrence; 4 = Northern New England; 5 = South
Women's occupations — 1 = Lawrence; 2 = Rhode Island; 3 = Northern New England; 4 = Philadelphia.

In another problem industry, namely, footwear, wages in New England are far from the highest. Thus, for women's cement process shoes (1949) wages were highest in New York City, second in Los Angeles, and important centers in New England varied from third to ninth place. (There were 10 areas in all.)

What of the wages in the apparel industries, which tended to migrate to New England in the thirties? In cotton garments, 1949 wages in New England were in excess of the national average but less than in the Pacific areas. In work clothing, wages in New England were close to the national average. But here the great potential advantages for the South are clear. The average excess of wages for ten occupations exceeds that in the South by 24 per cent; and in one job (pressers, finish by hand) by no less than 50 per cent. So far, most competition is with the Middle Atlantic States, and the wage structure favors New England. In men's and boys' suits and coats, Boston's wages were higher than those in St. Louis and Baltimore, lower than in Newark, Jersey City, and New York City, and roughly equal to the level in Chicago, Philadelphia, Cincinnati, and Rochester.

New England has marked advantages in some industries. A feature of the New England wage structure is the low wages (lower than in the South) paid to clerks, stenographers, and the like. This may reflect lack of organization, but primarily it results from the large outpourings of high school and college graduates, and the higher social status of the white-collar worker. Even manufacturing requires clerical assistance, and these low wages should offset to some extent other disadvantages. Industries that require much clerical and stenographic help — e.g., insurance, finance, distribution, education, medicine, and offices of all kinds — should gain greatly in labor costs by establishing in New England.

Finally, there are the industries that are most productive, require the highest type of labor, and pay the highest wages. Metal fabrication is an important example. New England's recent gains are suggested by a 1947 wage study. In six occupations for men in ferrous foundries, a study of 24 cities showed that wages in Boston and Hartford were relatively low. High skills and low wages are a strong magnet for an industry that requires large outlays for wages.

Average Rank for Six Occupations

Detroit	2
Portland, Oregon	5
Cleveland	5–6
Hartford	14
Boston	16

Again, consider these recent averages in high wage occupations:

	N. E.	Middle Atlantic	U. S. A.
Chemicals (per hour) $	1.35	1.46	1.51

7. DIFFERENCES IN WAGES ASSOCIATED WITH INDUSTRY-MIX

We are indebted to Professor Hanna, of Duke University, for an analysis of wage differences to be explained (1) by the "industry-mix" and (2) by differences in wage rates.[4] The composition of a state's activity, in terms of production worker man-hours by industry, may be called the state's industry-mix. Dr. Hanna finds that the industry-mix pulls New England wages down by 2.3 per cent; and that lower wage rates pull New England's average down 2.4 per cent. This means that New England harbors industries that pay less than the average wage and that in the same industries wages are less than the average. The reader will also observe that the industry-mix of the South Atlantic States pulls them down by 11.8 per cent and raises the East North Central by 6.8 per cent. Wage rates are 9 per cent less than the nation's average in the South Atlantic, 15.5 per cent less in the East South Central, and 13.5 per cent less in the West South Central.

The variations among states in a region are also large. Note the highly productive industries in Connecticut (industry-mix = +3.5) and the low productivity in Maine (−10.8); and the low wage rates in Vermont, Maine, and New Hampshire, as against Southern New

---

[4] F. A. Hanna, "Contribution of Manufacturing Wages to Regional Differences in Per Capita Income," *Review of Economics and Statistics* (February 1951), pp. 18–28.

England — this explains a tendency of industry to migrate to Northern New England from Southern New England.

Professor Hanna also shows the extent of the differences between wage income of production workers in particular industries computed from industry-mix, on the one hand, and from major industry group average hourly earnings, on the other. This table shows, for example, that the industry-mix in textiles accounts for the New

Percentage Differences from Average in Production Workers' Wages Attributable to

	Industry-Mix	Wage Rates
New England	−2.3	−2.4
Maine	−10.0	−6.8
New Hampshire	−8.8	−5.9
Vermont	−7.4	−11.4
Massachusetts	−2.8	−1.5
Rhode Island	−4.9	−3.8
Connecticut	+3.5	−1.1
Middle Atlantic	+1.3	+2.9
East North Central	+6.8	+2.8
West North Central	−1.7	−7.0
South Atlantic	−11.8	−9.0
East South Central	−9.2	−15.5
West South Central	−3.9	−13.5
Mountain States	−3.1	+0.1
Pacific States	−1.3	+16.5

Source: F. A. Hanna, "Contribution of Manufacturing Wages to Regional Differences in Per Capita Income," **Review of Economics and Statistics** (February 1951).

England wage level 4.8 per cent above the national and for the 4.4 per cent below average in the South Atlantic States. In other words, New England concentrates on relatively high-valued and high-productive textiles. We should note, however, that within the 20 major industry groups, in 14 the industry-mix in New England tends to reduce wages and in 6 to raise them. This is perhaps additional evidence of the influence of factors which make for low-wage industries. Hanna concludes that

an examination of the differences within each of the 20 major groups by the 9 geographic divisions indicates that the fraction of regional wage differences which may possibly be attributed to regional industry-mix differences is likely to be small . . . For a geographical division *with* an unfavorable industry-mix (based on all industries) also to have an unfavorable industry-mix *within* more than half the major groups would indicate that its industry-mix tended to be associated with the factors which made for low-pay industries, wherever they occur, rather than being just heavily weighted by the lower-pay major industry groups. Only in the South Atlantic divisions do the lower-pay industries predominate within as many as 15 of the 20 major industrial groups.[5]

It is also clear that the chief contribution to regional differences in industry-mix is to be found in the differences among the major groups and that the intra-group contribution to the differences is quite small.[6]

Percentage Differences between Production Worker Wage Income Computed from Industry-Mix and from Major Group Average Hourly Earnings, Major Industry Groups, 1947

	New England	South Atlantic
All groups	−2.3	−5.1
Textile mills	+4.8	−4.4
Apparel and related	−1.9	−13.4
Machinery except electrical	−0.2	−3.0
Leather and leather products	+0.4	+6.5
Paper and allied products	+2.0	+1.7

Source: Hanna, p. 23.

8. CONCLUSIONS

New England's major advantage lies in its experienced labor force, and its industry-mix requires relatively large outlays of labor. Although at one time New England was a high-wage area, unemployment, the outward migration of industry, and substantial cash transfers to other regions have produced a decline in New England wages, compared to those in other areas. Over the last generation, this trend has led to some improvement in New England's competitive position. The area has attracted growing high-wage industries: machinery; and also some low-wage industries from other regions with high wages — e.g., apparel from the Middle Atlantic. Although New England's wages are low compared to the industrial Middle Atlantic, Middle West, and Far West, wages in textiles and shoes are still above the national average for these industries.

[5] Hanna, "Contribution of Manufacturing Wages to Regional Differences in Per Capita Income," pp. 22–23.
[6] Hanna, p. 24.

CHAPTER 15

PRODUCTIVITY

1. ITS SIGNIFICANCE

What matters is the wage rate corrected for output. Higher earnings in New England are not necessarily a handicap if they are offset by higher output per man-hour. Let us see in what respect the wage differentials discussed in the previous chapter should be corrected for differences in productivity.[1]

2. PRODUCTIVITY, NATIONAL AND NEW ENGLAND

There are few accurate measures of general productivity in New England compared to that in the country as a whole. An indication of one important trend is given in the following table, showing changes over twenty years in man-hours, man-hour output, pay rolls, unit costs, and employment in all manufacturing output and in three industries important to New England. In each of these variables, the three New England industries lag behind the national average. Man-hour output rose much less; unit costs declined less; and total man-hours, employment, and pay rolls declined while pay rolls and employment actually rose in the country as a whole. The decline in unit costs, in these three industries, is substantial when it is compared to the very moderate gains in total man-hour output. This means that wage-earners in these industries have a severe adjustment to make in order to maintain employment.

The lag in productivity in these important New England industries is explained partly by the fact that they are older. Relatively small gains in productivity result in relatively high unit costs; but they also slow up technological unemployment. Had the rise in

[1] See W. A. Krause, "Regional Shifts in Industry," pp. 247–276 (doctorate thesis deposited in Harvard College Library); *Labor in the South*, pp. 83–84; and "Geographical Variations in Hours and Wages During 1933 and 1935," *Monthly Labor Review* (July 1938).

man-hour output corresponded to that for all industries, it is doubtful if total sales could have risen to maintain employment — as it was there was some decline. This slow increase in productivity,

Productivity and Related Variables, All Industries and Three Important New England Industries: Relevant Variables, 1919–40 (Percentage Change)

	All Manu-facturing Industries	Boots and Shoes	Cotton Goods	Woolen and Worsted
Man-Hours	−20	−25	−27	−37
Man-hour output	+140	+63	+84	+55
Pay rolls	+8	−19	−14	−14
Unit costs	−44	−34	−36	−12
Employment	+1	−3	−4	−14

Source: Calculated from U. S. Department of Labor, BLS, **Productivity and Unit Labor Costs in Selected Manufacturing Industries** (1919–1940, 1942).

therefore, is a further symptom of stagnant industries, on which New England is overly dependent.

In other industries, growing somewhat in New England, much greater increases in national productivity occurred from 1919 to 1940:

Rise of Productivity, 1919 to 1940	Per Cent
Agricultural implements	182
Chemicals	225
Glass group	211
Iron and steel group	162
Motor vehicles, bodies and parts	182
Non-ferrous metal group	164
Rayon	386 [a]

[a] 1923–1940.
Source: See last table.

Some scattered information is available for the years 1939–1947. Man-hour output rose as follows for several industries in which New England is interested:

	Per Cent
Footwear, except rubber	6.6
Leather	20.1
Rayon and allied products	96.8
Paper and pulp	13.6 (to 1946)
Machine tools	21.0

Source: U. S. Department of Labor, **BLS, Handbook of Labor Statistics** (1947 ed.), pp. 157–158, and also E. Clague, **Productivity, Employment and Living Standards**, June 4, 1949 (Mimeographed by Bureau of Labor Statistics), Charts, pp. 4–5.

More specific indications of New England's record can be obtained for some industries. A comparison of productivity in the shoe industry follows:

Hours Required to Produce a Pair of Shoes, in 1947 (1939 = 100)

	Men's Shoes	Women's Shoes	Juvenile
United States	101.7	90.8	98.2
New England	92.6	86.3	114.0

In general, New England's recent record stands up well in boots and shoes. But New England, with much excess capacity and producing on distribution orders, gained especially from the wartime increase in demand and the reduction of number of styles.[2]

For electrical equipment and supplies, New England's recent productivity record is also favorable. It should be observed, however, that in New England about one-half of the reporting companies were producers of insulated wire and cable — a product not subject to large losses of productivity in the war as were many others in this classification.[3]

Unit Man-Hours Required, 1947 (1939 = 100)

United States	82.8
New England	78.1
Middle Atlantic	92.0
Great Lakes — Midwest	74.5

3. THE CONTRIBUTION OF THE WORKER

It is often said that the low-priced worker produces less than the high-priced worker. This is not uniformly so. In chemically produced rayon yarn, hourly earnings in Southern firms were 6.1 per cent less than in the North; yet the value added in the former was $1.34 per man-hour, against $1.14 in Northern firms. Nevertheless, one New England asset is its large reservoir of highly skilled workers; but this advantage counts for much less than it used to as educational standards rise in the South and rural areas generally and as the training of workers continues to improve.

[2] BLS, *Trends in Man-Hours Expended Per Pair of Footwear, 1939 to 1947* (1950), pp. 21–23, 30–31.

[3] *Trends in Man-Hours Expended Per Unit, Electrical Equipment and Supplies, 1939 to 1947* (April 1950), pp. 8, 16.

The testimony of most observers is that there is not any great difference between the worker in the North and the South — I leave out of account the relative supply of skilled workers. The United States Steel Workers Union claimed that the average steelworker, wherever he works, has the same labor productivity — assuming the same technological conditions.[4] According to a prewar study by the TNEC, labor unit costs were less in the South in textile mills than in the North by more than the wage differential, the excess being explained by greater efficiency of Southern labor.[5]

Professor Lester asked a substantial number of firms:

How did labor in your Southern plant(s) compare with labor in your Northern plants with respect to efficiency or effectiveness under comparable conditions and supervision? (This is intended purely as a measure of labor effort, ability and speed, making allowances for any differences between the Northern and Southern plants in such non-labor matters as equipment, management, etc.) [6]

Labor efficiency was reported to be higher in the South by 4 firms employing a total of 25,900 workers in 35 plants in the North and 9 plants in the South; to be equal in both regions by 18 firms employing 489,000 workers in 126 Northern plants and 47 Southern plants; and labor efficiency was reported to be lower in the South than in the North by 18 firms employing 366,000 workers in 246 Northern plants and 107 Southern plants. Two firms reported greater efficiency in the South because of larger work loads.

These results suggest somewhat lower efficiency in the South. But there are large variations by industries: the South excels in textiles, hosiery, and clothing but is behind in rubber and food. Variations in the same industry suggest the importance of management.

Typical comments follow:

Have no reason to believe Southern workers are slower than Northern workers in similar circumstances. In fact, as a general statement based on experience, we would say there is no difference . . .

. . . . .

[4] J. W. Markham, "Regional Labor Productivity in the Textile Industry," *American Economic Review* (1943), p. 110.

[5] TNEC Monograph No. 5, *Industrial Wage Rates, Labor Costs, and Price Policies* (Washington, 1940), p. 57.

[6] The Lester study is discussed fully below: R. A. Lester, "Effectiveness of Factory Labor, South-North Comparisons," *The Journal of Political Economy* (February 1946), pp. 60–75.

We have found it impossible to expect the same continued output as in the North . . .

. . . . .

In 1937 and 1938, two plants were started, but the workers were not textile minded, so that it has required more and more supervision — at least three or four times the normal. There has been a terrific turnover because, after they make a little money, they quit . . . On account of their inefficiency and the extra supervision that is necessary the costs at present in the South are practically equal to what they were in our Northern Union plants . . .

. . . . .

Our Experience has been that, while there is some variation between plants in regard to efficiency, we have always considered it more or less due to plant layouts, our supervisory organization, and the type of manpower available, which we are sure is not brought about by the fact that the plant is located in any particular section of the United States . . .

Another interesting question put by Dr. Lester was: "In setting piece rates by time-study methods, has it ever been necessary to use different standards of achievement for fatigue, etc. in your Southern plants from the standards or allowances used for your Northern plants?" There were 34 answers: 27 — no difference; 2 set higher standards for the South, and 5 set lower standards for the South.

One consulting firm wrote:

We have made applications of our methods to all types of foundries in ten Northern states and prior to 1933, in (two Southern) foundries. We used the same data in those two instances as we apply to the North. Our standards were identical. Our records show that the response of Southern labor to our standards was in line with that of the North. I would say that the potentialities of Southern foundry mechanics and labor were on a par with those of the North.

Twelve consulting firms also replied on the question of labor efficiency under comparable conditions. Of twelve answers, two said Southern output was higher, six that it was the same, and four that it was lower. One consulting firm found that Southern output was 8 per cent higher in textiles and about 10 per cent lower for heavy manufacturing or durable goods and food packaging or preparing. In textiles, the explanation of higher productivity was held to be a better selection of workers, drawing from whole towns, whereas in New England textile workers were largely from "the lowest mental section of the population." The consulting firms also emphasized greater work-loads, and homogeneity of the labor supply in the South.

In general, the consulting firms were of the view that plant management was inferior in the South. "Management is a little more prone to procrastinate and is slightly less open-minded . . . "

"The greatest hindrance to good management in the South has been the plentiful supply of cheap labor . . . "

"Departmental supervision is less effective in the South . . . "

Labor officials generally contend that, given similar equipment, supervision, and other non-labor factors, labor is as efficient in the South as in the North. When there are differences, these officials stressed variations in management and equipment.

In general, we can conclude from the Lester study that there is not much evidence of substantial lower labor efficiency of the South under comparable conditions. The evidence is a little on the side of somewhat lower efficiency in the South. Even in textiles, where the south performs unusually well, the evidence is mixed. Variations in man-hour output should be associated more with incomparability of conditions: inferior management in the South, larger work-loads in the South. There is no clear evidence of a correlation of low wage rates and correspondingly low efficiency.

Productivity depends on many factors: management, size of plant, number of products turned out, use of capital, etc. A low man-hour output in particular instances in the South might be explained by less capital, by inferior management, by smaller plants (with a more restricted market to tap), etc. To cite an example: Total unit labor required per identical set was 2½ times as great for a plant one-tenth as large as another.[7]

4. SPECIAL REFERENCE TO WORK-LOAD

In an earlier chapter, we commented briefly on work-loads. Here is some supplementary discussion. The Cotton and Rayon Textile Mills of Massachusetts, in a report to the 1950 Special Commission on the Textile Industry of Massachusetts, dwelt on the unfavorable productivity of Massachusetts textile workers. They are too much concerned over accustomed work-loads, and refuse to adjust even when a rise in load is consistent with the output of less energy.

[7] U. S. Department of Labor, BLS, *Trends in Man-Hours Expended Per Unit Home Radio Receivers, 1939 to 1947* (December 1949).

There is little doubt that due to new and modern machines, improved methods and modern working conditions, additional productivity per worker can be obtained without additional "energy input" and with little or no increased physical strain. Although top management of the textile union is fully aware of the discrepancy of work assignments in New England as compared to the South and have publicly approved the principle of full man-hour productivity, the Northern textile operator through habit, tradition and the teachings of the old craft union and his father before him, has become accustomed to thinking of his work assignment in terms of number of machines which he is required to operate, rather than in terms of the actual time and effort required . . . A modern textile mill considers 85% of the worker's time to be a full-time job and allows 15% of the worker's time for rest, idle time, and personal needs. In many Massachusetts mills today not more than 40% to 50% of the worker's time is consumed in productive efforts.[8]

Because of the absence of work traditions in the South, management of new mills have found little or no opposition to work assignments greater than in similar occupations in the North. It was pointed out also that this variance in worker attitudes had, in the past, made easier the introduction of the new and more efficient machinery in established mills in the South, which in turn further improved the competitive advantage of manufacturers in that area.[9]

A firm of textile engineers recently made a survey of comparative work assignments in 21 Southern mills as compared to like assignments in New England mills. This is what they found: [10]

Machines Per Tender

	North	South
Pickers	2 to 7	2 to 9
Cards	18 to 26	24 to 52
Drawing deliveries	18 to 36	18 to 48
Combing deliveries	6 to 8	6 to 12
Roving frames (long draft)	2 to 3	2 to 6
Spinning frames (long draft)	8 to 20	8 to 26
Looms X-2	24 to 36	24 to 72
Looms	8 to 12	12 to 18

This same firm of textile engineers estimated that Northern labor costs on a modern mill of 450 looms, producing combed broadcloth, amounted to $44.44 per hour more in the North than in the South.

[8] Report *Cotton and Rayon Textile Mills of Massachusetts* (1950), pp. 7–8.
[9] Report *Cotton and Rayon Textile Mills of Massachusetts*, p. 29.
[10] Report, *Cotton and Rayon Textile Mills of Massachusetts*, p. 10.

Extending these results to the entire New England cotton and rayon industry, these engineers find that the North would require 70,000 operatives, the South 52,278; total pay (assuming equal wage rates), $77,770 and $58,080; and the excess of costs in the North over the South for a 40-hour 50-week year would be $39.4 million.[11]

Nor do these New England employers agree that larger assignments increase costs. Thus, one of the best running spinning jobs in New England is being operated on the basis of 18 sides per spinner with semi-specialized scheduling of work. An especially modern Southern plant producing the same count of yarn used in the same type of fabric has a spinning schedule of 22–24 sides per spinner. In the measurement of production efficiency in actual pounds per spindle hour, the output in the Southern mill exceeds that of the Northern by 6–7 per cent. For a typical fabric, three Southern mills produced the material at an average cost of 14.7 cents a yard; the Northern mill, at 21.1 cents a yard. The loom assignment was 82, 72, and 70 per weaver in the South, and 48 in the North.[12]

5. LABOR ON PRODUCTIVITY

In labor circles, the low productivity is associated with poor management and ruthless consumption of capital on the part of New England mills. This is the period of integration, of new products, of new methods. It is the failure of management to keep on its toes that explains the difficulties of New England mills.[13]

We wish to emphasize from the very start that there is no such problem as the "New England textile problem." . .

The problems which beset us now arise from the deficiencies of individual manufacturers who are showing lack of enterprise and who are refusing to build up through adequate modernization of equipment, management, merchandising, research facilities, product development and sales organization, the type of enterprise required in this day and age in the textile industry. The issue is that of the individual manufacturer rather than that of an area.

[11] Report *Cotton and Rayon Textile Mills of Massachusetts*, pp. 11–12.
[12] Report *Cotton and Rayon Textile Mills of Massachusetts*, pp. 14–15. Cf. Report of the 1950 Massachusetts Special Commission on Textiles, pp. 28–31.
[13] See, especially, *Statement of Solomon Barkin on behalf of the Textile Workers Union of America before the Massachusetts Special Commission on the Textile Industry on October 31, 1949.*

The competent New England manufacturer who is following current lines of progressive development will flourish. Those who are unfortunate enough not to have fully fathomed the fundamental changes taking place within the industry and reorganized their properties to meet these trends will not survive.[14]

Barkin puts the latest developments as follows: [15]

What is significant about the industrial giants is that they have radically altered the prevailing type of business organization. They are generally organizations which maintain their own selling houses; and in some instances actually convert the goods or manufacture apparel or industrial, or home furnishing products; maintain research facilities for the development of new products, investigate new processes; test their products; investigate new markets; establish brands; engage in national brand advertising and establish close relationships with the users of their products to keep abreast of trends and to expand the uses of their products.

The old image of the textile manufacturer who produced gray goods for the general market, which products were unidentified or undistinguished, and who could maintain his market only by underselling his goods in comparison to other producers has been reduced to relative unimportance . . .

In this state of affairs therefore, the enterprise engaged in the manufacture of traditional products, which is not seeking new products, which does not have its own brands and selling organization and which is not alert to economic trends is distinctly handicapped. In this new business era only the exceptional small enterprise can easily survive and grow. It does not ordinarily have the resources with which to cope with these developing trends or keep abreast of them.

Second, the industry is being radically transformed by technological changes affecting the methods of manufacture, the plants and the products. In this connection the most significant fact for New England is that the traditional woolen and worsted industry is facing competition from new fibres and new processes. Rayon tropical suitings have definitely established themselves and are now making progress in getting part of the all year round market. Despite this threat and actuality, the traditional woolen and worsted industry has retired resignedly in face of this foe. Its smugness and indifference to the radical changes in market have left it belatedly behind. The emphasis on patterned goods has handicapped the producer of piece dye fabrics . . .

The individual woolen and worsted company must reëquip itself with hundreds of thousands, to millions of dollars of new equipment and machinery if it is to remain in business. The excessive profits of the war period must be plowed back. Unfortunately, the industry is slow in

[14] *Statement of Solomon Barkin . . . October 31, 1949*, p. 1.
[15] *Statement of Solomon Barkin . . . October 31, 1949*, pp. 6, 7-8, and 9.

developing new uses for its products or adding those vital fabric finishes
which will reëstablish the superiority of the woolen and worsted fabric.

Technological developments have not been restricted to the woolen
and worsted industry. It is only being more radically shaken by them
because of its slow technological progress during the last thirty years.
The appearance of nylon is fast threatening many established cotton and
rayon products. Orlon is on the horizon and promises to make further invasions into the woolen and worsted market. Saran is substituting for
rayon and cotton duck. Fibre glass has made notable progress in replacing fine cotton yarns for wire insulation. Rayon tire fabric is fast
replacing cotton tire cords. Other illustrations of the radical changes in
fibre uses could be listed, but the above will suffice.

. . . . .

Every modern mill must have the new automatic winding machinery. In
each of the specific branches new machinery is being introduced at a rapid
rate. When the flow of new ideas for machinery is sluggish in this country, foreign countries move in to supplement the flow . . .

Industrial change has caught up with the textile industry. It has been
relatively slow to feel the impact of current industrial developments. But
now precision machinery, electronic controls, quality testing, new lay-
outs, labor saving devices and methods are flowing into it at a rapid rate.

The textile workers emphasize the failure of Northern mills to
reinvest their large profits. In New England for a recent year, the
average investment per employee was $261.90 and the Southern
average was 22 per cent higher.[16] It is possible to put too much into
these figures, for it might be expected that the more rapidly growing
area would necessarily spend more on investment. This, of course,
in turn helps explain the more rapid progress in the South.

6. CONCLUSION

Productivity varies with the industry; with the amount of investment, past and present; with the adaptiveness of management; with
the native ability, training, and coöperative spirit of workers. Taking
into account all of these considerations, we conclude that the North
still excels the South in man-hour output; and even in man-hour
output corrected for larger amounts of capital and more expensive
management. The advantages vary from industry to industry; and
when allowance is made for differences in wage rates, the South
excels in some industries — textiles in particular. In the training and
intelligence of workers, the North still seems to have an advantage

[16] *Statement of Solomon Barkin . . . October 31, 1949,* p. 14.

generally; but it is one that is being whittled down. In textiles, where the North draws primarily on below average workers, and the South on the aristocracy of labor, the latter is not far behind in training and intelligence and is far ahead in coöperative spirit. Where techniques and management are on a national basis, as in the new durable goods and investment industries, regional differences in productivity and wages are less than in other industries (e.g., soft goods). In the last generation, New England has concentrated on industries which have lagged in productivity gains. The result has been a reduction in the rate of job losses but also a relative decline in wage and income levels.

CHAPTER 16

VARIATIONS IN THE COST OF LIVING

The cost of living varies from region to region, though not so much as is popularly assumed. In large part the differences stem not from variations in prices of identical items but rather from unlike consumption patterns. Thus in the South, little warm clothing is needed and outlays for fuel and housing are relatively small. The Works Progress Administration in 1936 made a study of the cost of living in 59 cities. The range from high to low was 20 per cent overall. But whereas for food (which accounts for about 40 per cent of low-income budgets) the span was but 14 per cent, for clothing it was 24 per cent, for household operation, 44 per cent, and for rents, 54 per cent.[1]

This same study also suggests another reason for regional differences, namely, the size of the city. By regions, high and low were but 6.3 percentage points apart, with New England a maximum; but the extremes by size of city differed by 8 percentage points, the maximum being cities of ½–1 million population with 105.6 (all = 100) and cities of 25,000 to 100,000, a minimum with 97.6.[2] Variations in the cost of living between the large metropolitan area and small communities so frequently chosen for factory sites in the South are undoubtedly much greater than 8 percentage points.

The Works Progress Administration concluded: "Less was required per year for support of the maintenance level in the most expensive South Central city than in the cheapest New England or Middle Atlantic city." [3]

By now, it must be clear that the lower cost of living in the South is an obvious advantage, for wages below Northern levels can be

[1] Works Progress Administration, *Inter-City Differences in the Cost of Living* (1936), p. 5.
[2] WPA, *Inter-City Differences in the Cost of Living* (1937 ed.), pp. 132, 144.
[3] *Inter-City Differences*, p. xix.

paid without a reduction in the standard of living. A famous study by the Bureau of Labor Statistics revealed that in June 1947 it cost substantially more to provide a family of four with a reasonable standard of living in the North than in the South. The estimated cost was at a maximum $3111, in Washington, D. C. Boston was fifth from the top with $2981. The first Southern city to appear on the list was Mobile, Alabama which ranked thirteenth, with a cost of $2925. New Orleans had the lowest cost, namely, $2734, or 12 per cent less than in Washington. For the ten Southern cities included in this survey, the average cost was $2859; for the three New England cities, $2904, or but 2 per cent more.[4] This should not, however, be considered the measure of the South's advantage, for it is necessary to compare the particular cities which accommodate Southern and Northern industries.

As the newer industrial areas advance, their prices respond, for pressure on available housing, distributive facilities, labor, etc., increases. In other words, the underdeveloped areas gradually lose the advantage of cheaper living. Some indication of this appears in the increase in the consumers' price index in cities, which has tended to rise relatively in the South and fall relatively in New England. Thus,

(1935–1939 = 100)

	1923	1946
All	121.9	139.3
6 Southern cities	122.0	139.3
2 New England cities	119.7	134.6

the increase in the index between 1923 and 1946 was 14 per cent for six Southern cities; for the two New England cities, 12 per cent.[5] Although this is not a substantial difference, a more striking change occurs in the cost of food at retail. Here the average rise for 56 cities from 1935–1939 to October 1947 was 101.6 per cent; but Boston, next to the lowest, had a rise of but 91.8 per cent and in the three Southern cities the increase averaged 110.2 per cent.[6]

The pressure on living costs in Southern cities was especially evident during the war and postwar inflation. Thus, from August

[4] U. S. Department of Labor, BLS, *The City Worker's Family Budget,* Serial No. R 1909 (1948), p. 21.

[5] BLS, *Handbook of Labor Statistics* (1947 ed.), pp. 107–115.

[6] *Food Prices, Production and Consumption,* Senate Document 113 (1948), p. 33.

1939 to June 1946, the cost of living in seven of the ten largest Southern cities rose more than that for 34 large cities. From mid-1940 to early 1945, the average rise for the 34 cities was 26.2 per cent; the advance in all Southern cities but one exceeded the average, and for eight of these the rise was from 6 to 13 per cent more than the general average.[7]

In summary, living costs are lower in the South than in the North, a difference which gives the South an advantage. One reason for the South's advantage is greater concentration in smaller cities where costs are lower. The higher living costs in the North in part reflect higher standards of living, in part higher costs for roughly similar standards. The latter, in turn, is related to savings on clothing and fuel and the lower living costs in smaller communities in which Southern plants are located. In the last 10–20 years, the South's advantage in living costs has been reduced to some extent, particularly in the cities.[8]

[7] *Labor in the South,* pp. 110–117.

[8] Some authorities deny the importance of these considerations. E. M. Hoover, *The Location of Economic Activity* (1948), pp. 105–106, and Hoover and Ratchford, *Economic Resources and Policies in the South* (1950), pp. 397–399.

CHAPTER 17

LEGISLATION AND ECONOMIC MIGRATION

1. THE PROBLEM

So far we have analyzed costs in which New England may be at a disadvantage. But in part, the movement from old to new areas is not justified by the underlying cost and market conditions. The New England capitalist seeking the best possible return on his investment does not merely compare returns in New England with those in the Southeast. He seeks the state offering the lowest costs and the most desirable environmental conditions and within that state the community offering the most favorable conditions.

Older communities seeking to preserve their industrial position are confronted not only with fair competition, which is bound to result in relative and even absolute losses, but also "unfair" competition. The new areas, for example, offer subsidies to new industries or new plants, inclusive of free land, factories at low rents, and tax exemptions; they offer a tax structure which, on the whole, favors business against the nonbusiness groups; they offer anti-union legislation, niggardly social security programs, and lower wages which in part are related to low standards of living. The result of these concessions is a movement of industry into these areas beyond what might be justified by underlying economic conditions.

In a more general way, what I am saying is that the development of industry in the South, for example, means a reduction of standards of living in the nation. To the extent that the newer industrial area is unwilling to meet the national standards of social security, of trade unionism, and of tax equity, its standards of living are lower. New England's deserted textile towns and abandoned factories are in part the price of a transfer of the industry to an area where New England's high standards are not being met.

No easy answer to the problems raised by this migration is possible. Even subsidies may be justified on the grounds that unless subsidies are offered, the underdeveloped areas, without recourse to "infant industry" tariffs, can never establish themselves on a position of equality with the older industrial regions. The subsidy is a substitute for the temporary tariff. One may also contend that the South's wage levels are low, that plentiful labor is its important resource, and that low wages and standards of living merely reflect the advantage of its one rich resource.

Yet the older industrial areas are confronted with a serious problem. Can they afford to advance in social legislation when the newer areas are capturing their industries? Or should they retrace their steps? Should any one state or community be allowed to depress standards of living and thus attract industries and factories? Should South Carolina, for example, the magnet for at least two of the outstanding cases of migration (the Kendall Company and Textron), be allowed to pay unemployment compensation benefits of one-half or less of those paid in Massachusetts? (The benefits multiplied by weekly payments are less than one-half in the Southern industrial states than in New York, Connecticut, and Massachusetts.)[1]

A partial answer lies in increased federal determination of standards. In the international economy, the competition of countries with cheap labor is frequently a subject of consideration. But the comparative cost principle suggests noninterference, and stresses the gains to be had from free trade. Yet even here temporary difficulties suffered by American industries are a matter of legislation. Where, as in interregional trade, there are virtually no obstacles to movements of capital, management, and goods, the effects on workers injured by the free movements of other factors are serious indeed. The federal government can surely assume greater responsibilities in setting minimum standards of working conditions, of social legislation, of benefits under social security, of tax patterns. (The last, for example, might be accomplished by an increase in tax collection and distribution of proceeds by the Federal Government, a movement already on its way.) The question may be raised whether regions or communities should be allowed to induce vast losses, both private and public, in older industrial areas, without real underlying advantages.

[1] Massachusetts *Report of the Special Commission Relative to Textile Industry* (May 1950), pp. 16–17.

2. LEGISLATION

Social legislation, however justified on other grounds, may well be a disadvantage to progressive states in competition with others. In the struggle for industrial supremacy, the South has gained on the North and on New England in particular because it has lagged in social legislation. The older states have progressed in regulating wages and hours, in the protection of women and minors, in social security — but their advances have increased the relative costs of manufacture and selling. To some extent federal legislation, particularly in the field of minimum wages, has negated the differentials between states. A federal minimum wage of 50 and later 75 cents an hour makes inoperative the minimum wage of 25 cents in some of the Southern states. (The federal law does not, however, apply to industries whose output does not leave the state.) Yet other aspects of federal legislation have weakened the competitive position of the Northeastern states. Thus, under federal unemployment insurance, the pay-roll taxes (and benefits) are less and the costs less (because of relatively less coverage and less unemployment) in the South.

Here are a few examples of the disadvantages suffered by the North as a result of wage differentials. All Northern cotton textile mills had minimum job rates of 97 cents an hour or more for experienced men and women. In the South, about 88 per cent of the mills had minimum rates under 95 cents for men and 83 for women, the range being from 75 to 95 cents. The Massachusetts Commission on the Textile Industry estimated the average minimum rate for the South at 87 cents, a rate above the legal minimum.[2]

Too much weight should not, however, be put upon minimum wage legislation. For the most part, the legislation reflects existing wage rates, although it may exclude a limited number of inefficient or parasitic employees. Hoover and Ratchford contend that even the 75-cent minimum wage legislation has had little effect in the South, since wages were generally above this level. Southern manufacturers have to some extent resented federal minimum wage regulation, contending that the South could attract industry only by paying lower wages. In the opinion of these dissenters, the

[2] Massachusetts *Report of the Special Commission Relative to Textile Industry*, p. 28.

South's most valuable asset has been the plentiful supply of cheap labor. It is no more fair to raise artificially the price of this most potent factor than it would be to raise the price of coal for Pittsburgh or of capital for New York City.[3] Hoover and Ratchford are not sympathetic with this position, contending that labor is as productive in the same industries in the South as elswhere, and that the mix of capital, technology, and labor (despite a plentiful supply of labor in the South) will be similar to that in the North. Hence lower wages than in the North are not a condition for moving workers from the farms.

The slight progress made by the South in minimum wage legislation as compared with the North is suggested by what follows. It should be emphasized, however, that the state minimum wage laws need cover only intra-state industries, although the failure of some states to enact laws for industries that sell over state lines — e.g., textiles — is costly to the other states which cover such industries at wages above the federal minimum.

The Department of Labor publication, *Labor in the South*, includes the following:[4]

Since the first minimum wage law was passed 34 years ago (1912), State minimum wage legislation has been enacted in 26 States, Alaska, the District of Columbia, Hawaii, and Puerto Rico. In only 4 States (Connecticut, Massachusetts, New York, and Rhode Island) and in Hawaii and Puerto Rico does the legislation cover men.

. . . . .

Four, among the Southern States studied — Arkansas, Kentucky, Louisiana, and Oklahoma — have enacted minimum wage laws, and they apply to women or to women and minors. The Arkansas law, passed in 1915, applicable to women only, with specific industry coverage, establishes a statutory minimum wage of $1.25 a day for experienced workers. The minimum rate for workers with less than 6 months' experience is $1.00 a day. Time and a half pay is required after a basic 8-hour day and basic 6-day week.

In Kentucky, a minimum wage law of the wage-board type applies to women and minors. Under this authority a blanket order, covering all

---

[3] *Report of the Special Commission Relative to Textile Industry*, pp. 398–400, 414–416. Cf. the evidence of J. Van Sickle before the Sub-Committee of House Agricultural Committee, 80th Congress, *Study of Agricultural and Economic Problems of the Cotton Belt*, p. 688; Report of the Joint Committee on the Economic Report on *The Impact of Federal Policies on the Economy of the South* (1949), pp. 48–49.

[4] *Labor in the South*, pp. 121–122.

industries except laundry and dry cleaning and dyeing, provides for minimum wage rates ranging from 20 to 25 cents an hour, according to zone. A separate laundry, dry cleaning, and dyeing order establishes rates ranging, according to zone, from 20 to 28 cents an hour. A hotel and restaurant order passed subsequently to the blanket order provides for rates ranging from 20 to 30 cents an hour. Each order provides for payment of overtime rates.

The Louisiana law, which is also of the wage-board type, applies to women and girls. Although the legislation was enacted in 1938, no minimum wage orders have been issued to put the law into effect.

The Oklahoma law, also of the wage-board type, was written to cover men, women, and minors. The law has been declared unconstitutional as to its coverage of men and boys, owing to a defect in the title. Enforcement of the orders for women is prevented by injunction, so that the law is inoperative.

All four laws exclude agriculture; the Kentucky and Louisiana laws exclude domestic service. In Kentucky, persons subject to regulation by the public service commission, and in Louisiana, municipalities having a population of 10,000 or less, are not covered by the minimum wage acts.

Another type of social legislation that may be harmful to the state introducing it is that which protects the worker against long hours, women and minors against night work, minors against premature desertion of the schools. In discussing this problem, the statement of the Cotton and Textile Mills of Massachusetts concludes "that the difference in the requirements and provisions of state labor laws has been a factor entering into the consideration of a change in manufacturing location." [5] It is indeed unfortunate that the law which prevents women from working in factories after 11 P.M. frequently precludes the three-shift system and, therefore, tends to raise unit costs in the Northern mills and deprive them of much production in periods of high activity. According to a memo of the Boston office of the Bureau of Labor Statistics (April 1949), 8 per cent of the workers in the Northern textile mills were on a third shift; and 17 per cent in the Southern mills. The solution lies not in retracing steps as, for example, the recent extension of work in Massachusetts for women in factories from 6 P.M. to 11 P.M., but rather the pushing ahead of similar legislation in backward states.

[5] *Memorandum on the Cotton and Rayon Textile Industry,* before Massachusetts Special Commission Relative to Textile Industry, p. 16.

From the Massachusetts *Report of the Special Commission Relative to the Textile Industry*, we take the following: [6]

It was represented to the Commission that the hours for working minors and women are of major importance to the industry. Due to the high cost of equipment and machinery, the fact that the business is seasonal, and to operating practices in competitive mills in other States, it is essential to operate in many branches of the industry "around the clock." Chapter 149, section 66, of the General Laws of Massachusetts (Tercentenary Edition) provides that persons under eighteen years of age may not be employed in manufacturing or mercantile establishments after 11 P.M. and before 6 A.M.

Under union rules the choice of shifts becomes a matter of seniority, and while it is true that some individuals prefer the second and third shifts, the majority prefer daytime work hours, resulting in filling up the daytime shifts with senior workers, and if minors cannot procure work on the first or second shifts, there is little opportunity for them in the industry. This situation has resulted in the diversion of young blood. It was revealed that in thirty-one other jurisdictions there are no regulations relative to the working hours of minors between the ages of sixteen and eighteen years.

Under chapter 149, section 59, of the General Laws (Tercentenary Edition) Massachusetts regulates the hours of employment of women in the textile and leather industries in that no woman may work after 11 P.M. (this was formerly 6 P.M.) nor before 6 A.M. It was pointed out to the Commission that many mill workers are women, and that this regulation makes it difficult, if not impossible, to operate three shifts a day. Suspension of the laws regulating the working hours of women and minors is within the power and at the discretion of the Commissioner of Labor and Industries, but it has been represented that manufacturers find the situation unsatisfactory in long-range planning.

* * * * *

Evidence was heard to the effect that working conditions in the textile mill of today are far different from the conditions in former times; that the mills are clean, some air conditioned, there is adequate transportation and protection, yet hours of female labor in this industry are restricted. Chapter 149, section 100, of the General Laws of Massachusetts (Tercentenary Edition) provides that no minor or woman shall be employed for more than seven and one half hours without an interval of thirty minutes for a meal, which restriction causes a stoppage in machinery, which stoppage in turn marks some materials in the process of manufacture, and makes the employment of women in three eight-hour shifts impossible. It was represented that certain work, particularly that requiring finger dexterity, required female labor, as well as the fact there exists a repug-

[6] *Report of the Special Commission Relative to the Textile Industry*, pp. 31–33.

nance among male labor to perform certain jobs considered as "women's work."

That the South still has a long way to go is suggested by the following: [7]

North and South Carolina, in 1937 became the first of the Southern States to incorporate a 16-year minimum age standard in their child labor laws. Florida followed in 1941, Louisiana in 1942, and Georgia in 1946. Four of these five States — Georgia, Louisiana, North Carolina, and South Carolina — have a 16-year minimum age for employment in factories at any time and for any employment during school hours except in agriculture and domestic service. The fifth State — Florida — also has a 16-year minimum age for factory employment at any time, but requires a minimum age of 14 for all other employment during school hours.

A 15-year minimum age requirement obtains in factory and related employment in Texas. A 14-year minimum age standard applies to factory employment at any time in the remaining seven States (in Kentucky only during school hours), and to all other work during school hours, except in Mississippi, Oklahoma, and Virginia. In Virginia, work in agriculture and, in Mississippi and Oklahoma, work in agriculture and certain other occupations are not covered. . . . . .

None of the 13 States protects minors up to 18 years of age from excessive hours of work to the extent recommended by the International Association of Governmental Labor Officials — a maximum 8-hour day, 40-hour week, and 6-day week. Louisiana, which has an 8-hour day, 44-hour week, and 6-day week for minors under 18, comes nearest. Few of the other States have limited maximum hours for both boys and girls of 16 and 17.

Five States, in addition to Louisiana, have adopted for children under age 16, a maximum workweek standard of less than 48 hours. These are Florida, Georgia, and North Carolina, with an 8-hour day, 40-hour week for children under 16, and Mississippi and Virginia with an 8-hour day, 44-hour week, for such children. Except for South Carolina, the remaining States have an 8-hour day, 48-hour week, applicable to children under 16 (in Texas to children under 15). South Carolina has no maximum hours of work provisions applicable to minors only, but has an 8-hour day, 40-hour week, 5-day week for most employees of any age in silk, rayon, cotton, and woolen mills. For girls in stores the maximum is a 12-hour day, 60-hour week.

3. COSTS OF SOCIAL SECURITY

Under the American system, the responsibility for social security rests largely on the states. Under the Social Security Act of 1935 and

[7] *Labor in the South,* pp. 135–136.

later amendments, the federal government provides for collection
of taxes and sets minimum standards. Nevertheless, in some areas
— e.g., workingmen's compensation — the responsibilities lie wholly
with the state governments; and in others — e.g., unemployment compensation — the state governments retain a large degree of discretion.

One of the major complaints made by New England businessmen
against doing business in New England is the high cost of social
security programs. For example, Mr. Kendall, the Chairman of the
Kendall Company, one of the large textile firms in New England,
wrote a series of articles for the *Boston Herald* (March 18–20, 1951)
in which he complained of the high taxes which were driving industries out of Massachusetts. The high social security burden especially
received his attention. For workingmen's compensation, Mr. Kendall
claimed that his firm paid $32,910, or 113.78 per cent more than in
comparable plants in four non-New England states where he
operated — South Carolina (6 plants), North Carolina (1 plant),
Illinois (2 plants), Indiana (1 plant). For unemployment taxes, his
firm paid 227.27 per cent more than in the four states outside of
New England. He estimated that the costs of the latter would be
$108,000 in Massachusetts (in 1951, at 2.7 per cent rate), $20,000 in
Illinois and Indiana, $40,000 in North Carolina, and $52,000 in South
Carolina. (The comparisons were for plants of similar size.)

Undoubtedly, the burden of social security is greater in New
England than in the South. In the three southern New England
states, which account for most of the industry of New England, the
average weekly benefit under unemployment compensation in 1947
was $20.10; in the seven most important Southern industrial states,
$13.17. In the three New England states, the maximum duration
of benefits averaged 24 weeks; in the seven Southern states, 17½
weeks. In the years 1942, 1945, and 1948, the contribution (tax)
rates as a percentage of covered pay rolls were:

	1942	1945	1948
3 New England states	2.50	1.90	1.03
7 Southern States	1.87	1.33	1.10

The differential in the tax rate has tended to decline, but as a result
of depleted reserves associated with substantial unemployment,
the New England rates in 1951 once more exceeded those of the
Southern states. In the ratio of benefits to taxable wages, the advan-

tage of the South is once more evident. Benefit schedules are more generous in New England and, with large amounts of unemployment, it might be expected that benefits as a percentage of taxable wages would be higher.[8]

Ratio of Benefits to Taxable Wages, by States

	1938	1939	1940	1941	1945	1946	1947	1948 [a]	Average of 8 years
3 New England States	3.0	1.6	3.1	0.8	1.0	0.8	1.4	1.5	1.65
7 Southern States	1.7	1.3	1.5	0.7	0.4	1.4	0.7	0.6	1.04

[a] 12 months ended September 30, 1948.

A comparison of New England and the rest of the nation also reveals more generous benefits and higher costs of social security for New England. On the basis of amount of qualifying earnings, of maximum weekly benefit amounts (New England, $25.83, and the United States, $23.50), total benefits in benefit years (average New England = $597; average of United States = $510), and maximum number of weeks (23 and 21½, respectively) — in all of these the burden is greater in New England. But it is not clear that there is much difference between New England and its important Northern industrial rivals.[9]

Recently the government issued a history of unemployment insurance from its inception in 1938 to December 31, 1950. Several interesting points may be gleaned from this comprehensive survey:

1. The amounts collected for the country over 13 years were $15,361 million; for New England, $1180, or about 7–8 per cent, an amount somewhat greater than its proportion of workers or income.

2. In cumulative benefits paid, New England accounted for $845 million, or more than 10 per cent of the $8369 million paid out.

[8] Material in last two paragraphs calculated from U. S. Senate Document No. 208, *Recommendations for Social Security Legislation: The Report of the Advisory Council on Social Security to the Senate Committee on Finance* (1949), pp. 227–232.

[9] For relevant information, see U. S. Department of Labor, *Handbook on State Unemployment Insurance Laws* (1950), and *Comparison of State Unemployment Insurance Laws,* as of September 1949.

This burden has been disproportionate in New England, and especially in Massachusetts, which had paid out $465 million.

3. Funds available for payment at the end of 1950 were $6972 million for the nation and $343 million in New England, or less than 5 per cent of the nation's total. In Massachusetts, there was available but $92.6 million, or only 1⅓ per cent of the nation's total (its income is about 3.5 per cent of the nation's total). In contrast Connecticut, with more than 2 per cent of the nation's reserves available, receives about 1½ per cent of the country's income.

4. For each dollar paid in, the average benefits received in the country over these 13 years amounted to 64 cents. For Massachusetts, the corresponding figure was 97 cents; for Rhode Island, 96 cents; and for Connecticut, 59 cents. In 1950, the benefit payments for each dollar paid in were $1.15 in the United States, $1.29 in Massachusetts, $1.26 in Connecticut, and $1.15 in Rhode Island.

5. Over the five postwar years, the average ratio of benefits to taxable wages was 1.55 per cent. The corresponding average for Massachusetts was 2.14; for Connecticut, 1.54; for Rhode Island, 3.16.

6. The federal government also estimated the per cent employed covered workers who could be paid benefits for maximum duration under existing law out of funds available December 31, 1950:

For the nation, 48.9 per cent; for Massachusetts, 12.8 per cent; for Connecticut, 51.8 per cent; for Rhode Island, 17.8 per cent.

Under a uniform benefit law (26 weeks' benefit, payments amounting to 1/20 of high-quarter income, with a minimum of $5 weekly and a maximum of $25 weekly), the *percentage* of covered workers who could be paid would be less than under existing law:

New Minimum Standard

United States	39.1	(under existing law = 48.9)
Massachusetts	11.3	(" " " = 12.8)
Connecticut	46.7	(" " " = 51.8)
6 States in South (Region VI)	39.2	(" " " = 72.4)

Source of all figures in these paragraphs: U. S. Department of Labor, **The Labor Market and Employment Security** (April 1951), p. 36.

The low ratio of covered workers payable under the proposed schedule, relative to numbers payable under the present benefit schedules in the South, suggests (compare New England) the low standards in the South.

In general, these summary figures show that the burden of un-employment has been greater in New England than in the country and especially in New England vis-à-vis the South; and more so in Massachusetts, Rhode Island, and New Hampshire than in the other New England states.

In workingmen's compensation, the benefits are more generous and the costs higher in the North than in the South. In employee coverage, in medical and hospital care, in diseases covered, and in numerous other respects, the New England states are ahead of the Southern states. The difference between New England and 13 industrial competitors (inclusive of three Southern states) is not, however, large.

	Maximum Percentage of Benefits to Average Wage		Benefits Maximum	Payments Per Week Minimum $	Payments Maximum $ per Week	Maximum Payments $
	Widows	Widows and Children				
New England States	57	59	362	11.50	25.17	6,900
Average of 13 Competitive States	52	61	362	9.34	25.10	7,600

Source: Calculated from U. S. Department of Labor, **State Workmen's Compensation Laws** (September 1950), p. 13.

It is clear that the burden of social security in New England and the Northeast, generally heavier than in the South, aggravates the industrial disadvantage of the Northeast. Yet too much can be put into this aspect of the problem. It is well for the hard-pressed businessman to realize that the pay-roll tax or the payments out of gross receipts for insurance against workmen's compensation are part of the cost of doing business; that according to the accepted theory of incidence, these costs are passed on to workers in lower current wages.[10] Only in so far as these costs are passed on to con-sumers in higher prices for commodities and services subject to interregional competition does the region suffer from the excess costs of social security.

A second point is that the differential of, say, one-half of 1 per cent of pay rolls, even if passed on in higher prices, is not a substan-tial factor. The third point relates to the position taken by Mr.

[10] Cf. my *Economics of Social Security* (1941), Part III.

Kendall. Differences in tax burdens for individual businesses may exceed the average differences. For example, Mr. Kendall's tax advantage in the Southern states rests largely on the fact that his firm receives large tax concessions under merit rating in the Southern States. Furthermore, with the large depletion of reserves in New England states, tax rates were high in 1951. By using 1951 as a basis of comparison, Mr. Kendall exaggerates differences in rates; and by generalizing from his firm's experience, he gives the impression of variations for all greater than they actually are.

The fact remains, however, that more generous formulae for benefits and a greater amount of unemployment increase the burdens on New England industry and especially vis-à-vis the South. A true index of the burden should, however, take into account the incidence of the tax and relative coverage of pay rolls and the taxes in relation to pay rolls over the years, not merely for one year.

CHAPTER 18

UNIONIZATION AND STRIKES[1]

1. UNIONIZATION

Before the war, under the stimulus of the Wagner Act, unionism made great strides in the North and was making progress in the South. The Department of Labor summarized the situation as follows in 1946:[2] "It is clear that union organization in the South is substantial in character and is no longer restricted to its traditional spheres in railroading, printing, and a few other industries."

Yet at the time of the enactment of the Taft-Hartley Act, the North was at a great disadvantage because unionization had gone so much further there than in the South. For example, whereas only about 20 per cent of the cotton textile workers are unionized in the South, they are predominantly unionized in the North and the unions are much stronger. Of cotton garment establishments investigated recently, 19 out of 24 were unionized in New England, 79 out of 97 in the Middle Atlantic States, and but 9 out of 32 in the Southeast. Furthermore, the same unions will generally exact less onerous terms in the South than in the North.

Trade-unionism makes a difference because, among other reasons, wages are generally high in union shops. Just before the war, labor in unionized meat packers' shops received 62.7 cents per hour while in the nonunionized shops it received but 56.6 cents.

The Taft-Hartley Act has had the effect of freezing New England in its current *relatively* unfavorable unionization position. By guaranteeing employers freedom of speech, by changing rules of evidence, by outlawing the closed shop, and by introducing numerous other changes, the authors of the Taft-Hartley Act have substantially retarded unionization in the South where the largest advances remain to be made. The companies frequently intimidate

[1] Parts of this chapter are from a memorandum written by the author for Governor Dever of Massachusetts.

[2] *Labor in the South,* p. 173.

workers, use their freedom of speech to threaten workers who wish to join a union, fire organizers, refuse to abide by National Labor Relations Board decisions, introduce all kinds of delays as a means of flouting collective bargaining — in fact, frequently do not bargain collectively.[3] In some cases, by the time an employer has finally yielded, the union has disappeared.

The effects of the Taft-Hartley Act are suggested by the following:

Elections Lost by Textile Workers Union of America

	No. of Elections	No. of Employees
Before Taft-Hartley (June 1945–June 1947)		
Total textile elections	143	64,544
Lost	67	41,672
Per cent lost	46	64
After Taft-Hartley (June 1947–June 1949)		
Total textile elections	61	38,834
Lost	33	33,730
Per cent lost	54	87

Source: Memorandum TWUA.

The Textile Workers of America (CIO) are clear about the effects of the new legislation: not only are their unions losing more elections, but agreements follow in a much smaller percentage of cases once an election is won. It was the general contention of the CIO that mill control was much more on monopolistic lines than by collective bargaining: of 645,594 textile workers in the South, 299,238 were employed by 42 firms who operated 417 out of a total of 2051 plants in the South. The TWUA accounted for only 41,341 of the employees in these mills. The union has furnished dramatic evidence on the recent difficulties of trade unions in the South.

Some of these cases include stories of violence as in the Itasca and Hillsboro cases. Union members were beaten when they returned to work after a strike. There are stories of strikes which caused much loss of money to both employer and employees because the employer had gotten the idea that workers would no longer protest exploitation after the passage of the Taft-Hartley Act. In some of these situations the local unions actually did fold up for all practical purposes when the workers

[3] The reader will find plenty of evidence of illegal and immoral activities by Southern employers in hearings of Senate Committee on Labor and Public Welfare on *Labor-Management Relations in the Southern Textile Industry*, Parts 1 and 2 (1950), and especially the evidence of I. Katz, I, 71 *et seq.*

found themselves without legal protection against the worst forms of despotism. There was no way for even a strong International Union to assist these isolated workers short of moving an army into the area.

We wish to point out that this group of Texas cotton mill manufacturers has been and is still selling its products on the national market at the same prices all other producers are able to realize. However, these employers pay their workers even now from 20 to 40 cents per hour less than the unionized employers in Texas pay, and these manufacturers pay somewhat less than the prevailing rates in the cotton textile industry as a whole. These law-resisting employers have reaped considerable profits as their reward for thumbing their noses at the NLRB and the courts.

CIO Counsel summarized abuses as follows: [4]

It is difficult to assess the degree of animosity to unionization which possesses the controlling interests of textiles in the South. Some are more violent in their reaction than others. But, with one or two exceptions, none of them gives hospitable reception to the union. Alabama Mills, Inc., relies on armaments to smash the union, as it did at the Anchor-Rome Mill in Rome, Ga.; American Thread Co. puts its trust in slavish employees who indulge in kidnaping of organizers and gun play; while Burlington Mills and Deering-Millikin just close up the mill and move the equipment elsewhere. Bibb Manufacturing Co. relies upon hate sheets and community control; Clark Thread Co. devotes itself to appeals to prejudice through letters to the employees.

In fact the greatest opposition emanated from the Burlington Mills, which controlled 45 mills. From 1938 to 1949, the CIO was unable to complete a single collective-bargaining agreement, although relations with 16 mills were involved.[5]

The concerted nature of the attack against unionization is suggested by the contributions of some doctors and particularly of some of the local churches.

A physician castigated the Chamber of Commerce, which had already discouraged the union from coming into the area, for feeble opposition: [6]

And if you look into the CIO organization with an unbiased attitude, you will find it is shot all to hell with irregularities and rottenness and crime of all kinds and that it all stinks to high heaven. What can persuade anyone to believe that the CIO will smell any better from this point onward? I know a great deal more about this set-up than perhaps you think I know,

[4] *Labor-Management Relations in the Southern Textile Industry*, p. 88.
[5] *Labor-Management Relations*, p. 88.
[6] *Labor-Management Relations*, p. 7.

and it is my opinion that we in Anderson, are at the very threshold of a catastrophe.

If you will only reflect for a few minutes at the millions of dollars invested around Anderson in textiles within the last 8 years. Do you think for one moment that these millions of dollars would have been invested around there if we had had a lot of these slick, slimy, putrid, crooked, vicious CIO organizers and sympathizers here? No. These mills would never have come here. And many of these men in our chamber of commerce who are so infernally afraid to speak out against the CIO put up a veritable din or clamor to bring in these new enterprises. The enterprises came. Now what are these men doing? They are afraid to take a positive stand against the malignant cancerous activity of an organization that will spell death or ruin to our prosperous textile industry.

It seems to me that the very least the Anderson Chamber of Commerce can do, is to make the operation of our great textile plants smooth and easy by whatever means in its control. The present situation offers the chamber of commerce such an opportunity. The textile industry here deserves it. The CIO doesn't deserve a single bit of consideration from any of us.

Some churches also seem to be involved in anti-union activity:[7]

. . . My testimony deals with churches and ministers in textile villages of the South.

We cannot understand this problem unless we first know something of the pattern of employer paternalism in the textile industry. From the early beginnings of the industry in the 1880's through the present day, paternalism is the characteristic of labor relations in the industry. The average textile employer owns the houses and the streets of a village; he dominates the politics and the law; and he influences when he doesn't acually dictate what happens in the schools and the churches. The average minister of mill towns is hardly free to preach the gospel unafraid. Over him is the employer who will have donated the land on which the church stands, and have given substantially to the building fund, paid for the lights and water, contributed the parsonage, and paid a large proportion of the minister's salary. Under these circumstances, the minister is too often the captive of his benefactor; and consequently, when the workers begin to organize, he remains judiciously silent or attacks the CIO loudly and often hysterically as the "mark of the beast."

Three recent studies reveal the extent of company donations to churches. In his book, *Life in Mill Communities* (Presbyterian Press, Clinton, S. C.), William Hays Simpson, professor in the department of political science at Duke University (1943), states the following about mills in South Carolina:

"As a general policy, the mills donate the land on which the (mill) churches are located; for, out of 71 plants replying, 65 had made such a contribution . . .

[7] *Labor-Management Relations*, II, 167–168.

"The most common practice is for the mill to give one-half the total cost (of the church construction), promising to give its check when a similar amount has been raised by the church members . . . Complete records of church contributions are not kept by the mills, but the management of 56 plants have built or have contributed to the building of 112 churches, at a total outlay of $1,067,160.

"In a number of instances mills donate electricity or fuel to the churches, or furnish these supplies at greatly reduced prices. Many give directly to the support of the churches and Sunday schools, the annual gifts of 61 plants amounting to $54,370 in 1941 . . .

"Of the 74 plants reporting, 50 supply parsonages free, often including free water and electricity."

. . . . .

A similar study was made of mill communities in North Carolina by Miss Harriett Herring (*Welfare Work in Mill Villages*, University of North Carolina Press, 1930):

"Of the mills included in the study (322), 43 built churches for the workers, 78 mills aided the churches regularly, 126 contributed toward running expenses."

Dr. Liston Pope, now dean of the Yale Divinity School, substantiates these findings in regard to the city of Gastonia, N. C. (Liston Pope, *Millhands and Preachers*, Yale University Press, 1942):

"Nearly every mill in Gaston County has donated one or more lots for the erection of churches and has given appreciable percentages of the costs of construction. Conversely, there are practically no mill churches in Gaston County that were not partially built by mills of their vicinity" (p. 37).

As to current operating expenses of churches, Pope says:

"Gifts from mills comprised only 6 percent of the total amount received by Methodist pastors (20) in the county, but accounted for 20 percent of the total amount received by the ministers to whom subsidies were given" (p. 38).

In evaluating the motives which lay behind these gifts, Dr. Pope concludes that they were exceedingly mixed. Employers wanted to help the churches because they loved the church and wished to help their fellow man. But at the same time, the employers, often unconsciously, had a selfish motive in mind.

Here are some excerpts from the evidence of a Congregational Church minister, commenting on the church publications used to restrain the advance of trade-unionism.[8]

A typical example is found in the case of the Bibb Manufacturing Co. and its use of the *Gospel Trumpet* edited by Preacher Jack Johnson of

[8] *Labor-Management Relations*, II, 168.

Columbia, Ga. (National Labor Relations Board Case No. 10-C-1995-Bibb Manufacturing Co. and the Textile Workers Union of America, CIO). The Bibb Co. operates a typical company town at Porterdale, Ga., where all town property, except the churches and the railroad right-of-way are owned by the company; where all town officials are company employees; and where evidence brought out in the NLRB hearing shows that the mayor instructed the local police to spy on union meetings. In such an atmosphere, the company sent each employee a copy of the *Gospel Trumpet*, at the company's expense. This religious hate sheet according to Trial Examiner Thomas S. Wilson, "utilized every conceivable propaganda device from fear, hatred, race discrimination, bias, and prejudice, to loyalty to country and to the employer, to promises and inducements of better wages and better working conditions purporting to come from manufacturers, in order to prevent textile employees from joining the union . . . At least 90 per cent of the space of each issue of the paper was devoted to vicious attacks upon the union and the CIO, based purportedly upon religious grounds" (p. 6). The Board finally ruled that the Bibb Manufacturing Co. must cease from using the *Trumpet*. Today Parson Jack is still editing the *Trumpet* and is pastor of the Robert Memorial Church, valued at $100,000, in Columbia, Ga.

Despite these witnesses, it is probably too soon to judge the full effects of the Taft-Hartley Act. According to Professor de Vyver, unions in the South made roughly as much progress from 1938 to 1948 as in the rest of the country: about 88 per cent new members were added in both areas. But de Vyver suggests that legislation in 14 states which provides the right to work (anti-closed shop legislation) is a hindrance, as is the attitude of employers.

2. STRIKES[9]

If New England is at a disadvantage because unionization lags in the South, it has an advantage in that fewer strikes, with the accompanying losses of output, occur than in the country generally.

Thus, the Massachusetts Development and Industrial Commission of 1947 noted that on a five-year average (1939–1943) the man-days lost per employee were lowest in Massachusetts among ten leading industrial states — 0.56 days lost per employee (the highest was 2.16 in Pennsylvania).

The table below shows that in the years 1943–1949 the percentage of man-days lost was less than one-half the percentage of manu-

[9] For earlier statistics on strikes, see BLS, *Strike Data in the United States, 1880–1936.* New England's record was not always as good as it has been in recent years.

facturing employment in New England in relation to total manufacturing employment in the United States.

This is a favorable factor in the New England situation. But we
note that the explanation in part is the absence or limited importance
of certain industries which account for much of the industrial strife
— e.g., coal and automobiles.

Work Stoppages Caused by Labor-Management Disputes — New England

	% of Total Workers Involved	% of Man-Days Lost	% of Total Manufacturing Employment in N. E. in Relationship to Total Manufacturing Employment in the United States
All States	100.0	100.0	100.0
New England			
1949	1.6	2.0	9.5
1948	3.0	4.2	9.9
1947	4.1	5.1	9.6
1946	4.3	5.8	10.3
1945	4.1	4.9	9.8
1944	5.2	7.4	9.7
1943	4.1	2.8	10.2

Source: Boston Regional Office, Bureau of Labor Statistics, U. S. Department of Labor.

3. CONCLUSIONS

It is clear that New England has been injured by the Taft-Hartley
Act in so far as unionization has been slowed up in competitive areas
where it lags behind the North. At least from this viewpoint New
England would gain from a repeal of this act. What is needed to prevent the South's capturing other industries because of lower standards of living and of social legislation is an equalization of working
conditions. That means legislation by federal government and state
governments in the South which will raise social legislation to the
levels of an enlightened state like Massachusetts.

So long as Southern employers continue to oppose trade-unionism
by enlisting the support of the church, members of the medical
professions, the police, and thugs, and under the Taft-Hartley Act
can abuse the right of freedom of speech, it will probably be long before unionization will advance much in the South. Less unionization
means higher work-loads, greater freedom for managers, and wage
differentials. The unfortunate Southern textile strikes in the early
part of 1951 have further weakened the textile unions in the South.

PART IV

FISCAL POLICY

INTRODUCTION

In Part III, the major issue has been labor costs, the most important single element of costs. It is clear that the supplies of labor, working conditions, wage rates, work loads, the cost of living, and the contribution of management are all relevant; and together they help explain the disadvantages in labor costs that beset New England's industry. From these major problems we turn to one that is of much less importance but, from the attention given it, is still worth a thorough discussion.

I have devoted much space to the tax issue in the following chapters. In the struggle for industries, state and local governments use their taxing power as a means of enticing industries or of discouraging them.

As a *cost*, taxes are not very significant. As a *differential* cost, they are even less so. Since the heaviest taxes are federally imposed and businessmen can avoid local taxes by relocating, *differences* in state and local taxation become matters of secondary and possibly tertiary importance. Finally, the actual differences in tax costs between New England and its competitors are surprisingly small.

Indeed, not only the *total* amounts involved but the tax *structure* is of importance. The burden of taxes is greater on Massachusetts corporations than on corporations in competing states. Yet when allowance is made for the fact that these taxes are not largely passed on in higher prices, that in the years of greatest development the rise in tax yield has been very small compared to the gains of corporate income, that about two-thirds of the tax is in fact borne by the federal government (through deductions in arriving at federally taxable income), that the federal corporate tax is about seven times that of the Massachusetts tax, that against the corporation taxes levied in Massachusetts should be placed the heavy taxes on consumption levied elsewhere (which are an indirect burden on business) — when allowance is made for these factors, then the claim that heavy taxes on New England business are a major factor in inducing migration, is not supportable. I have considered the Massachusetts situation here (and in a separate chapter), because taxation in Massachusetts is a subject of widespread discussion.

The propaganda associated with this charge is possibly much more detrimental to the maintenance of business in the area than is the actual burden of taxes. Another safe conclusion is that in imposing heavier burdens on business than some of its competitors, the Massachusetts government provides a tax system which can much more easily be supported on reasonable principles of public finance than the tax systems of competitors which spare business and hit the relatively poor.

It is nevertheless arguable that in the light of the 1952 federal tax burden and the precarious position of the textile industry, New England should seek to lighten the tax burden on industry.

CHAPTER 19

TAXES

1. THE SIGNIFICANCE OF THE TAX PROBLEM

Differences in the competitive power of states and regions are often ascribed to differences in taxes. The true burden of existing taxes must be measured in terms of tax capacity and the extent to which taxes are a cost of doing business. The structure of the tax system influences both these factors: does business pay a disproportionate share of total government receipts or, conversely, is it exempted from tax payments? Undoubtedly the greatest significance of the problem lies in the fact that businessmen themselves claim that taxes are a *decisive* factor (mistakenly, as it will be shown). In this chapter we consider all of these elements and their effect on New England compared to other parts of the country.

2. TAXES AS A COST OF DOING BUSINESS

In a prewar study of manufacturnig costs, the Federal Trade Commission estimated tax *costs* at about 3 per cent of the total. Although since the war taxes have increased greatly, it is doubtful that they are any more important as a cost element. National income has tripled, and the heaviest taxes now are on surpluses. Income taxes, unlike excise taxes, are not a cost item.

On the other hand, the survival of business enterprise depends not only on costs but also on the profits retained after taxes. The location of new business may be greatly affected by differences in taxes which are not part of costs. Neither New Jersey nor Connecticut levies personal income taxes, and the prospective entrepreneur may, if costs and markets are similar, prefer to locate in these states rather than in New York or Massachusetts. The continued absence of personal income taxes undoubtedly indicates a deliberate policy of attracting industry into Connecticut and New

Jersey.[1] In a similar fashion, the existing tax structure may be a locational factor, if firms try to avoid a heavy general property tax.

The effect of the tax structure on competitive strength must be carefully analyzed, however. With a given amount of total receipts, heavier taxes on corporate income mean lower taxes on property and consumption. Prices are therefore lower than in other areas relying on, for example, sales and excise taxes, and business gains from increased purchases. But this differential is important only in competition with outside sellers. A large part of total income in a state is spent on domestic commodities and services where the differences in taxes among states make little difference in competitive position. In New England about two-thirds of total income is spent on regional goods and services; in a large state like Connecticut or Massachusetts the proportion is somewhat smaller. In the competition for sales outside the area (and about one-third of New England production is sold outside) low excise taxes in New England are significant.

Another relevant consideration is that taxes are not necessarily borne by those who pay them in the first instance. Thus, the taxes on business are in part on corporation income, and in part upon gross receipts and similar indices of tax capacity. To some extent, these taxes are considered as costs and shifted to the consumer. For example, taxes on public utilities tend to be passed on, for, *in practice*, regulations of public utilities guarantee 6–7 per cent on capital. The tax on corporate income is, in pure theory, assumed to be borne by business. In practice, rises in these taxes are an opportunity for increasing prices, where, as is often the case and especially for larger firms, the consumer is not charged what the traffic will bear. The pay-roll tax, which seems to irritate Masachusettes busi-

---

[1] Cf. State of Connecticut, *Report of the Connecticut State Tax Survey Committee* (1948), pp. 109–119. In opposing a personal income tax for Connecticut, the Committee does not mention the problem of interstate competition. There does seem to be a little lack of candor here. Its main points against the tax are (1) that the federal government has preëmpted the personal income tax; (2) that in paying a heavy income tax to the federal government, government considers capacity to pay adequately; (3) that in state and local services, the benefit principle and contributions by all should be emphasized; (4) that the payment of a tax by Connecticut residents doing business in New York might involve double taxation; (5) and that savings on federal income tax for Connecticut citizens resulting from deductions for state income tax, though a factor, would continue only so long as the federal tax remained high.

nessmen more than any other, is not borne primarily by the business unit. Its long-view incidence is generally held to be on wages.[2] Since the worker obtains what he produces (marginal productivity theory of wages), the more the employer pays out in pay-roll taxes, the less he pays out in wages. The actual incidence will to some extent vary from that suggested by this oversimplified theory.

A third reservation is related to the above. In so far as taxes are on surpluses and not on costs they do not affect the competitive position of industries or firms. Even where the tax is on costs, it can often be absorbed out of profits and, therefore, not require increases in prices.

Fourth, the businessman thinks in terms of taxes paid directly by him and not in terms of the taxes paid by others which in fact indirectly affect him. A case in point is the sales tax, levied on consumers in other states but a depressant on demand and hence also felt by business.

Fifth, the taxpayer emphasizes the increase of state and local taxes without considering adequately the economic milieu in which he operates. (The opposition to state and local taxes seems even greater than to federal taxes — undoubtedly in part because interstate competition is a real threat and, therefore, differences in tax burden are of concern, whereas federal taxes are equally depressive.) It would be well for the businessman to consider the rise of taxes in the postwar period in relation to the rise of prices, income, population, and services. Their significance as a cost item may then be somewhat lessened.

Another relevant factor is that excessive burdens resulting from local taxation are of declining importance, the explanation of this fact being the inelasticity of the sources of revenue of local government, with resulting greater dependence upon state and federal government. (This is important because differences in local tax burdens are especially great.) Thus, from 1890 to 1932 state taxes increased twice as much as local taxes; and from 1932 to 1946, about ten times as much (see table, page 186).

With the decline in the relative contribution of local taxes and with the failure of property taxes to respond to rising prices and incomes (these two are related, of course), property taxes are of

[2] Cf. my *Economics of Social Security*, Part III (1941).

much less importance than in the past. Even in Massachusetts, property taxes accounted for 22.9 per cent of all tax receipts in 1950 as compared with 57.3 per cent in 1936. Of total tax receipts for state *and* local government in Massachusetts, the contributions of property taxes were 62 and 78 per cent, respectively.[3]

	State Taxes	Local Taxes
	(Multiple of 1890 receipts)	
1932	20	11
1946	63	13

Source: Calculated from U. S. Census, **Historical Review of State and Local Government Finances** (June 1948), p. 13.

3. TAX CAPACITY AND TAX BURDEN[4]

Comparative tax burdens must be related to comparisons of taxable capacity. Our most detailed information on this point comes from studies of prewar years, and, as will be argued later, the position may have changed somewhat since then.

In the table below, each of the New England states is ranked according to various measures of taxable capacity. In Column 1 the measure is the potential yield of a uniform tax system, on a per capita basis. (Under such a system, Massachusetts' receipts would have been large; only seven states would have raised more revenues.) In Column 5 tax capacity is shown by six weighted indices: the proportion of urban population, the value added by manufacture, the farm cash income per inhabitant, postal receipts, motor-vehicle registration, and retail sales. Here Rhode Island, Connecticut, and Massachusetts rank ninth, fifth, and eighth out of the forty-eight states. If all the indices are averaged, Massachusetts would rank about sixth or seventh, Connecticut fifth or sixth, and Rhode Island ninth or tenth. These three states account for 80 per cent of New England's population: the other three have a much

[3] Computed from the Commonwealth of Massachusetts, *Report of the Special Commission on Taxation: Part I. The Tax System Today* (1951), p. 43.

[4] The figures used in this section are based on data in these publications: *Industrial Location and National Resources,* p. 322; Social Security Board, *Measurement of Variation in State Economic and Fiscal Capacity* (Washington, Government Printing Office, 1943), pp. 62, 65, 97; Social Security Board, *The Measurement of State and Local Tax Effort* (Washington, Government Printing Office, 1944), p. 42; National Resources Board, *Problems of a Changing Population,* pp. 207, 218; and U. S. Census, *Financing Federal, State and Local Government* (1941), pp. 106, 108.

lower tax capacity — they fall midway between the richest and the poorest of the forty-eight states.

Tax Burden.[5] Next there is the question of the proportion of tax capacity used: the larger the proportion, the greater is the relative tax burden and the more dangerous are further rises in tax rates. The Social Security Board has calculated state ranks for proportion of tax capacity used for the fiscal year 1938–39. This over-all index

Variations in Ranking of States under Eight Indices of Fiscal Capacity, for Specified Years (State with highest per capita amount ranked first)

	Yield of Uniform State Tax System, 1930		Wealth and Income, 1930	Series of Economic Resources [a]				
	(By New-comer)	(By Chism)	(By Blough)	1930 (By Norton)	1930 (By Mort)	1932, 1933 1935 (By SSB)	1935 (By SSB)	Income, 1935 (By SSB)
Rhode Island	10	18	8	9	9	9	7	8
Connecticut	5	4	6	7	5	5	4	5
Massachusetts	8	7	4	11	8	3	5	6
Maine	31	26	25	29	18	26	23	20
New Hampshire	29	21	16	21	27	16	13	16
Vermont	35	34	29	16	19	24	26	21

[a] These four series are in each instance based on various indices of economic well-being, e.g., retail sales, property tax assessment. The indices used differ in each series.
Source: Social Security Board, Measurement of Variations in State Economic and Fiscal Capacity (Washington, Government Printing Office, 1943), pp. 20, 26 (by P. Studenski).

is based on a study of degree of exploitation of the individual tax base in terms of prevailing state and local revenue structures.

(For 1938–39 each tax is related to its base: thus receipts from the general property tax are figured as a percentage of property values, sales taxes and retail licenses as a percentage of retail sales, and so on. States are then ranked in order of the percentages, a high precentage indicating that taxes were close to tax capacity.) The results are subject to a substantial margin of error, and yet are not without usefulness. The ranks for the New England states (the higher the rank, the more tax capacity is used up) are: Maine, 1; New Hampshire, 4; Massachusetts, 5; Vermont, 7; Rhode Island, 41; and Connecticut, 48.

On the basis of this study, the state and local tax burden of Maine, New Hampshire, Vermont, and Massachusetts relative to tax capacity

[5] The next few paragraphs are adapted from my "New England's Decline in the American Economy," *Harvard Business Review* (1947), pp. 363–365.

was severe indeed. Rhode Island and Connecticut, on the other hand, seem to have had large amounts of untapped tax resources.

A large part of the explanation of the heavy tax burden in the four high-ranking states lay both in the heavy reliance on the general property tax and the severe rate of this tax. This is one of the most unfortunate aspects of New England's fiscal system; for the property tax is to a substantial degree a cost which has to be paid irrespective of profits. It is, therefore, a depressant. Of fifteen states without income taxes at this time, three were in New England (each ranked forty-eighth). The last three columns show the relatively minor place of consumption taxes, except for gasoline taxes which exploit the tourist in Maine and Vermont. The capacity to pay, in terms of the major taxes (those listed account for 86 per cent of all state and local tax revenues) is given in the table below:

States Ranked on Basis of Ratio of Specified State and Local Revenues to Capacity Measures, Fiscal Year, 1938–39 (Rank among 48 states; highest state is 1)

State	Property Taxes	Income Taxes	Gasoline Taxes	Employer Unemployment Compensation Taxes	Retail Sales License Taxes
Massachusetts	3	4	36	17	45
Connecticut	37	48	38	34	37
Rhode Island	31	48	25	47	42
New Hampshire	7	18	29	43	47
Maine	1	48	18	36	39
Vermont	9	10	21	24	46

Source: **The Measurement of State and Local Tax Effort**, pp. 26, 34.
Note: Of all the revenue of state and local governments, property taxes accounted for 51.2 per cent, income taxes for 10.8 per cent, gasoline taxes for 9.1 per cent, employer unemployment compensaiton taxes for 8.7 per cent, and retail sales and license taxes for 5.9 per cent.

How valid are these indications at the present time? The only index of present taxable capacity is figures on income and economic growth. These suggest that while tax capacity in Connecticut, Rhode Island, and Massachusetts may still be high, it is exceeded by· capacity in many other areas.

The per capita income of these states, for example, rose by only one-half as much as that in the country as a whole from 1933 to 1949. Average incomes in these states were only 10 to 11 per cent higher than the national average in 1949: a contrast to the 1933 excess of 76 per cent.

The Massachusetts Special Commission (1951) also presents some indicators of economic growth: from 1939 to 1949 New England expanded less than the nation. In five important indices, New England's growth was 3/4, 3/4, 7/10, 3/5, and 3/4 that of the country as a whole.[6] These general indications of a smaller capacity to meet rising tax bills may be supplemented by details for 1948.

The accompanying table shows the percentage of state and local taxes, on a per capita basis, to per capita income. The percentages are computed for ten industrial states (including Massachusetts, Connecticut, Rhode Island, and New Hampshire) which had the highest percentage of manufacturing employment to total employment.

Industrial States, Taxes as Percentage of Income, 1948

	State Taxes	Local Taxes	State and Local Taxes
10 industrial states (inclusive of 4 New England states)	3.6	2.5	6.1
3 competitive Southern industrial states	5.2	1.5	6.7
New York (maximum output of factory output, but not in 1st ten in percentage of manufacturing employment)	3.4	3.0	6.4
California — new competitor	5.1	1.5	6.6
Massachusetts	3.7	3.6	7.3
Average of 4 industrial New England states	3.8	3.0	6.8

Source: **Survey of Current Business** and **Facts and Figures of Government Finance,** 1948–49.

We conclude from these figures:

1. That the *state* tax burden per capita in New England is lighter than in the competitive South and California, somewhat heavier than in New York, and roughly equal to that in the ten most highly industrialized states.

2. That the New England states are at a substantial disadvantage in the heavier burden of *local* taxes, and especially in comparison with the South and California.

3. That the net relative burden of both state and local taxes is somewhat greater in New England than for their competitors. The ratio of per capita state and local taxes to per capita income in four industrial New England states is 0.7 points, or 11.5 per cent

[6] *Massachusetts Special Commission on Taxation,* Part I, pp. 22–23.

above that in all ten industrial states (possibly 1 point or 16.4 per cent above that in the six other highly industrialized states), roughly equal to the ratio in the three Southern states and California, and 0.4 points or 6.3 per cent in excess of the New York ratio.

A more limited comparison made by the *Connecticut State Tax Survey Committee* reveals that in comparison with New York and New Jersey, tax burdens are light in Connecticut and about equally heavy in Massachusetts. Connecticut's burden is somewhat greater than is here indicated, since Connecticut residents transacting business in New York are subject to income taxes in New York. In comparing New York with Massachusetts, Connecticut, or even New Hampshire, the greater size of New York State should be considered. Undoubtedly there are economies of operation in a large state like New York, which are, however, offset to some extent by the high income level (and costs) in New York City and extension of services as the communities become larger.

State and Local Taxes, Per Capita, and in Relation to Incomes and Retail Sales, Five States, 1947

	Connec-ticut	New Jersey	Massa-chusetts	New York	New Hampshire
State and local taxes, per capita	$79.93	$103.94	$102.21	$118.62	$84.21
State and local taxes, as per cent of income	4.8	6.5	6.9	6.3	7.0
State and local taxes, as per cent of retail sales	8.5	10.9	12.0	13.6	10.7

Source: State of Connecticut, **Report of the Connecticut State Tax Survey Committee** (1948), p. 53.

4. TAX STRUCTURE

How burdensome a tax system is depends in part upon the structure. A crude comparison of tax structure of New England and the South, for example, shows that New England relies more on property and income taxes and the South more on consumption (e.g., sales) taxes. Both because of its inflexibility as revealed in its slow response to falling or rising incomes with unfortunate effects upon the public authority, and because of its dissociation from capacity to pay with troublesome effects on business and consumers, the general property tax is archaic. It is especially troublesome for older regions where any exodus of industry and population does not bring corresponding savings in cost of government and where the burden of the tax has to be apportioned over a smaller income or output; rates or (and) assessment will then have to rise.

We present (page 193) a recent view of the tax situation. These figures relate to state revenues primarily, and may be summarized.

1. The per capita governmental *expenditures* of the four New England industrial states are greater than the national average, are somewhat higher than those of the six other heavily industrialized states, are substantially less than those of California and New York, and are greater than those of Maine. (We include Maine as a state reflecting the tendency of industry to move from Southern New England to Northern New England.)

2. Per capita *state taxes* are roughly equal in the four New England industrial states to the average for all other groups of states listed, but somewhat above 6 non-New England industrial states and above those for the Southern states. (Note, however, the higher incomes in New England.) The reader is reminded of the more extensive discussion of pay-roll taxes in Chapter 17.

3. The tax structure in the four industrialized New England states varies (a) From the six other heavily industrialized states as follows: Lighter pay-roll taxes, license and privilege taxes, and heavier individual income and corporation taxes. (The last apply almost exclusively to Massachusetts.)

(b) From the three Southern competitors, the variations are: Heavier relative reliance on pay-roll taxes and license and privilege taxes and relatively less on sales, use, and gross receipts taxes.

(c) In relation to the country, the four New England states have relatively low individual income taxes and higher license and privilege taxes and corporate income taxes.

(d) In relation to New York, pay-roll taxes are low; sales, use, and gross receipts, and license and privilege taxes are high; individual income and corporation taxes are low.

In general, the differences in tax structure between the New England and other states is not great. In relation to competitors, the large differences are in pay-roll taxes — lower in relation to some, higher in relation to others. (But the *relative* burden of pay-roll taxes varies from year to year, depending upon the amount of unemployment and the state of the reserves.) Taxes on corporations are probably higher vis-à-vis the other industrial rivals, though here the taxes on corporations in Massachusetts are especially important.[7]

5. LOCAL TAXES AND THE GENERAL PROPERTY TAX

In the discussion of relative tax burdens, we shall show that the large differences between New England (and Massachusetts) and other regions and states are in local tax burdens. But the greater weight of differences in local tax burdens is not so important as it seems to be for two reasons.

First, the tax burdens vary greatly from locality to locality. A business depressed by heavy rates in one locality can move to another within the same state or region; and the incoming business firm can avoid the high tax cost area (e.g., Boston). Thus, for 1949 the direct tax per capita on property in 39 cities in Massachusetts varied from a minimum of $42.44 in Chicopee to a maximum of $118.69 in Boston. Four cities experienced taxes in excess of $75 per capita: Beverly ($77.63), Gloucester ($87.07), Newton ($91.64), and Boston. There were seven cities with taxes less than $50: Chicopee ($42.44); Gardner ($46.85), Lawrence ($47.10), Marlborough ($49.88), Newburyport ($49.89), Taunton ($44.32), Woburn ($47.36).[8]

---

[7] Cf. State of Connecticut, *Report of the Connecticut State Tax Survey Committee* (1948), p. 57. The Commission compares the structure of state and local taxes of Connecticut, Massachusetts, New Hampshire, New Jersey, and New York. General property taxes contribute a high percentage of total receipts in the three New England states; but in New Jersey the percentage of 67.9 greatly exceeds that of the three New England states (57–58), and in New York the percentage of 50.4 is much smaller than in the others. The percentage of receipts for business taxes varies greatly: Connecticut, 12.8; Massachusetts, 12.8; New Jersey, 10.3; New York, 14.6; New Hampshire, 4.4. The burden varies according to the type of business and the importance of the industry. Thus, insurance companies account for a large percentage in Connecticut, in part no doubt because of the importance of insurance. Unincorporated business is taxed in New York and Connecticut, but not in the other states (as special taxes on business). Utilities are heavily taxed in New Jersey and Connecticut, but lightly in Massachusetts. Though the percentage of business taxes to all taxes was identical for Massachusetts and Connecticut, the burden on the latter was less: total taxes were less per capita.

[8] Data compiled by Bureau for Research Municipal Government, Harvard Graduate School of Public Administration. I am indebted to Morton G. Schussheim for this material from a study, *The Revenue Expenditure Pattern in Massachusetts* (1950), made for Governor Dever under my supervision.

...ate and Local Taxation ... 4 New England Industrial States, 13 Rivers, and the United States

	Per Capita State Expenditure 1948 $	Per Capita State Taxes 1948 $	Percentage Distribution of General Revenue, 1948					Receipts & Local Tax Collections 1945 $ Million
			Unemployment Compensation	Sales, Use & Gross Receipts	License and Privilege	Individual Income	Corporation Income	
I. Ten States with 30 or More Per Cent of Income Accounted for by Manf. Payrolls, Average								
Mass.	64.56	55.21	11.9	26.0	20.2	12.0	9.1	252
Conn.	86.68	57.79	5.1	52.4	10.3	...	11.0	88
Delaware	85.38	54.86	5.7	25.5	31.2	9.0	...	5
Indiana	55.94	45.28	5.2	56.7	9.5	...	...	103
Michigan	121.37	70.16	12.5	47.7	10.0	...	...	195
New Hampshire	71.74	41.70	10.3	32.3	14.1	2.3	...	20
New Jersey	62.80	48.80	34.1	25.0	15.8	...	...	271
Ohio	55.90	51.70	9.8	55.5	11.9	...	...	258
Penn.	54.68	41.23	9.8	32.2	18.2	...	10.1	326
Rhode Island	80.00	66.68	16.3	45.9	9.6	...	11.1	31
II. Average, 4 New England States	75.74	55.34	10.9	39.1	13.2	3.6	10.4	...
III. Average, 6 Leading Ind. States Other than 4 N.E. States	72.68	52.01	12.8	40.4	16.1	1.5	1.7	...
IV. Three Southern Industrial States								
Alabama	53.26	36.07	5.0	41.4	6.8	3.5	3.7	38
North Carolina	60.86	57.85	7.3	40.3	10.5	9.5	13.8	48
South Carolina	67.68	48.80	6.0	43.7	5.7	7.7	13.8	27
Average	60.60	47.57	6.1	41.8	7.7	6.9	10.4	...
V. Other Relevant States								
California	96.19	84.06	12.3	45.5	5.5	4.9	6.8	344
New York	89.49	64.91	21.4	23.3	9.2	12.7	15.7	810
Maine	70.48	49.89	9.9	35.6	12.8	...	...	30
Vermont	76.14	53.75	8.0	32.6	18.7	6.8	4.8	11
United States	72.96	54.65	10.6	40.3	9.8	5.0	5.8	4,778

Source: U. S. Census, **Compendium of State Government Finances in 1948**; and The Tax Foundation, **Facts and Figures of Government Finance, 1948–1949.**

These figures give only the roughest indication of the relative burden of the general property tax (GPT) upon industry in different localities. First, because assessed valuation varies greatly in relation to true valuation. Second, because the over-all per capita GPT does not reveal the extent of the tax upon industry. Here the problem is partly one of the distribution of the GPT between residences and industry. In Massachusetts, for example, special exemptions are provided for manufacturing firms. In Boston, there is a tendency to overassess business and favor residences. Finally, differences in property holdings per capita, are relevant.

Nevertheless, in New England as a whole the general property tax constitutes a real problem, accounting as it does for far more governmental revenue than in other states. Of all the New England states, Massachusetts raised the maximum proportion of its revenue from this tax: 64.5 per cent. Vermont used it least, obtaining 38.0 per cent of total revenues from the GPT.

When communities throughout the country are compared, it is obvious that New England cities depend more on taxes, and more on GPT, than cities elsewhere.

A summary of city revenues and taxation for the nation and the country is presented in the following table:

Revenue, Taxes, Cities with Population of 25,000 and Over, 1948

	No. of Cities		Taxes, % General Revenue		Property Taxes, % All Taxes	
	U.S.A.	N.E.	U.S.A.	N.E.	U.S.A.	N.E.
All cities, 25,000 or over	397	52	69.9	...	78.4	...
1 million or over	5	..	71.0	...	70.8	...
500,000 to 1 million	9	1	70.3	72.2	82.7	96.2
250,000 to 500,000	23	1	69.5	81.2	70.1	95.7
100,000 to 250,000	55	10	68.3	69.7	86.6	96.8
50,000 to 100,000	105	12	70.1	63.1	84.1	97.5
25,000 to 50,000	200	28	66.4	74.6	85.9	96.2

Source: Calculated from U. S. Census, **Compendium of City Government Finances in 1948** (1950).

The reader will note that taxes as a percentage of general revenue are higher in New England for cities of 100,000 to 1 million and 25,000 to 50,000, but lower for cities of 50,000 to 100,000. New England's greater reliance on taxes reflects largely a smaller recourse to charges for current services and contributions from enter-

prises (6.8 per cent for all cities 25,000 and over). Of more significance is the relatively heavy recourse to the general property tax.
Property taxes account for a much larger percentage of all taxes
than in the country generally; and the difference is especially large
for Boston and Providence. All cities receive 15.5 per cent of general
revenues from sales and gross receipts. New England cities do not
rely on such taxes and hence have to depend more on the GPT.
Although, in general, these taxes are regressive and discourage consumption, a case can be made out for some local sales levies, or
better, income levies, where the GPT has become unbearable.

6. FEDERAL TAXES

Perhaps a word should be said here concerning the burden of
federal taxes (cf. also Chapter 10). The relevant variables were as
shown in the accompanying table.

Taxes, per Capita Income, Federal Income Tax per Capita and % Change in Collections,
1945–49

| | Per Capita Income Payments, 1949 | | Federal Income Tax | |
	Payments	Index (U.S.A. = 100)	Taxes, Per Capita of Population, 1945	Percentage Change, Tax Receipts, 1945–49
United States	$1,330	...	128.45	+6.1
New England	1,395	105	152.19	−5.7
Massachusetts	1,417	106	159.08	−8.4
Connecticut	1,591	119	191.07	−3.3
Middle East	1,565	117	183.10 [a]	+10.6 [a]
New York	1,758	132	217.90	+17.8
Central	1,414	106	148.24 [b]	+8.1
Pacific	1,610 [c]	121 [c]	187.46	−9.0
California	1,665	125	199.96	−8.5

[a] New York, New Jersey, and Pennsylvania only.
[b] East North Central.
[c] Inclusive of Nevada.
Source: **Massachusetts Report of Special Commission on Taxation**, Part I; **Survey of Current Business** (August 1950).

The reader will remember that while New England's per capita
income is above average, it is substantially less than that of other
regions. What of federal tax burdens relative to New England's
somewhat higher per capita burdens? Federal tax payments per
capita are higher in New England than in the country; relative to

other high income areas, its tax burden under the federal income tax is a little high even when allowance is made for differences of income. For example, the per capita income in the Pacific states exceeds that in the nation by 21 per cent; but its per capita federal income tax exceeds that in the nation by 47 per cent. For the Middle East, the respective figures are 17 and 43 per cent; for New England, 5 and 20 per cent. Also of interest is the high income and federal tax burden for Connecticut vis-à-vis Massachusetts; and the reduction of federal tax receipts in New England vis-à-vis the nation from 1945 to 1949.

7. THE BURDEN ON THE INDIVIDUAL ENTERPRISE: GENERAL VIEWS

The businessman is not particularly interested in over-all estimates of tax burdens. He wants to know more about the taxes *he* has to pay in one state against another, for this reveals to him the structure of the tax system as it affects his business. Even if such studies do not reveal large differentials in taxes assessed in New England, he will tell you that the tax problem is still a serious one — in part, because this ailment is one of several minor ones injuring business in New England and, in part, as a leading Massachusetts businessman wrote me, because what counts is not the actual state of affairs but what the businessman *thinks* his taxes are.

In this connection, a study of the Boston Reserve Bank, based on a questionnaire sent to 663 New England manufacturers, revealed that businessmen in larger numbers reported taxes as a competitive disadvantage than any other of 21 location factors. In Connecticut and Vermont, more manufacturers reported taxes as an important advantage rather than a competitive disadvantage; but in Rhode Island, five times as many reported taxes as an important disadvantage than an important advantage; and in Massachusetts, eight times as many.

The results of this questionnaire may suggest merely that New England businessmen may be misinformed. Surely the statistical studies of tax burdens do not suggest that taxes constitute an important disadvantage. As a matter of fact, 34 per cent of all responding (9 per cent not reporting) said that taxes were not a matter of importance. (Forty-two per cent reported taxes as an important disadvantage, 16 per cent an important advantage.)

An examination of the replies given on other locational factors —
e.g., efficiency of machinery and adequacy of power — may suggest
the limited significance of these replies.[9]

An examination of the movement of industries into the South
suggests that the tax differential has not been an important factor.
In previous chapters we have noted the advantages in the South,
particularly the large supplies of labor available, the lower labor
costs, the material resources, and the special concessions to incoming
industry. Most of the special studies and reports on Southern industrialization minimize the importance of tax differentials. While tax
rates are lower, and subsidies to business include exemption from
taxes, many businessmen are aware that they yield independence
in accepting these favors, that they give up services and will later
have to pay more taxes.

McLaughlin and Robock, on the basis of a survey of 88 new
plants in the South, conclude that:

> The great bulk of the concerns included in this survey pointed out that
> they received no special inducement whatsoever in selecting their plant
> locations. Usually, however, manufacturers accepted short-term exemp-
> tions from state taxes, whenever they were available to new industrial
> ventures. Corporate executives are generally convinced that it would be
> a poor business on their part to accept any special concession from a local
> community. Similar statements will be found in references cited below. [10]

In the most thorough survey of shift of industries yet made, the
National Resources Planning Board concentrated on three factors:
markets, wage rates, and availability of raw materials.[11]

In an address before the New England State Tax Officials Association, Mr. Norman MacDonald, Executive Secretary of the
Massachusetts Federation of Taxpayers Association and a member of
the Massachusetts Commission studying the tax problem, supported
the position taken by the experts on the Southern economy.

[9] *Monthly Review of the Federal Reserve Bank of Boston* (September 1949),
pp. 1–6.

[10] G. E. McLaughlin and S. Robock, *Committee of the South,* National
Planning Board, 1949, pp. 107–108, 122, 125; see also *Economy of the South,
Report of the Joint Committee on the Economic Report* (1949), pp. 71–72;
State Planning and Economic Development in the South, A. Lepawsky, Com-
mittee of the South (NPA), 1949, pp. 70–81; *Why Industry Moves South,*
p. 112.

[11] *Industrial Location and National Resources* (1943), p. 104.

Admitting that business migration is a problem, Mr. MacDonald said it was due to other factors than taxes. Among these, he said, were the desire to be nearer mass markets and sources of raw materials, rising transportation costs in this region, and high wages.

He also said that preliminary findings showed that taxes had substantially the same total impact on manufacturing in such states as New York, New Jersey, Michigan, Ohio, and Georgia as in Massachusetts.[12]

8. RELATIVE TAXES ON IDENTICAL TAXPAYERS

In a memorandum to the Governor, of November 21, 1949, Tax Commissioner Long took a similar position. Mr. Long applied the tax rate in competing states to 25 Massachusetts corporations, assuming that real estate and machinery were assessed at 85 per cent (as in Massachusetts), other tangible property at 50 per cent, and intangible property at 20 per cent. (Mr. Long applied the taxes according to rates of several cities in each state.) The taxes of 25 corporations with a taxable value of $21 million would have been as follows:

$000
Massachusetts = 874

In Excess of Massachusetts		Less than Massachusetts	
California	1,644	Illinois	780
New Jersey	1,399	Rhode Island	760
Florida	1,144	Ohio	608
Indiana	1,092		
North Carolina	994		
Pennsylvania	904		
New York	893		
Connecticut	886		

On the basis of these figures, the record of Massachusetts seems to be rather favorable, but the validity of the assumption concerning assessments is questionable. New England cities depend more on taxes, and more on the general property tax, than do cities elsewhere in the country. (Whereas city property taxes in the entire country range from 70 to 86 per cent of total taxes, in New England cities they range from 95 to 97 per cent of total taxes.) That the burden of taxes on corporations seems to be much less in Massachusetts than in eight other states points to higher assessments in New England.

[12] *New York Times,* October 6, 1950.

It is possible to obtain a crude guide of the relation of assessment to true value by comparing per capita income and per capita assessed values. Obviously, these two variables are related, though the relation will vary to some extent according to dependence on manufacturing and agriculture and other factors. These estimates suggest less difference between assessed and actual value among heavily industrialized states in the East and Middle West than in the South and in California.

Per Capita Assessed Value as a Percentage of Per Capita Income, 1940

Massachusetts	195
Connecticut	221
7 Heavily Industrialized States [a]	190
5 Industrial Southern States [b]	166
California	153

[a] New York, New Jersey, Pennsylvania, Ohio, Illinois, Indiana, and Michigan.
[b] Alabama, Georgia, North Carolina, South Carolina, and Tennessee.
Source: Income — **Survey of Current Business** (August 1945); Assessments, **Facts and Figures**, p. 165.

The Connecticut State Tax Survey Committee has also studied the tax burdens of identical individuals and corporations in various states.

First, a comparison was made of the tax (state and local) borne by three individuals, with incomes of $2600 (A), $10,200 (B), and $60,000 (C) in four states.

Tax Burden in Four States, Federal (Income Tax), State, and Local, 1948

	Connecticut	New Jersey	Massachusetts	New York
Taxpayer A ($2600)	61	70	38	51
Taxpayer B ($10,200)	1,314	1,291	1,392	1,374
Taxpayer C ($60,000)	16,709	16,653	17,143	17,670

Source: **Connecticut State Tax Survey**, p. 62.

Clearly the differences in tax payments are not large enough to induce movements from one state to another on the part of individuals. The lowest payments, it will be noted, are in Massachusetts for A, in New Jersey for B and C. Surely even the *extreme* difference of $101 for B (1 per cent of income) and $1117 (2 per cent of income) for C will not result in large-scale migrations. These differences would be somewhat larger if taxpayers in Massachusetts and New

York, with state income taxes, did not receive abatements in their federal income taxes. Actual migrations (say) from New York to Connecticut by those in the high income group (with a saving of $1000 out of $60,000 income) may well be explained by exaggerated views of the gains to be had.

Another study relates to four corporations with sales of $2.066 million (A), $2.635 million (B), $184,000 (C), $612,000 (D), and net income before taxes of $533,000, $395,000, $8000, and $50,000, respectively. These four metal-working corporations are assumed to operate in Boston, Bridgeport, Newark, and Philadelphia. For the four corporations, the lowest average relative taxes (Bridgeport = 100) were in Philadelphia (90 per cent), the highest in Boston (155), the next highest in Newark (143), and the next, Bridgeport (100). The reader will note that the tax disadvantage varies with the corporation — e.g., Boston's relative tax burden varies from 84 per

Comparative Indices of Total State and Local Taxes for Four Corporations, 1948

	Bridgeport, Conn.	Boston, Mass.	Newark, N. J.	Philadelphia, Pa.
Corporation A	100	161.9	50.2	103.9
Corporation B	100	83.8	121.3	63.0
Corporation C	100	153.5	202.5	82.6
Corporation D	100	220.4	200.3	109.7

Source: **Connecticut State Tax Survey, p. 66.**

cent of Bridgeport's (Corporation B) to 220.4 (Corporation D). It is well also to keep in mind that this comparison is not valid for Massachusetts as a whole because of the abnormally high tax rate in Boston. It is interesting that Corporation A in Boston pays 9 per cent of net worth and 7 per cent of net income, whereas Corporation B pays 3 per cent of net worth and 6 per cent of net income. Another disturbing feature of this analysis is that from 1944 to 1948, the percentage rise of taxes for the four corporations operating in Boston averaged 54 per cent; for Philadelphia, no change; for Bridgeport, 24 per cent; for Newark, 15 per cent.

Finally, the Connecticut Committee received information on 29 manufacturing corporations operating in more than one state. In general, Illinois seems to offer the lowest taxes to its corporations, whatever the variable to which taxes are related. Taxes are highest in Massachusetts, except in relation to pay rolls, where the state ranks fifth. Ohio averages second, Connecticut third, and New York and Pennsylvania roughly tied for fourth.

Lest too much be put into these comparisons, the Connecticut Committee wisely concludes:

As shown in Table 42, comparisons between taxes paid in Connecticut and taxes paid in each of five other states indicate that taxes paid in Connecticut are generally lower than those paid in New York and Massachusetts and higher than those paid in Ohio and Illinois. The results obtained, however, are not conclusive evidence that all manufacturing corporations in any state are taxed more heavily than are all manufacturing corporations in another state. On the contrary, they indicate that tax liability is largely conditioned by local circumstances and operating practices of individual corporations. Within wide limits, manufacturers can and do find both "favorable" and "unfavorable" tax environments within all states and any attempt to generalize is in the main futile.[13]

Tax Payments of Selected Manufacturing Corporations, Total State and Local Taxes Reported as Per Cent of Gross Receipts, Net Income, Net Worth, and Payroll Allocated to Selected States, 1948 (Per Cent)

	Gross Receipts	Net Income	Net Worth	Payroll
All states	1.36	10.67	2.97	3.42
Connecticut	1.41	10.86	3.26	3.69
New York	2.22	14.17	2.05	4.10
Ohio	1.54	9.10	2.54	2.35
Pennsylvania	2.61	12.14	3.74	3.06
Massachusetts	7.45	15.72	5.26	3.05
Illinois	0.23	5.19	0.66	1.18

Source: Connecticut State Tax Survey, p. 143.

The next chapter deals further with the problem of identical corporations, as a problem of Massachusetts tax burdens.

9. CONCLUSION

Tax differentials among New England states and of more importance between New England and competitors, especially the industrial South, are not so large as they are claimed to be by some businessmen here. In fact, a calculation based on taxes as a percentage of costs and tax differentials suggests that variations in taxes are a matter of secondary importance in the determination of location.

[13] *Connecticut State Tax Survey*, p. 144.

It is important that the views of businessmen should conform more nearly to the facts. Indeed, the tax structure, in New England and notably in Massachusetts, is less favorable to businessmen than in competing states. But it is well to distinguish the taxes on costs from those on surpluses; the small differences in present income taxes, only in part a tax on business; the heavier differential in local than in state taxes, a matter of great importance, since entrants can seek the towns with low tax rates, and those disposed to move may migrate within the state or region. Even studies of taxation of identical individuals and corporations which emphasize the heavier taxes in Massachusetts at any rate are not by any means conclusive on the importance of tax differentials.

The reader should also consider the following: Tax *differentials* are irrelevant for a large part of the employment and enterprise of a state: for the purely domestic and service industries. The burden on business is not measured merely by the taxes paid by business. It is necessary to take account of the incidence of the tax; of heavy taxes on consumption elsewhere which put business at a disadvantage in other regions; the benefits received in better education, health, protection, social services for the money expended, all of these of some importance for business.

We shall discuss remedial measures in the next chapter, where we concentrate on the Massachusetts problem, for it is particularly in Massachusetts that the tax problem is discussed with vehemence.

CHAPTER 20

THE PROBLEM OF MASSACHUSETTS' FISCAL POSITION

1. INTRODUCTION

Grumbling about taxes is especially loud in Massachusetts, the state which accounts for one-half of New England's population and income. The reasons are obvious, and justify a separate chapter. Taxes on business are heavier than in the other major New England state, Connecticut; and Massachusetts suffers more from economic maturity than does Connecticut.

It will be recalled from the preceding chapter that business taxes accounted for a larger part of Massachusetts taxes than in other New England states [1] and in the nation generally; that the proportion of state and local taxes to per capita income was 7.3 per cent in Massachusetts, 6.8 per cent in four New England industrial states, and 6.1 per cent in ten leading industrial states; that Massachusetts businessmen more than in the other New England states considered taxation a factor of locational disadvantage; that Massachusetts' burden on an individual corporation is not heavy on the assumption that assessed value equals true value; that the differences in personal income taxes are not adequate to account for migrations; and, finally, that the Connecticut study of tax burdens on identical corporations suggests an unfavorable tax situation in Massachusetts.

In a statement published in the *Boston Herald* in May 1950, General Wood, President of Sears, Roebuck and Company, said: "Taxes in Massachusetts are the highest in the country and I am in a position to know. Taxes in this state amount to 2.24 per cent on retail sales as against 1.1 per cent in the country."

A similar attack was made by Henry P. Kendall, a large textile manufacturer, who operates in Massachusetts, Indiana, Illinois,

---

[1] Except Connecticut, where, however, total taxes are substantially less.

Rhode Island, North Carolina, and South Carolina.[2] His contention was that unemployment (pay roll) taxes for plants of comparable size in Massachusetts exceeded those in the four states outside New England by 227.27 per cent; income and excise taxes, by 207.42 per cent; property taxes, by 1.87 per cent; the average of such taxes, by 124.52 per cent; and workmen's compensation taxes, by 13.67 per cent.

Against these appraisals of the Massachusetts tax burden, we should recall the statement of Mr. MacDonald, who minimizes the significance of taxes, the conclusion of the Connecticut Committee that no generalizations are safe on the basis of studies of samples of corporations, and the study of Tax Commissioner Long.

The Wood statement seems particularly unconvincing. It is obvious that Mr. Wood related his study only to states in which he operates and included only part of the taxes. For example, he surely must have omitted the sales tax. In 1947, there were 26 states with sales taxes with rates generally at 2 per cent (5 at 3 per cent, inclusive of Connecticut, and 2 at 1 per cent). New York City, with a 2 per cent sales tax (now 3 per cent), and Illinois, with a 2 per cent tax, California, with a 2½ per cent tax, are all places in which Sears does much business. Only by excluding sales taxes could Mr. Wood arrive at his conclusions. Massachusetts has no sales tax.

The Kendall case is subject to a different interpretation. Obviously, the Kendall Company has expanded on the basis of careful consideration of costs. Their greatest expansion seems to lie in South Carolina, where taxes are relatively low, but, more important, where other significant costs seem lower. In comparing unemployment taxes in 1951 in Massachusetts and Rhode Island with those in other states, Mr. Kendall exaggerates the difference in tax costs. The 1951 rate reflects the exhaustion of reserves and excessive concessions under merit rating from which Massachusetts had profited earlier. Allow me to add, whatever the weight of the payroll taxes there can be no doubt that businessmen are greatly disturbed by them. *The Blanchard Report* makes that clear.

[2] *Boston Herald*, March 18, 19, 20, 1951; and see especially R. M. Darrin, *Massachusetts — A White Elephant?* (Distributed by Massachusetts Foundation, May 31, 1951).

2. RESERVATIONS

As is true for all of New England and elsewhere, federal taxes are the major burden in Massachusetts. In a recent year, of a total of $782.1 million paid as individual income taxes in Massachusetts, approximately 95 per cent went to the federal government; of a total of $358.8 million paid in corporation income taxes in Massachusetts, the federal government received $343.6 million or 95 per cent. This trend is not likely to be reversed. From 1936 to 1950 federal taxes rose from 3.6 per cent to 15.1 per cent of total income payments in Massachusetts, while state and local taxes declined from 9.9 per cent to 8.8 per cent of the total.[3] The federal government collected roughly $1 billion in Massachusetts in 1950, while state and local taxes amounted to $600 million. Even these figures understate the rise in federal taxes, because they omit taxes levied elsewhere but paid by consumers in Massachusetts.[4]

The general discussion of taxes in the previous chapter may also be recalled: that taxes on surpluses are not cost items, that if consumption taxes were substituted for business taxes sales would be depressed, that business does not bear the cost of pay-roll taxes (which are largely shifted to workers), and that some other taxes can be shifted to consumers in the form of higher prices.

One final reservation may be made about the general increase in expenditures and taxes, which has caused such comment.

In the past three decades the cost of state and local government in our Commonwealth has risen from about $150,000,000 to almost a half billion dollars a year. The limit does not appear in sight.[5]

. . . For example, overall state and local expenditures in Massachusetts increased from $81,000,000 in 1913 to $326,000,000 in 1942. These expenditures required a fourfold increase in current requirements over a thirty-year period.

But the economy has grown as well, and many new services have been added. The rise of taxes was even greater than expenditures — from $90 million in 1913 to $449 million in 1942. Almost 40 per

[3] *Preliminary Report of the Special Commission on Taxation* (March 1949), p. 32.

[4] The Commonwealth of Massachusetts, *Report of the Special Commission on Taxation.* Part I, *The Tax System Today* (March 1951), pp. 42–43.

[5] The Commonwealth of Massachusetts, *Report of the Special Commission. . . Public Expenditures. . .* (December 3, 1947).

cent of the increase was associated with the new pay-roll taxes (10 per cent), taxes associated with motor vehicles (8 per cent), and 12 per cent for corporate and income taxes, introduced in part to relieve the growing burden of the general property tax (GPT). These new taxes for the support of new services accounted for almost 40 per cent of the thirty-year increase.[6]

It is well to note that in these thirty years, while *state* expenditures increased by 303 per cent, the national income rose by 225 per cent, prices by almost 60 per cent. Unfortunately, the income of Massachusetts rose by less than the nation's,[7] and, therefore, we conclude that relative to income the burden of taxes has increased.

More recently, the Massachusetts Tax Commission compared state taxes of $91 million in 1930 with $231 million in 1950. Over this twenty-year period, the tax increase was more than 150 per cent, whereas the increase in income payments was only 100 per cent. Again, the sizable increases which have taken place since 1947 are worth noting. State expenditures (excluding soldiers' bonus) rose by almost 60 per cent, exceeding the rise in prices and incomes. But all *state and local* taxes as a percentage of Massachusetts income declined from 1936 to 1950;[8] and for postwar years, allowances should be made for underspending during the war years, when state and local government expenditure was far smaller than the normal proportion.

3. TAXATION AND GOVERNMENT EXPENDITURE IN MASSACHUSETTS

Recent fiscal developments in the Commonwealth as compared to the country must be viewed. From 1939 to 1950, all state taxes, per capita, increased 101 per cent; those in the Commonwealth by 98 per cent. Increases in income per capita over the same period were 247 and 197 per cent. It is clear that Massachusetts taxation has become more of a burden than state taxes in the rest of the country. This is true despite a lag in Massachusetts expenditures. From 1942

---

[6] The Commonwealth of Massachusetts: *Preliminary Report of the Special Commission on Taxation* (March 1949), pp. 26–27.

[7] The rise of population from 1910 to 1940 was 44 per cent for the nation and 12 per cent for Massachusetts, and the increase of value added in manufacturing from 1909 to 1947 was 8 times for the nation and 4 times for Massachusetts. *Statistical Abstract* (1948) and *1947 Census of Manufactures*, I, 35.

[8] The Commonwealth of Massachusetts, *Report of the Special Commission on Taxation*. Part I, p. 43.

to 1949, expenditures *for operations* in all states rose by 102 per cent; in the Commonwealth by 51 per cent. The rise for Massachusetts was little more than the increase in prices. If state expenditures including debt and aid to local governments are examined, the increase for all states was 160 per cent; for the Commonwealth, 118 per cent.

The absolute level of Massachusetts taxes is, however, high. In 1949 the per capita tax burden in the state was $57.80 as compared with that in the country of $57.51. By 1950 per capita taxes in Massachusetts were $59.30, compared to $60.52 in the nation. The data in the table below show more details.[9]

Per Capita Taxes and Expenditures, United States Average and Massachusetts, 1948–1950

| | Per Capita Taxes | | % Income Payments | | Per Capita Expenditures | |
	All States	Mass.	All States	Mass.	All States	Mass.
1948	55.18	55.19	4.2	3.8	72.96	64.56
1949	57.51	57.80	...	...	79.56	68.86
1950	60.52	59.30	4.6	4.5	87.38	90.69

Sources: U. S. Census, State Government Finances in 1948, 1949, 1950. State Tax Collections, 1948, 1950; Compendium of State Government Finances in 1949.

There is, therefore, reason for concern. The debt of the Commonwealth has been rising rapidly, and a state and local tax burden amounting to about 9 per cent of the total income in the Commonwealth (on top of federal taxes amounting to 15 per cent) is serious indeed. Under these circumstances it is important to scrutinize expenditures and to improve the tax structure. Since 1950, the burden of federal taxes has greatly increased.

In the table (page 209) I have summarized the results for a longer period. In general, these figures reveal that the rise of taxes and expenditures in Connecticut has equaled or even exceeded that of the nation. I have included Connecticut to stress the contrast of growth with Massachusetts. These two states, of course, account for four-fifths of the income of New England. Here we note once more the lag in Massachusetts taxes, expenditures, and growth.

In Massachusetts, the rise of the property tax yield from 1860 to 1922 was substantially less than in the country or in Connecticut,

[9] Several paragraphs based on the author's memorandum (unpublished) to Governor Dever, December 27, 1949.

though, from 1922 to 1942, the gain in Massachusetts exceeded that of the country. An unfortunate aspect of the development and clearly one of the depressing factors in the Massachusetts tax situation is the large part still played by the GPT (in *local* rather than *state* taxation). The failure of Massachusetts to adjust to the national tendencies is verified by the trends of the GPT as a proportion of all tax receipts from 1913 to 1942.

Yield of General Property (GPT) as Percentage of All Taxes

All state and local government — declined from	80 to 47	per cent	
Connecticut	"	"	67 to 49 " "
Massachusetts	"	"	77 to 60 " "

By 1947, the GPT accounted for 58.5 per cent of tax revenues (state and local) in Connecticut and 57.5 per cent in Massachusetts. In 1949, it represented 62 per cent of these revenues in Massachusetts. Both tax yield and operating expenditures in Massachusetts show a substantial lag behind those of Connecticut and the country. Massachusetts' rate of growth in these items over the years 1913 to 1942, was roughly two-thirds that in Connecticut and the country. In 1913, per capita taxes in the Commonwealth were about 1.8 times the national average; in 1942 only 1.3 times. Does this reflect a wise diminution of government activity or is it another symptom of decline? It will be recalled, for example, that from 1910 to 1940 the population rise in Massachusetts was less than that in the nation, and the increase in value added by manufacture (1909–1947) in the state was only half that in the country.

Finally, state taxes did not rise *vis-à-vis* local taxes in keeping with the national trend. Undoubtedly the increased dependence on local taxation, with its burden of general property tax, injures Massachusetts' fiscal position. In recent years, (1941 to 1948) however, income taxes have accounted for almost one-half the total increase in tax receipts. On this score, the structure of the Massachusetts tax system changes along the lines supported by modern theories of public finance.[10]

In summary, the facts presented in this section suggest that the rise of state and local taxes in Massachusetts has exceeded the increase in income over some recent periods and has fallen short of income

---

[10] *Report of the Connecticut State Tax Survey Committee*, p. 50.

rises in other recent periods. They also reveal that the rise of taxes and expenditures in Massachusetts has lagged behind those of the country and Connecticut, as might be expected from the slower rate of growth in Massachusetts. The relative contribution of the property tax also remains too large, a fact associated with a slower expansion of state (with greater dependence on non-property taxes) relative to local taxes in Massachusetts.

Items of General Revenue and General Expenditure by State and Local Governments, Various Years, 1860–1942   ($ Million)

	1942	1922	1902	1860
Property Taxes				
All States	4,544	3,504	725	94
Connecticut	82	48	8	1
Massachusetts	241	156	49	7
	1942	**1932**	**1913**	
Total Taxes				
All States	9,512	6,358	1,351	
Connecticut	167	106	21	
Massachusetts	400	308	90	
States Taxes				
All States	5,015	1,890	300	
Connecticut	82	30	5	
Massachusetts	170	90	15	
Local Taxes				
All States	4,597	4,468	1,051	
Connecticut	85	76	16	
Massachusetts	233	219	74	
General Operation Expenditures, State and Local				
All States	7,216	5,533	1,174	
Connecticut	117	92	19	
Massachusetts	326	265	81	

Source: Bureau of the Census, Historical Review of State and Local Government Finances (June 1948), pp. 28–29.

4. BUSINESS TAXES

In view of the historical trends in taxation elsewhere in the country, as evidenced in the greater recourse to state aid, in the reduced dependence on the GPT, in the increased outlays of government, and in the inflationary bias in our economy which increases the need for taxes responsive to rising prices and incomes — in view of all these, the case is strong for the growth of personal income taxes, corporate and noncorporate income taxes, and other taxes which impinge on business and other income. These, more than any other levies, reflect capacity to pay and respond to changing price and income levels.

There is indeed some substance to the point of the Connecticut Commission that state (and perhaps local) government must be protected against taxes that respond well to changing business conditions. With a highly elastic tax system, receipts tend to fall excessively in periods of depression, with disastrous results upon governments without credit. Some reliance on inelastic taxes is therefore necessary. (The Committee urges the use of the sales tax. Other taxes on consumption may do as well and not be so regressive; and the GPT is the ultimate in revenue stability during depression.) But since one means of coping with economic decline is to lower taxes, the answer must lie in part in more productive revenues (surpluses) during prosperity and recourse to federal help during depression. The best solution is, of course, to avert depression.[11]

Hence we conclude that the Massachusetts tendency to rely upon business taxation is in the right direction. The failure of other states (e.g., Connecticut) to follow this lead may be explained by various facts: ignorance of correct fiscal principles; control of government by groups excessively friendly to business (the rotten borough system of Connecticut may be relevant here); the determination to capture business from other states by freeing business of its fair share of taxation (e.g., the South).

On this score we should comment on Part IV (*The Comparative Impact of Corporate Taxes in Massachusetts in the Report of the Special Commission on Taxation*), a document which appeared after these chapters on taxation were written.

The Commission emphasized the point that corporate income taxes are heavier in Massachusetts than in any of the 33 states with corporate income taxes but Oregon. But the comparative position of Massachusetts corporations, based on a study of taxes on 20 Massachusetts corporations (*not randomly picked, may I add*) in Massachusetts cities and the taxes that would be levied on these 20 corporations in 7 competing states, is more satisfactory, when the basis of comparison is *all local and state* taxes on corporations than on the basis of state taxes alone. Indeed, there are genuine difficul-

[11] Cf. *Connecticut Tax Survey*, pp. 113–115.

ties in comparing property taxes, as the Commission readily admits. Actually total taxes on corporations in New Haven, Connecticut and Charlotte, North Carolina were heavier in 1948 than taxes on corporations domiciled in the Massachusetts towns; and taxes in the five cities in the other five states were less (see especially pages 30–41).

But even these apparently unfavorable conclusions are subject to reservations. First, as the Commission notes, there are some advantages in relying on income taxes which are sensitive to business conditions. (In this respect Massachusetts, New York, and Pennsylvania tax systems are preferable to those of New Jersey, Indiana, North Carolina, and Michigan.) Second, and related, the apparently heavier burden on Massachusetts corporations would change to an advantage in depression — not a negligible matter. In fact, as the Commission wisely elaborates, tax burdens vary greatly from year to year depending on the tax structure. (The Commission compares movements in four relevant variables, that is tax bases, over 13 years, and shows the wide relative movements.) Third, so far as competition is concerned, it is well to note that Massachusetts corporations are not taxed on the business done outside the Commonwealth. Fourth, for the most part corporation taxes are not passed on in higher prices, and hence to that extent do not impair competitive strength. Fifth, even in relation to states with appreciably lower tax burdens, many of the 20 corporations pay less taxes in Massachusetts. Thus taxes in Lansing, Michigan vary from 23 per cent of the Massachusetts taxes for one corporation to 295 per cent for another. Massachusetts corporations may select a site in one city with taxes of $18 per $1000 or in another with a $75 tax.

The last paragraph is perhaps an adequate comment on the strong statement made by Ralph M. Darrin of the General Electric Company (see footnote 2). He comments on the heavy taxes to which his corporation has been subjected in Massachusetts.

Finally, the Special Commission has made out a case for some relief of manufacturing corporations. The relief should be had in moderating the rise of taxes on these corporations rather than in reducing them. The discussion in this chapter does not suggest that the over-all tax burden on corporations in Massachusetts is a *serious* competitive factor.

In re the Report of the Special Commission, we should here note another approach: the percentage of business taxes to all taxes.[12] Results vary greatly according to the taxes included.[13]

According to the Massachusetts Tax Commission, corporate income taxes, inclusive of excise taxes on corporations, in 1950 amounted to $73 million, or 12 per cent of the total state and local taxes.[14]

The Connecticut Survey reveals the following percentages of business taxes to all state and local revenues, 1947.

Tax Revenues (Exclusive of Unemployment Compensation Taxes) [15]

Connecticut	Massachusetts	New Jersey	New York	New Hampshire
12.8	12.8	11.6	14.6	4.4

On this basis, Massachusetts stands up well against important rivals. But we should note that the *total* burden of taxes is relevant here. On that basis, Connecticut's taxes on business, for example, are less than those of Massachusetts. Furthermore, the burden varies according to the type of business. Connecticut and New York tax unincorporated businesses; the others do not. (Unincorporated business is subject to the income tax in Massachusetts.) Connecticut relies heavily on taxation of insurance companies and public utilities, industries which on the whole are well established and not easily moved. In concentrating its taxation of business (exclusive of GPT) largely on public utilities, New Jersey also indulges in the practice of taxing heavily industries that cannot move.

Finally, note the table on the following page.

The reader will note that the Massachusetts burden in 1947 was 0.31 per cent, 0.39 per cent, and 0.25 per cent of total income payments more than Connecticut's, New Jersey's, and New York's, respectively. The differences certainly do not seem to be a matter of major importance, and especially if consideration is paid to the lower burden of indirect taxes in Massachusetts and to the theory

[12] The Tax Foundation, *Facts and Figures on Government Finance, 1950–1951*, p. 155.

[13] *Facts and Figures on Government Finance, 1950–1951*, p. 157; *cf.* Bureau of the Census, *Sources of State Tax Revenue in 1950* (November 1950), p. 13.

[14] *Report of the Special Commission on Taxation*, Part I, p. 43.

[15] *Report of the Special Commission on Taxation*, p. 57.

of incidence discussed above. My approach differs from that of the Massachusetts Commission, and is not without significance.

Finally, while both the effective rate upon corporation income and total corporation tax receipts have increased substantially since prewar years (2.5 per cent in 1936 to 6.2 per cent in 1947, and 6.765 per cent of income in 1950 plus .615 per cent of capital invested),[16] corporation incomes have increased even more. We can estimate gross corporate profits in Massachusetts by assuming that they are roughly the same proportion to the national total as federal corporate taxes in Massachusetts are to the total of federal corporate

Comparative General "Business" Taxes in Five States, 1947

	Conn.	N. J.	Mass.	N. Y.	N. H.
Total all business taxes, inclusive of tangible personal property, except real property and unemployment compensation as					
Per cent of all state and local taxes	13.8	8.8	13.8	11.2	10.2
Per cent of income payments	0.65	0.57	0.96	0.71	0.72

Source: **Connecticut Tax Survey,** pp. 140–141.

taxes. The rise in corporate profits in Massachusetts since the prewar period then becomes approximately $1.5 billion by the end of 1950, compared to an increase in corporation taxes in the state of roughly $70 million. Before taxes, corporate profits increased about 20 times as much as state corporate taxes; profits after taxes, ten times. These facts should be considered when businessmen protest the "expelling" force of Massachusetts taxes upon business.

5. THE BOSTON PROBLEM

A major issue is the financial plight of Boston, which in 1949 spent around $125 million, or about 21 per cent of all state and local tax receipts in Massachusetts. In Boston, the economic problems of a major metropolitan center and those of a mature area are merged. There are various explanations of the serious losses of Boston: the decline of manufacturing industries; heavy tax rates associated with Boston's economic decline and inefficient government; the general

[16] *Preliminary Report of Special Commission on Taxation,* p. 41; and Part IV, p. 23.

tendency for industry to move from large metropolitan areas. Whatever the explanation, the net result has been a heavy burden of taxation.

In many ways, Boston faces a more serious problem than any other large metropolitan area. Whereas in most large metropolitan areas the central city population is around two-thirds of the total, in Boston it is but one-third. The percentage, in 1940, of central city population to total metropolitan population was 72.2 per cent for New York, and averaged 63 per cent for nine major metropolitan areas exclusive of Boston. Hence the city's services, which are in no small part available to the two-thirds living in the metropolitan area outside Boston, are a burden on those who remain in Boston. Yet the city is not in sufficiently strong position to impose a tax burden on neighboring residents. These "outsiders" need not pay sales taxes on Boston goods in the same sense that a White Plains resident pays sales taxes in New York City. In part, the stronger position of New York City rests on the larger proportion of population within the city and the unique selling and other service facilities in New York City.[17] In 1950, Boston still accounted for but one-third of the population in the Metropolitan area and New York City two-thirds.

Boston's unfortunate financial position makes it very difficult to attract new businesses, and stimulates the exodus of old firms. Taxes are a crucial issue in Boston, for the local tax burden is severe and that disadvantage on top of the slow rate of growth of New England and metropolitan areas dependent on manufacturing generally means severe pressures on Boston.

Her financial plight is evident in: (1) The large amount of annual expenditures – $123 million. In 1950, Boston was the twelfth city in order of population. Yet in expenditures in 1949 it was fifth, its outlays exceeding those of Los Angeles ($85 million), Cleveland ($50 million), Baltimore ($94 million), St. Louis ($39 million) – all larger cities on the basis of 1950 population. The per capita outlays in 1949 were: Boston, $160; Baltimore, $109; Los Angeles, $57; Cleveland, $55; St. Louis, $48. The per capita outlays in New

---

[17] For a discussion of the factors determining relative growth of metropolitan areas and the distribution of population within these areas, see especially Bureau of the Census, *The Growth of Metropolitan Districts in the United States, 1900–1940* (1948).

York, Chicago, Philadelphia, and Detroit, the four largest cities, were: $141, $50, $60, and $114 respectively. The average for all eight cities other than Boston was $79. In other words, Boston's disadvantage was $81, or more than 100 per cent of the per capita outlay of the nine cities. The amounts involved are sizable indeed.

Lest the reader conclude that the comparison of Boston with eight larger cities is unfair, I have compared Boston with the eight largest Southern cities (population 250,000 – 500,000 in 1940), a comparison of particular relevance because of the threat of Southern competition. In the smaller cities, the overhead costs of government have to be spread over a smaller number. Yet for these eight cities, per capita outlays were but $67, or 42 per cent of the Boston level.[18]

(2) Boston is similarly at a disadvantage in taxes ($80 million in 1949) exceeding those in Los Angeles ($55 million), Cleveland ($28 million), Baltimore ($53 million), and St. Louis ($33 million). All these cities had larger populations in 1941 than Boston.

Per capita taxes in Boston amounted to $104 as compared with $50 for the eight larger cities. Whereas taxes accounted for 69.2 per cent of general revenues in the 37 largest cities, 70.7 per cent in 5 cities with population in excess of 1 million in 1940, and 68.7 per cent in 9 cities with population of 500,000 – 1,000,000, in Boston the percentage was 73 per cent.

In her heavy dependence upon GPT, Boston also suffered under a severe handicap. The GPT yielded $81.8 million in 1949, 96 per cent of all taxes. For the 37 largest cities, the percentage was 77 per cent. Only Detroit, Indianapolis, and Providence among the 37 largest cities depended as much or more on the GPT.

Tax rates in Boston in 1949 were $56.80 per $1000 of assessed value. The only cities with higher rates were St. Paul and Minneapolis. Average rates for the cities in Group I (in excess of 1,000,000 persons in 1940) were $17.82; in Group II, exclusive of Boston (500,000 to 1,000,000), $23.29; in the eight large Southern cities, $18.79. These differences are striking, especially in view of the high assessments in Boston.[19]

[18] Material from the Bureau of the Census, *Large-City Finances in 1949* (September 1950), pp. 6–7, and *Statistical Abstract of the United States* (1950). (My calculations.)

[19] Statistics, *Large-City Finances in 1949*, and *Summary of City Government Finances in 1949*.

(3) With heavy taxes and with a tax structure which greatly hampers adjustments to lower incomes and declining business, Boston's economic status is bound to suffer. To some extent, the load is lightened by contributions from other governments. Thus, in 1949 Boston received $32.8 million from other governments, almost exclusively from the Commonwealth. The amount involved was larger than that received from other governments by any city but New York and Chicago. Per capita aid amounted to $43 for Boston and averaged $16 for the other eight cities among the first nine. In other words there was a difference of $54 in per capita taxes unfavorable to Boston and $27 more intergovernmental aid to Boston. In this manner, the whole state was forced to share the disabilities of Boston. There was some justice, in this sharing, since part of Boston's large outlays are on behalf of citizens outside the city. But those living, say, outside of the metropolitan district, undoubtedly have a grievance, since all do not share greatly in the services of Boston.

6. REMEDIAL ACTION

What is to be done to improve the fiscal situation of New England and particularly of Massachusetts? As a preliminary, let us stress the point that any competitive disadvantage suffered by Massachusetts is the result in part of the failure of competing states to depend as much as they should on income and business taxes.

New England, Massachusetts, and Boston are all handicapped by the excessive recourse to the GPT. Undoubtedly, this is another penalty of maturity. New England's tax structure reflects her age, for until recently the GPT has been the almost exclusive source of revenue for state and local government. In the last fifty years, new tax sources have gradually displaced the GPT. As the federal and state governments assume larger spending responsibilities, the importance of the GPT will continue to decline.[20] The movement can be accelerated by even greater recourse to income and business taxes and even to selective excise taxes, and by an increase of state and federal taxes. Recourse to some consumption taxes might help Boston, but these are opposed by the mercantile groups. Why not a Boston income tax in place of part of the oppressive general property tax?

[20] Cf. earlier statements in this and the last chapter.

Other suggested improvements are the following: There should be less tie-up of taxes with particular outlays — e.g., the gasoline tax and outlays on highways. All taxes should be pooled, and expenditures determined according to a scale of priorities rather than by receipts from a particular tax. State aid to local government should be determined by need, rather than by tax capacity — as is the practice with about two-thirds of the funds distributed in Massachusetts. New England states, and particularly Massachusetts, could increase their revenue by taxing unincorporated businesses; and, where competitive taxation is relevant, rely more, as New Jersey does, on taxation of industries that are not easily moved — e.g., utilities.

Finally, there is much to be said for better integration of state and local taxation with federal taxation. In the inflationary fifties, for example, taxes should rise as a means both of reducing private outlays and providing reserves for depression periods. The case for selective excise taxes is stronger than usual, in view of the high rates on income taxes and the desirability of cutting the consumption of luxuries. In these years, economies of spending are even more necessary than in normal times. Furthermore, in view of the high taxes in 1951–52 and particularly in Massachusetts, and of the textile crisis, further increases in state and local taxes which might weaken the competitive position of Massachusetts should be avoided.

The Boston problem is especially perplexing. Taxes on hotel rooms and on sales of nonessentials could be used to force the residents of the metropolitan area outside of Boston proper to pay a fair share of the city's expenses. Some greater assumption of the city's responsibilities by the Commonwealth might also help, although Boston has already succeeded in shifting some expenses in this way.

7. CONCLUSIONS

Having said all of this, I am not ready to agree that the tax system of Massachusetts is worse than that of other states. In many respects it is better. The difficulties lie more in the tax systems of competing states than in that of Massachusetts. In view of the limitations put upon the Commonwealth by the provincial charter of 1691, which is still substantially in force, it is surprising that our system is as good as it is. Since the adoption of the Massachusetts

Constitution of 1780, the only important change has been the income tax amendment of 1915.

We have not consciously planned a tax structure to meet the changing conditions of an industrialized state. We have not readily abandoned methods of taxation suited to conditions of an earlier day; nor have we been quick to substitute new methods designed to reach changing tax resources of the industrialized economy . . .[21]

No better evidence of the superiority of the Massachusetts tax system is to be had than a comparison of the tax structure of five industrial rivals:

Percentage of Tax Receipts, Five States, 1948–49

	Mass.	N. J.	N. Y.	Penn.	Conn.
1. Direct taxes upon individuals	10	2	10	8	3
2. Indirect taxes upon individuals and taxes upon motor vehicles and fuel	19	20	24	29	30
3. Taxes upon business	15	10	16	20	13
4. General property, etc.	56	67	49	44	56

Source: Computed from **Report of the Special Commission on Taxation**, p. 48.

On the score of the use of direct tax (primarily income), certainly the most equitable and most productive tax of all, Massachusetts is in the lead along with New York. In its reluctance to use onerous taxes on consumption, which weigh disproportionately on the low-income group, Massachusetts also has an excellent record in comparison with Pennsylvania and Connecticut. The Massachusetts taxes on business are roughly equal to the average of all five states, though heavier than those in New Jersey and Connecticut. Even the burden on property is little more than average. These comments relate to the *structure* of the tax system, not the amounts of money raised. The main cure for Massachusetts' competitive disabilities lies in heavier taxes on business and income elsewhere.

In all the Massachusetts Special Commission has published four major reports, all full of interesting and valuable material. Many of their suggestions are valid and supportable. They do not understand why rental income should be exempt from the income tax, and they are disposed to eliminate deductions under the Massachu-

[21] *Report of the Special Commission on Taxation*, Part I (1951), p. 12.

setts income tax for federal taxes paid. They would also reduce the exemptions of taxpayers without dependents and increase them for those with dependents, and provide exemptions for those with unearned income.[22]

Yet I would not agree with all the recommendations of the Commission. The tax on higher income and unearned income is indeed higher than for low incomes, but in so far as high income and unearned income are associated, this element of progressivity is not to be regretted.

Under the present law, taxpayers with under $5000 of adjusted gross income represent 52 per cent of all such income in the Commonwealth, but pay only 28 per cent of the individual income tax. Those with $5000 or more of adjusted gross income represent 48 per cent of such income, and incurred 72 per cent of the total tax liability.[23]

Though we would allow exemption on *all* income irrespective of how earned, we do not see that the present distribution of tax burdens is unfair. The proportion paid by high-income groups relative to their income is not excessive.

The argument against reducing the progressivity element in the income tax is as follows:

(1) The present tax is regressive for adjusted gross incomes up to $5000.

(2) The burden of the Massachusetts income tax has declined over the years. Thus, from 1929 to 1949 income payments rose by 82 per cent and receipts of the income tax by 29 per cent.

(3) The *over-all tax system of the country*, despite the advances in federal taxes, is still regressive over a large range, as Dr. Musgrave showed before the Joint Congressional Committee on the Economic Report (1951). This regressiveness is the result of the heavy recourse to consumption taxes by state and local governments and the failure to apply genuine progressivity in their income taxes.[24]

(4) The Commonwealth needs additional revenue to meet commitments already incurred. Early in 1950 the Commonwealth

[22] *Report of the Special Commission on Taxation,* pp. 54 *et seq.*

[23] *Report of the Special Commission on Taxation,* Parts I and II, *The Taxation of Personal Incomes,* p. 40.

[24] *Report of the Special Commission on Taxation, The Taxation of Personal Incomes,* pp. 31–57.

required $261 million and taxes anticipated were but $206 million.[25]
Under these circumstances, it would be a mistake to move even
further towards a regressive system. The case is much stronger for
increased progression. The tax differential against unearned income
is, however, probably too great even if allowance is made for
substitution aspects of the tax — i.e., the tax is a substitute for the
personal property tax. Progressivity may be applied to total income
rather than according to type of income, a change that requires a
constitutional amendment.

In summary, the best kind of tax from a competitive viewpoint
is a tax on surplus, not on cost. A 1930 Committee of the Massachusetts House seemed to be aware of this fact, whereas authorities
now seem to be blind on this point:

> Every dollar of tax laid on the real estate and machinery of industry
> is a direct burden in competition but the taxes raised from intangibles are
> not a burden on industry. Just as water diverted from a stream above the
> wheel diminishes the water power, while water diverted below the wheel
> does not affect the power, so taxes levied where they are a direct element
> in the cost of industry diminish the competitive power of industry, while
> taxes levied on the realized profits of industry are not a direct burden on
> its productive power.[26]

[25] *Report of the Special Commission on Taxation,* Part I, p. 18.
[26] House Document No. 1324, *Report of the Committee on Taxation,* The
Commonwealth of Massachusetts (1930), p. 4.

PART V

FUEL COSTS AND RESOURCE DEVELOPMENT

INTRODUCTION

In successive chapters I deal with fuel, power, and river development (Chapter 21) and with the St. Lawrence Seaway (Chapter 22). Fuel and power costs are not a large item in total costs, except for industries which use much power. New England reacts against high fuel and power costs by concentrating on industries and subindustries which do not require large outlays for these purposes. Here again a hostility to public enterprise has resulted in a failure to make the most effective use of resources in this region at the same time that federal funds collected in part here were developing resources and reducing costs in competitive areas.

The separate chapter on the St. Lawrence Seaway is justified not because the outcome of the enterprise is going to influence substantially New England's economic strength, but rather because we question the wisdom of New England's opposition to a program which is almost certain to aid the country and is likely to help this area.

CHAPTER 21

FUEL, POWER, AND RIVER DEVELOPMENT

1. INTRODUCTORY

On no issue has there been so much controversy as on power. The major problem is the high price of fuel, which largely accounts for the high costs of power and for a somewhat higher cost of living. But we do not intend to pass over the hot issue of hydroelectric power.

In recent years, the Passamaquody project, the St. Lawrence Seaway, and the fuller exploitation of the Connecticut, Merrimack, and other New England rivers have been widely discussed, both in the region and in the nation.[1] The importance of the issues is suggested by a message from the President, May 22, 1950, when he signed H. R. 5472:

A second, and even worse, example of inadequate planning provided for in this Act relates to New England. The Act places responsibility on the Department of the Army to survey the Merrimac and Connecticut Rivers and their tributaries, and such other streams in New England when power development appears feasible and practicable to determine the hydroelectric potentialities, in combination with other water and resource development. This assignment of responsibility, like that in the case of the Arkansas, White, and Red River Basins, obviously involves the work of other Federal Agencies, and of the States, as well as that of the Department of the Army. And these other agencies and the states should participate in the planning work.

In this case, moreover, the Act does not specify the several other purposes aside from the development of power, which should be considered in order to prepare proper development plans.[2]

[1] See *Letter from Federal Power Commission to Senator Saltonstall*, February 28, 1949, p. 7.

[2] The danger of excessive authority to the army lies in their opposition to multi-purpose projects. For a vigorous criticism of the army engineers, see R. de Roos and A. A. Maas, "The Lobby that Can't be Licked," *Harper's* (August 1949).

This statement by the President, as well as many other official statements, highlight some of the issues. In fact, earlier (February 9, 1950) the President had urged the Senate to amend H. R. 5472 and to support S. 3707 actually introduced on June 6 — this was the Green Bill providing, as the President proposed, for the treatment of "real and serious problems [of New England and of New York] of soil and forest conservation and management, and of controlling and using water to prevent floods, to provide domestic and industrial water supplies, and to furnish low-cost hydroelectric power." Ultimately the President appointed a New York–New England Inter-agency Commission to study resource and river development.

That New England has no federal hydroelectric development, whereas the rest of the country has 156 projects, is of much significance. The funds expended by the Bureau of Reclamation on its projects from the fiscal year 1903 through fiscal year 1950 amounted to $2.05 billion. These funds were used for power development, irrigation, flood control, etc. For the fiscal years 1950–1956, authorized projects under construction amount to $5381 million, and $329 million in addition has been authorized but not under construction. Not a dollar of these 5–6 billion dollars was allocated to New England. The largest items under construction are Missouri River Basin ($2834 million), Columbia Basin ($773 million), Central Valley, California ($581 million), and Boulder Canyon ($174 million).[3]

The omission of New England suggests first an aloofness towards federal participation in the life of the region;[4] second, strong opposition to federal power and multi-purpose projects partly instigated by propaganda from well-organized power interests; and third, the absence of federal competition which might depress rates and force private power companies to experiment more with low prices and quantity sales. Surely federal competition accounts in some part for the much greater reduction of rates in the Southeast than in New England in the last twenty years. I am not, however, suggesting that a New England TVA would help our region as much as it has helped the South.

[3] Memorandum to author from Assistant Secretary of the Interior Davidson, 1950.

[4] For an example of New England's attitude, see Editorial, "Trumanizing, N. E.," *Boston Herald*, May 24. 1951.

2. MULTI-PURPOSE DEVELOPMENT AND UNDEVELOPED HYDRO-ELECTRIC POWER

This brings us to our next problem, multi-purpose development. Such projects are often feasible when single-purpose ones are not. Moreover, they are cheaper because part of the costs can be allocated to each purpose. For example, TVA costs are estimated at $786 million; but if equivalent navigation, flood control, and power benefits were achieved by single-purpose projects, the cost would have been 40 per cent greater.

On the gains from federal financing, the following is revelant:

For example, analysis of the Enfield power and navigation project shows that the total cost of the project, including navigation facilities, could be repaid and amortized by power revenues if federal financing is considered. The ratio of annual power value to the total annual cost, including maintenance and operation would be about 1.7. On the other hand, the Enfield project considered on the basis of nine per cent annual charges (the average figure for private financing considered in the NEC report) would have a corresponding benefit-cost ratio of about 0.8 and, upon that basis, would not be considered economically feasible.[5]

It is important in our view that multiple-projects be given careful consideration, and it is hoped that under H. R. 5472 this will be done. Not power alone, nor flood control alone, but protective forestation, recreation, etc., should be considered; and the relevant federal and state agencies should participate in the planning. (This is provided in a request made of federal agencies in a letter of October 11, 1950 by the President.) It does not follow that the distribution of power should necessarily be denied to existing public utilities; nor should plans be made which disregard the legitimate interests of the public utility companies. But since the problem is more power and cheaper power, arrangements should be such as to assure that the gains of cheaper power are passed on to the ultimate consumer.

What is especially germane is the amount of power capacity needed in the years to come, and the sources from which this capacity is to be derived. There are two recent sets of estimates on these points: one made by the Power Survey Committee of the

[5] *Letter from Federal Power Commission to Senator Saltonstall*, pp. 9–10; N.E.C., *Power in New England*, 1948, p. 61. Cf. G. H. Arris, *New England Water Power — Myth or Fact?* 1949.

New England Council, and one by the Federal Power Commission (FPC).

Requirements. According to the New England Council Report of 1948, New England would require 1.1 million kilowatts of additional generating capacity in the next ten years. In its study of power requirements, the FPC concludes that New England exclusive of Maine will require 774,000 additional kilowatts (dependable capacity) by 1955, 1,832,000 by 1960, and 3,899,000 by 1970. (Assumption of partial coördination.) These estimates are higher than those of the New England Council. The FPC conclusions are based on the following assumptions: [6]

Rise of population in fifties — 4.6 per cent
"   "   "   " sixties — 2.8 per cent

On the basis of these and various assumptions concerning the use of electricity for appliances and the like, the FPC estimates that annual sales per residential customer will increase from 1171 KWH in 1947 to 3060 in 1970. For the average commercial customer, the rise is estimated from 6110 in 1947 to 10,930 KWH in 1970; and for *all* industrial customers, 7047 in 1947 to 11,645 million KWH in 1970.

The total estimated requirements are as follows:

(*Million KWH*)
1940 = 7,629
1947 = 12,014
1960 = 20,980
1970 = 26,640

This gain of 14.6 billion KWH from 1947 to 1970 exceeds the total amount in use in 1947, and the average annual rise is to be 3.53 per cent. From 1940 to 1970, residential sales are to increase from 20.6 to 32.6 per cent of total consumption and industrial sales to fall from 43.5 to 35.2 per cent. It is interesting that from 1945 to 1970, the increase of industrial consumption is to be from 7.05 to 11.65 billion KW hours, or almost two-thirds. Even textiles are to increase their consumption by 50–60 per cent. These figures reflect, of course, increased mechanization as well as rises in output. They do not necessarily suggest a rise of factory jobs, and they do not

[6] Material from FPC, *Power Requirements in New Hampshire, Vermont, Massachusetts, Connecticut, and Rhode Island,* 1949.

reflect any deterioration for New England.[7] My general impression is that the projections were optimistic, though mobilization may make them a closer estimate.

Capacity. It is clear that increases in hydro capacity can play a significant part in filling these requirements. Hydro capacity in use now is but 800 million KW, or 20 per cent of the total, and its relative contribution has greatly declined in the last twenty years.

Against its estimated requirements of 110,000 KW annually for the next ten years, the New England Council estimated that capacity would increase by 1,000,000 KW before 1951. It suggested that 420,000 KW could be furnished by hydroelectric projects, although 263,000 of this would originate in Maine. Under the Fernald Law, the exportation of Maine power is precluded, and yet a large part of the potential contribution of hydro to New England is to come from Maine.

The FPC, however, estimates new hydro power capable of economic development at 3,119,000 KW (including 220,000 KW from Passamaquoddy). The differences between the two estimates are sizable. The FPC assumes a multiple and integrated development, the inclusion of capacity available only 10 per cent of the time, (the NEC report assumes capacity which is available 20 per cent of the time), and a different rate of return. The NEC report assumes an annual charge against capital of 8 to 10 per cent, although federal financing could cut the capital charges by one-half, and thereby increase the number of possible projects. Finally, the FPC estimate included projects not considered by the NEC: e.g., 258,000 kilowatts installed capacity in the St. John River basin.[8]

According to the FPC estimate, the Connecticut River is to provide the largest addition to new capacity — 749,000 kilowatt installed capacity, or about 20 per cent of the total. Recently a Presidential Commission eloquently pleaded for the development of the Connecticut River.[9] At present, there are 415,000 kilowatts capacity installed, all privately owned. In view of the need of adding 3.5 million kilowatts for New England by 1970, an amount equal

[7] *Ibid.*
[8] See footnote 5.
[9] The Report of the President's Water Resources Policy Commission, *Ten Rivers in America's Future* (vol. 2), pp. 467–522; also see the excellent statement by L. Olds, *Comprehensive Development of the Connecticut River*, March 18, 1949.

to existing capacity, it is important to use potential sources in the Connecticut River — approximately 20 per cent of the total additional required. The *Water Resources Policies Committee's* estimate of undeveloped hydroelectricity in the Connecticut River Basin is 952,600 kilowatts, or about 25 per cent of the total additional requirements for New England by 1970, and about one-half the hydro potential outside of Maine.

The Connecticut River is an excellent example of the possibilities of multiple-purpose development. So far flood control has been the major objective, and it is imperative that action be taken before the flood control projects are so far along that there will be no possibility of adequate multi-purpose development. The Connecticut River, through up-stream storage, should provide recreational facilities, treat pollution, and deal with forestation and fishing. Pollution from Holyoke, Massachusetts to Long Island Sound from industrial wastes is one of the most difficult problems. As the Commissioner points out, the complications are great and there are serious conflicts among possible uses. In a well-populated area, with great pressure for recreational facilities, and limited amounts of farm lands, with local governments in Northern New England strongly opposed to loss of land and of tax capacity, the many problems raised are not easily solved. Southern New England, the main beneficiary, should compensate Northern New England for losses.[10]

Hydroelectric power is an important issue: one great contribution would be the repeal of the Fernald Law preventing the use of Maine power elsewhere in New England. There are other obstacles: much of the unexploited capacity is far from the main industrial centers and is therefore likely to be costly; many object to flooding the land; and new hydro can provide only part of the additional capacity required. Nevertheless, water power is a valuable resource, and one which should be exploited to the utmost, especially since our great industrial rivals in the South and West profit abundantly from cheap power. With prices and demand at the levels required by mobilization, the case for development in New England is very strong. Even the Passamaquoddy project, declared uneconomic in 1941 by the Federal Power Commission, may become practicable. The potential contribution of the St. Lawrence Seaway will be discussed in the following chapter.

[10] *Ten Rivers in America's Future*, pp. 478–483.

3. FUEL AND POWER COSTS IN NEW ENGLAND

Hydroelectric projects are discussed because fuel and power in New England cost so much. In a pioneering study for the Boston Federal Reserve Bank in 1950 Mr. Arthur A. Bright, Jr. claimed that the high cost of coal in New England was the most important single factor and this, in turn, resulted from high transportation costs.

Average Production Expenses of Major Steam Electric Plants in New England and the United States, 1947 (Cents per kilowatt hour generated)

	New England (15 plants)	United States (200 plants)
Fuel	.52	.33
Maintenance	.08	.05
Labor, supervision, and engineering	.07	.05
All other	.01	.01
Total	.68	.44

Source: Compiled from **Federal Power Commission** data.

This conclusion is well brought out in the above table. The average production expense (cents per kilowatt hour generated) for major steam electric plants is as follows:

$$\text{New England} = 0.68 \qquad \text{United States} = 0.44$$

According to this study, roughly 80 per cent of the difference is explained by variations in the cost of fuel, about 8 per cent by differences in maintenance costs, and 8 per cent by variations in labor, supervision, and engineering. Relevant to the latter two are the following:

	United States	New England
1. Number of employees per 100 million KW hours generated	22	31
2. Per cent of turbo-generators installed before 1926	39	48
3. Cost of plant per KW of installed capacity	$97	$115
4. Plant factor (per cent of actual to generating capacity)	61	51
5. Efficiency of fuel utilization in major steam electric plants (average BTU per kilowatt hour generated)	14,640	15,650

Source: **Federal Power Commission** data.

In New England, required labor is high, plant and equipment are old, the cost of plant high, and plant factor unfavorable. Fuel is utilized less efficiently in New England than in the United States.

A somewhat different breakdown is the following: (Production expense is the major factor in explaining differences in costs; administration and taxes of secondary importance.)

Revenues and Expenses of Electric Utilities in New England and the United States,[a] 1947
(Cents per kilowatt hour of total sales)

Item	New England	United States
Operating revenue	1.93	1.61
Operating expenses:		
Production	.79	.50
Transmission	.02	.03
Distribution	.14	.14
Customer acctg. and collection	.06	.05
Sales promotion	.02	.03
Admin. and gen'l	.12	.10
Total operating exp.	1.15	.85
Depreciation	.14	.14
Taxes	.31	.28
Total deductions	1.60	1.27
Net Operating Revenue	.33	.33

Note: Details may not add to totals because of rounding.
[a] All privately owned utilities with annual electric revenue of $250,000 or more.
Source: Compiled from Federal Power Commission data.

These items do not exhaust the costs. Taxes, for example, are a relevant item; and taxes seem somewhat higher in New England than in the country. But as Mr. Bright observed, though taxes in New England exceeded those in the nation, taxes as a percentage of investment and operating revenues were lower in New England than elsewhere. Differences in wage rates are of secondary importance; but it will be noted that the number of employees per unit of output in New England exceeds that in the country by 41 per cent. Older equipment in New England, underutilization, labor and management differentials — these and other factors explain the 41 per cent higher labor costs in New England.

Mr. Leland Olds, the able ex-chairman of the FPC, suggests various attacks on low productivity. One obvious approach is replacement of old equipment and greater recourse to hydro capacity, in which New England has lagged. (See the next table.)

The obstacle to the infusion of new plant and equipment is the high costs of these items. Construction costs in the twenties were twice those of pre-World War I and the costs of the late forties twice those of the middle thirties. With heavy capital charges, the gains of reduced labor, fuel, and maintenance costs may be offset by higher financing charges. The fact that depreciation charges in New England were roughly equal to the nation's is relevant, the explanation in part being low cost of older investments.

Growth of Generating Capacity, 1929 to 1947 — Percentage

4 Pacific Northwest States	74
6 New England States	15
7 TVA States	79
United States	40

Growth of generating capacity in New England was but 38 per cent of the national growth, though New England's expansion of population, income, and manufacturing value added were 67, 71, and 82 per cent of the national average.

New England suffers also from a failure to integrate its power resources. Maine's large output, actual or potential, is denied to the rest of the country. Connecticut's main company, apparently in part to escape scrutiny of accounts by the FPC, is also not tied up with facilities outside of the state. These isolationist tendencies may contribute to higher unit costs.

Mr. Olds raises some relevant questions concerning the relative costs of fuel. Why should the cost of fuel to large purchasers in New England exceed costs to the nation generally by 40 per cent? Apparently one-half the difference is associated with higher transportation costs. What puzzles Mr. Olds is the ability of other regions, farther from sources of supply, to move coal at lower costs than New England. Why does not New England more effectively use its cheap water transportation, especially as a means of obtaining cheaper rail rates? Is there a possibility that the utilities and railroad companies coöperate in shunning low-cost water transportation? Mr. Olds also contends that the higher coal prices could be responsible for only about one-third of the difference of rates between New England and the United States "when recognition is given to relative efficiency of fuel utilization and to the fact that coal prices would not affect the hydro part of the New England economy."

Analysis of FPC steam plant data suggest that relative efficiency of steam plants is about as important a factor in fuel costs of such stations as price of fuel. Thus in 1947 the Arkwright Station of Georgia Power Company used $6.90 coal to generate electric energy at a fuel cost of 2.89 mills per kilowatt hour. For the Somerset Station of Montaup Electric Company coal at $7.97 meant 4.47 mills per kilowatt hour fuel costs. If differences in prices of coal had been the only factor, the Somerset plant should have been able to generate for about 3.35 mills per kilowatt hour, or at a saving of over one mill as compared with its actual fuel cost.[11]

Cost and Consumption of Electric Power by Manufacturers in New England and Some Competing States, 1947

Area	Average Cost of Purchased Power (cents per kilowatt hour)	Consumption Per Establishment (000 of kilowatt hours)	
		Purchased	Total [a]
United States	0.93	427	585
New England	1.48	300	428
Rhode Island	1.69	267	312
Massachusetts	1.57	264	347
Connecticut	1.57	371	469
Vermont	1.46	205	248
New Hampshire	1.44	258	514
Maine	0.83	486	1,043
New Jersey	1.30	313	440
Michigan	1.13	618	880
Ohio	1.01	730	1,012
Pennsylvania	1.00	559	773
New York	0.87	243	282
North Carolina	0.79	548	676
Tennessee	0.41	1,504	1,676

[a] Includes power generated for own use.
Source: Calculated from **Census of Manufactures** (1947).

Another memo. of the FPC of July 16, 1950 showed that differences in coal prices accounted for a difference of but 1 mill per KW hour between rates in New England and the Southeast and 2 mills in relation to the TVA area. Actual differences in residential rates were 7 and 13 mills per KWH over these areas, respectively; in commercial rates, 8 and 12; in average industrial rates, 2 and 4.

[11] *Memorandum to Committee on New England Economy*, February 8, 1951, by Leland Olds, Advisor to the Secretary of the Interior.

Since labor, construction, and operation and maintenance costs are approximately the same, the differences (other than in coal prices) must originate in variations in efficiency of operation and management, inclusive of age of equipment and failure to exploit hydro.

High cost of fuel and power is a matter of some importance. Costs of power per unit are 59 per cent higher in New England than in the country, 70 per cent higher than in New York, 87 per cent higher than in North Carolina, and 261 per cent higher than in Tennessee (see the table, page 234).

These are differences in *cost per unit*. The cost of *electric power* depends upon both the *amount of consumption in a given period and the level of applicable rates*. Consumption patterns here push rates above national averages (see tables below). But the applicable rates are also higher. The average charge per 200,000 kilowatt hours of monthly use in large New England cities as of January 1, 1948 exceeded the national average for similar cities by approximately 20 per cent (somewhat less today). On the average, New England costs are about 59 per cent higher than the national average.

	Average Cost of Purchased Power, N. E. as % of U. S. (per kilowatt hour)	Estimated Cost of Total Power to Value added by Manufacture, N. E. as % of U. S.	U. S. Cost of Electricity as Per Cent of Value Added by Manufacture	
			1939	1947
All manufacturing	159	109	2.85	1.70
Apparel	101	106	0.89	0.47
Leather and products	114	106	1.37	0.72
Machinery (nonelectric)	123	117	1.52	1.01
Rubber	139	91	3.67	2.46
Textiles	148	121	3.85	1.86
Chemicals	184	87	3.34	2.60

Source: Calculated from **Census of Manufactures** (1947).

Apparently in relation to the average value added, New England costs are not so high as is suggested by the cost per KWH. The explanation undoubtedly is the high value added in New England, and adverse effects on output requiring much power. On the other hand, in particular industries where power costs are large compared to value added, then the high cost of New England power is a sizable disadvantage.

These costs are especially high in paper (4.39), primary metals (4.02), stone, clay and glass (3.21), chemicals (2.60), and textiles (1.86).

Higher costs are reflected in less consumption in New England than in the rest of the country. In the next table, the reader will observe that the higher the relative New England cost for a particular consumer, the less is relative New England use.

Revenue and Consumption, by Classes, New England and United States, 1949

	N. E. as Per Cent of U. S. Revenue Per KW Hour Sold	KW Hour Sales Per Customer
Residential	128	81
Rural	133	73
Small commercial and industrial	138	65
Large commercial and industrial	162	61

Source: Electric Institute.

No matter how the comparisons are made, New England's fuel and power costs are high.

The three states with highest cost for industrial electric service (cities of 50,000 or over) are Rhode Island (1.78 cents per KWH), Massachusetts (1.77), and Connecticut (1.75). New Hampshire is fifth (1.64). The three low-cost states in 1948 were Tennessee (0.94), Oregon (0.83), and Washington (0.81).

In residential rates in 1949, the important industrial states ranked as follows: Connecticut, 24; Massachusetts, 40; New Hampshire, 38; Rhode Island, 43.

In commercial rates, the figures were 47, 46, 37, 44; and for industrial rates, 42, 43, 35, and 47.

Here is a comparison of Boston and a Southern and Western city:

Monthly Bill, in Dollars, 1948

	Residential Consumers, 100 KWH	Commercial Customers, 1,500 KWH	Industrial Customers, 200,000 KWH
Boston, Mass.	3.35	49.66	2810
Chattanooga, Tenn.	2.50	27.50	1810
Tacoma, Wash.	1.70	20.10	1180

Source: Release of FPC, 1949.

New England's consumption per customer relative to others was as follows, in 1947:

Residential: 1/3 of 4 Pacific Northwest States and 2/3 of 4 TVA States
Small Light and Power Consumers: Less than 2/5 of 4 Pacific Northwest
States and 2/3 of 4 TVA States.
Large Light and Power Industrial Consumers: 1/4 and 1/3 of the North-
west and TVA States, respectively.

Average cost per KWH in manufacturing industries per KWH
(cents): New England, 1.48; 4 Pacific Northwest States, 0.38; East
South Central States, 0.54. (Since 1939, New England's costs rose
by 10 per cent, Pacific Northwest declined by more than 40 per
cent, and East South Central States by more than 20 per cent.) [12]
The importance of power is suggested by the following:

Cost of Purchased Power

	Percentage of Wages	Percentage of Net Earnings
Leather and products	1.94	21.11
Lumber and wood	2.73	40.0
Metal products, etc.	4.41	16.54
Paper, pulp, etc.	8.33	35.34
Textiles and products	4.21	48.74

4. THE SIGNIFICANCE OF HIGH FUEL AND POWER COSTS

It is difficult to evaluate the significance of these high costs. For
example, the following correlation is suggestive:

Economic Growth, 1929 to 1947 — Relative Growth (%)

	4 Pacific States	6 N. E. States	7 TVA States
Income	202	91	198
Electric power — utility generating capacity	146	48	140

Source: Federal Power Commission.

These figures are of some significance; but the inference should
not be drawn that the more rapid increase of generating capacity
accounts for the greater gains of the Pacific and TVA States. Indeed,
the large advantages in power are of some importance. Mr. Little,

[12] Material of preceding paragraphs from Memorandum of Office of Secretary of the Interior, *Selected Economic Data*, No. 73454, April 17, 1950; *Release
of FPC*, No. 70,940; and other items.

in his evidence on the *Investigation of the Closing of Nashua, N. H. Mills and Operations of Textron,* emphasized the large differential in power costs: 7.1 mills average per KW hour in his four Southern mills and 12.4 and 17 mills in two New England Mills.[13]

Another approach is to dismiss differences, as of secondary importance. A survey by the Boston Reserve Bank indicated that 24 per cent of 663 New England manufacturers felt that power costs and fuel costs were an important comparative disadvantage, 13 per cent that power costs were an advantageous factor, and 9 per cent that fuels costs were a comparative disadvantage. These results may be questioned partly because many respondents probably did not know too much about the relative costs of power and partly because the essential problem is the industries lost because of high power costs. The importance of the campaign to associate public power with the threat of statism is also relevant here. The New England Council ended its report with a statement that "the question of cheap power is not a determining factor of management plans except for certain heavy industries." [14]

5. CONCLUSION

Fuel and power costs are high in New England. We should use every means to get them down: cheaper fuel through greater use of low-priced fuel (e.g., natural gas) or through stimulating imports (no tariffs on oil); through the maximum use of hydroelectric power when the net result is a reduction of cost (inclusive of *fair* allocation of costs to navigation, flood control, etc.); through improved plants and more efficient operation; and through savings on taxes. Fuel and power costs are high enough to keep some industries from coming here. We do not insist that this differential is a major factor; but we stress again that our New England problem is made up of numerous small handicaps as well as a few large ones.

Power costs are a substantial part of value added — almost 2 per

[13] Senate Hearings of Subcommittee on Interstate and Foreign Commerce, *Investigation of Closing of Nashua, N. H. Mills and Operations of Textron, Incorporated,* p. 32; cf. p. 68.

[14] Cf. New England's Power Problem, *A Conference on the Economic Development of the New England States,* Washington, D. C., March 31, 1949, and address by Assistant Secretary of the Interior, G. G. Davidson, at 10th Banquet of TVA, May 14, 1949, for an appraisal of New England's attitude towards public power.

cent for New England. For some industries, power costs are much more important — power outlays were close to one-half of earnings in the textile industries. Tax *costs* are probably a somewhat larger part of value added than power; but as a competitive matter, power may well be much more important. Differences in tax costs between New England and the nation or Southeast and Northwest are much less than those in power.

There are many disconcerting aspects of the power problem. In some industries, along with other locational disadvantages, high power costs may be a cause of migration or a deterrent to entry. Future requirements will be large and may be costly if full use is not made of hydro potentials. The hydro potential seems to the writer to be much closer to the 3 million KW estimate by the FPC, given their reasonable assumptions, than the 500 million KW estimated by the New England Council. Private attempts recently to exploit hydro considered unexploitable by the New England Council's Committee support the official estimate. Indeed, there are serious problems to be solved before full use can be made of this hydro. A greater use of hydro through multi-purpose development is one approach to lower the average costs of power and fuel; but there is much opposition by New England leaders to multi-purpose development.[15] Another is reduced transportation costs which the area might achieve. But most important is the high costs associated with management, low labor productivity, age of equipment, failure to integrate and pool resources.

Growth of capacity in recent years has been at a disconcertingly low rate. The ratio of new capacity relative to the nation's has been only about one-half the region's *relative* average growth in population, income and value added in manufacture. In recent years, New England's cost of power has tended to rise relative to important competitors. The high price of power is reflected in much less than average use. In relation to the Southeast and Northwest, New England's consumption in industry is ½–⅓.

---

[15] Cf. Materials in footnote 14 and the NEC, *Power in New England.*

CHAPTER 22

THE ST. LAWRENCE SEAWAY[1]

1. THE GAINS FOR NEW ENGLAND

New England's continued economic security depends upon free trade and its ability to sell, primarily in this country and secondarily abroad. Like England, it must export or die. Its percentage of employment in agriculture, mining, forestry, etc. is but one-quarter that of the rest of the country. Its population per square mile is three times that for the country as a whole. It must do everything possible to stimulate trade and the expansion of income. While New England's main weapons are its industry, intelligence, good schooling, and selling capacity, these can be used to best advantage with free trade and the absence of trade barriers.

We are prone to forget that we have had free trade in scientific discoveries: that our great technical advances, the very foundation of our prosperity, rest upon advances in pure science which have been made primarily by foreigners, not Americans, or, for that matter, New Englanders. Our manufacturing superiority and high productivity depend upon these gains. It ill becomes New England, then, to stand in the forefront in the opposition to the St. Lawrence

[1] This chapter is based largely on a paper presented before the New England Council, September 12, 1947.

In writing this chapter I have relied especially on: U. S. Department of Commerce, *The St. Lawrence Seaway*, N. R. Danielian, Director (1941), 7 Parts; U. S. Department of Commerce, *Domestic Transportation: An Economic Appraisal of the St. Lawrence Seaway Project*, P. M. Zeis (1947); Hearings, Senate Subcommittee of the Committee of Foreign Relations on S. J. Res. 111 on St. Lawrence Seaway Project (May–June, 1947); Senate Report No. 810, *Great Lakes-St. Lawrence Seaway Project* (January 1948), Majority and Minority Reports, Digest of Hearings on S. J. Res. 111, St. Lawrence Seaway Project (1947); Hearings, House Committee on Public Works, *Great-Lakes-St. Lawrence Basin*, H. J. Res. 192, Part I (July 1947); Great Lakes-St. Lawrence Association, *Fact Book on St. Lawrence Seaway* (1951, Preliminary Ed.); *New England News Letter*, Supplement, "Should the St. Lawrence Seaway be Built?" Debate by Seymour E. Harris and Henry E. Foley, 1947.

Seaway, a great and important application of engineering science for the production of transportation services and power.

Henry I. Harriman, in the early twenties, prepared a report in support of the Seaway Project. And early in 1947, he wrote:

New England is distinctly a manufacturing center, producing manufactured goods which it ships to all parts of the country and importing from other sections the major portion of the food which it requires. This means that New England is particularly dependent upon the freight it must pay on incoming and outgoing goods . . .

If the Seaway is finished, boats from six to twelve-thousand tons' burden can ply between western ports, such as Chicago, Duluth, and Detroit, on the one hand, and Boston, Portland, and other seaports, on the other hand, and while the distance by water is twice as long as by rail, I believe that water rates between the interior lake ports and the coastal ports of New England and New York will be materially lower than if shipped by rail.

Mr. Harriman then goes on to discuss the power aspects of the problem, emphasizing the need for cheap power. At a meeting of the New England Council on June 20, 1947, Governor Gibson elaborated on this point. Vermont, short of power, is not disposed to use up any more of its limited farm lands in conjunction with hydroelectric development or flood control dams.

It seems to me that we have come to the point where we have exhausted practically all the possibilities for hydroelectric power development in Vermont. We are desperately short of electricity in Vermont, and uses for electricity are increasing daily. That is why I and a lot of other citizens of Vermont believe that the St. Lawrence Seaway should be built. (He adds other reasons later.)

At an earlier date, the Joint New England Committee on the St. Lawrence Seaway Project, which included among its members three ex-Governors of New Hampshire, published a thorough survey of the problem. After examining the relative advantages of the St. Lawrence Project, the proposed Lake Ontario–New York Waterways, and the All-American Seaway, the committee decided in favor of the St. Lawrence Project. It concluded as follows:

The committee looks upon the proposed expenditure for developing the waterway as in the nature of a capital investment of a national character upon which exceptionally liberal dividends will be returned in the form of reduced transportation costs and the general benefit and prosperity of a large and important section of the country which at the present time is laboring under most serious and difficult economic handicaps. It further believes that the net result of the development of such a waterway will incidentally be of considerable advantage to New England and the surrounding community, both from a broad national standpoint as well as that of purely local self-interest.

Senator Aiken is another supporter of the project, as had been his fellow Vermonter, Calvin Coolidge. His support is unqualified. Recognizing the interrelationship of national income and New England income, he said in a speech before the Boston City Club, November 14, 1945 (reprinted in *Congressional Record*, December 4, 1945):

Shall we, through political sabotage, prevent the development of other sections, thereby permanently impairing the industrial vitality and military strength of our Nation?

Or shall we adopt measures to help our section of the country at the same time as we assist the betterment of other areas, thus increasing wealth and industry all around?

Quoting the Harriman study, Senator Aiken enumerated the following advantages to New England: lower transportation costs on much of its food and raw materials; lower freight rates to many markets for its finished products; a supply of export grain and flour at prices as low or lower than can prevail in other North Atlantic ports, hence a revival of export business in the port of Boston, and other New England ports; the disappearance of rail differentials following the completion of the St. Lawrence; and finally, cheap power.

2. ARGUMENTS OF OPPONENTS

Witnesses who appeared to testify against the project in the 1947 hearings before the subcommittee of the Senate Committee on Foreign Relations were primarily representatives of (1) port authorities; (2) mining companies; (3) steamship companies; (4) some labor groups; (5) railroads.

In each instance, the opposition represents a vested interest which might suffer, or which believed that it might suffer, as a result of the Seaway development. Power interests who are not friendly but seem to have refrained from making a public statement, dread government offer of cheap power, though if the retailing is done by

private companies, their opposition is softened. Port authorities —
New York, Boston, Baltimore, Buffalo, New Orleans — all of these
envisage the Seaway as a development tending to divert traffic from
their ports. In mining the threat is of foreign competition. Within
twenty years this country must depend substantially either on low-
grade ore, or imported ore from Labrador, Venezuela, and other
places. Some companies are beginning to experiment with low-grade
ores. Threatened with increased imports, via the Seaway, of iron
from abroad, these companies warn that they will not undertake
the large investments required if they have to meet this foreign
competition. Coal companies also object to the possibility of reduced
landed costs of foreign coal. Steamship companies are in opposition
because, in their view, foreign vessels will capture a large part of
the waterway business at the expense of their business from eastern
seaports. To the United Mine Workers, the Seaway offers increased
competition of foreign workers. Since the Seaway will obtain some
traffic at the expense of eastern railroads, the country's eastern
railroads are opposed. (It is a mystery why all railroads, including
those which would gain directly, should object.) Senator Saltonstall,
who also appeared against the bill, is not friendly to the project in
part because of the alleged losses that will be inflicted on the Boston
Port.

Most of the opponents are frank that they do not like the Seaway
because it will injure the interests that they represent. They do not,
however, restrict themselves to the points related to their interests:
The Seaway will not be self-liquidating; it will not contribute to
defense; it will support foreign labor, not American; technical difficulties will prevent significant use of the Seaway; government
should not be allowed to subsidize one method of transportation
against another; savings to shippers will be negligible — these are
the main arguments adduced by the opponents, the more important
of which we shall discuss presently.

Here it is necessary to note that for the most part, the opposition
comes from vested interests who cannot speak for the national
interest. If they appear to, what they say must be accepted with
reservations. Against them, the Joint Chiefs of Staff, ex-Presidents
Coolidge and Hoover, Secretary Marshall, the Secretaries of Commerce, Jesse Jones and Averill Harriman, the Secretary of the
Interior, the Chief of the U. S. Engineers, all of whom presumably

represented all of us, have spoken decisively in favor of the project.

In his speech before the City Club, Senator Aiken said as follows:

The opposition is engendered by the Eastern Trunk Lines and power companies, both intimately connected with the higher echelons of finance in New York . . .

The Eastern roads fear competition in their rates, and the power companies fear cheap public power, and this opposition has been consolidated since public development of this project was enunciated by Governor Roosevelt, of New York, in 1931 . . .

They have initiated hostile and false propaganda through the country from coast to coast, and unfortunately, many well-meaning and public-spirited citizens have fallen for it.

3. SELF-LIQUIDATING ASPECT

One of the most persistent criticisms of the project has been that it would subsidize shipping at the expense of the railroads and the taxpayers. To meet this criticism, particularly since there was much concern over the public debt, Senator Vandenburg introduced S. Res. 111, in May 1947, which provided for a toll system and self-liquidation. Unfortunately, this proposal had little effect: the opposition insists that the project cannot be made self-liquidating.

There is evidence to suggest that it can be made self-liquidating, yet even if the Seaway could not pay for itself directly, the federal outlay and receipts from a project are only part of the complete picture. Even if losses were $5 million a year, it does not follow that the project should be abandoned. It is necessary to take into account any gains of income associated with the building of the project as well as gains associated with reduced costs of transportation and power. Out of this additional income, the government might well finance any losses.

On this score, it is well to point out to Senator Saltonstall, and others that the railroads profited from vast subsidies; that they were not very solicitous of the hundreds of canal companies they put out of business; and that temporary subsidies to an infant industry is an established method of doing business.

4. FINANCES OF THE SEAWAY

But let us look at the finances of the problem. I can quote ex-President Hoover. His estimate was 30 million tons of traffic per year. Secretary of Commerce Harriman put it at 12 million tons initially, rising to 30–40 million tons. The Canadian government disposed of the theory that the Welland Canal would be a serious bottleneck; its present theoretical capacity is 75 million tons, its practical capacity 30–35 million tons. In the estimates of revenues in 1947 (cf. Harriman), it was generally assumed that dry cargo would pay the full $1.25 per ton and cargo competing with the 14-foot canals considerably less. Should the Waterway obtain 10 per cent of the total dry cargo (export and import) and 2 million tons of Canadian and domestic traffic, it would obtain 6 million tons, or 7½ million dollars. In addition, there is the grain trade. The Waterway would get a large part of the Canadian grain — 300–500 million bushels and ½–¾ of our exports, or another 400 million bushels. These estimates leave out of account the possibility of iron ore and petroleum traffic and the continued growth of this country to a $300–700 billion-dollar income level. Later estimates (1951) by the Great Lakes-St. Lawrence Seaway Association, an organization very friendly to the project, put traffic at 50 million tons.

The best available finance estimate is from Chief of Engineers Lieutenant General Wheeler.

A. *Costs*

		$ Million
1.	Costs (middle 1947)	674
2.	United States share	492
3.	Of which New York State pays $161 million for specific power costs and ¼ of combined power and navigation costs: Deduct	258
4.	Cost of navigation, U. S.	234
5.	Add interest, period of reconstruction	21
6.	Total U. S. costs of navigation	255

B. *Annual Costs*

1.	Interest and amortization at 4.33%	11.07
2.	Cost of operation and maintenance	1.23
		12.30

Ratio of costs to benefit (income):

$$1941 = 1 \text{ to } 2.25$$
$$\text{May, } 1947 = 1 \text{ to } 1.46$$

Mr. Harriman used similar figures and showed, however, that with a 2½ per cent rate of interest and 40 years' amortization, the total annual cost would be $18 million, and the American share, only $10.8 million. The Wheeler estimates are on the gloomy side. Why should the Seaway be required to amortize in 53 years when railroads do not; and why amortize the entire investment when a large part (e.g. dredging) is not to be depreciated?

These are the official figures, and let us stand by them. By inflating the cost, raising the interest rate and maintenance costs, or shortening the amortization period, opponents can show much larger costs. Mr. Sabin, vice-president of the Lake Carriers Association, for example, puts capital outlay at $600 million and arrives at total costs of $32 million per year. At 20 million tons and tolls of $1.25, Mr. Sabin then gets a deficit of $7 million. I shall quote 1951 figures presently.

5. DEFENSE ASPECTS

It has been noted that the project may well pay for itself out of receipts from tolls, and charges for power. For many years, supporters of the Seaway underlined the contribution to defense. In 1941, defense was a major consideration, as an examination of the excellent St. Lawrence Survey prepared by Dr. Danielian for the Department of Commerce will show. Even in 1946, the Chiefs of Staff strongly urged that the work go on, because the Seaway was essential for defense. Developments since 1946 further emphasize the defense aspects.

In his testimony for the Army, in 1947, Kenneth C. Royall, the Secretary of War, was less enthusiastic on the defense issue than his predecessors had been over a long period. He was not so enthusiastic as Secretary of State Marshall, whose experience was of much longer standing. Yet even Secretary Royall agreed that the Seaway would be helpful to national defense; that it would contribute toward mobilization for war; that industrial congestion on the Eastern Seaboard and vulnerability to attack would be reduced; that bottlenecks in rail transportation would be of less concern if the Seaway were available; and that it would provide increased facilities for shipbuilding. When one considers how important defense is in this kind of world, even a $10 million deficit should not stand in the way of building the Seaway. In 1950–1952, the military authorities once more stressed the contribution to defense.

6. POWER

Power is a significant cost element, particularly relevant to areas like New England and New York which are losing ground industrially, which are lagging behind the rest of the country in power development, and which in addition pay much more for power than do competitive areas.

New England's disadvantages in power costs and supplies were discussed in the preceding chapter. Governor Dewey, the head of the Power Authority of New York, and Senator Aiken have both urged more and cheaper power through the St. Lawrence Seaway. Estimates of its generating capacity range from 700,000 to 1,000,000 kilowatts, of which New England might obtain 100,000 to 200,000 kw. Power and navigation are joint products, the outlay for one reducing the other. The government's legal power rests largely on the navigation project, with power being made available through building dams to provide an even flow of water. It is not a practical matter to give New England and New York the power, and having provided a large part of the navigation outlay, to deny use of the Seaway for navigation.

It was pointed out by the head of the New York Power Authority that the St. Lawrence Development would annually save 5 million tons of coal or 20 million barrels of oil, both wasting assets, and would reduce the pressure upon transportation facilities. Hydropower has the advantage over atomic energy, moreover, in that it requires no fuel costs.

7. GOVERNMENT CONTROL

On the issue of government intrusion and control of industry, this should be noted. Certain developments simply cannot be expected of private enterprise. The amounts involved are too large; the public interest paramount; the rights to water power belong to the people, not private interests. It is interesting on this score that a famous engineer, Colonel H. L. Cooper, proposed in 1921 (acting on behalf of Alcoa, the General Electric Company, and du Pont), to make a gift of the navigation facilities if the governments of the two countries would give his clients the right to develop the electricity on the river from Ogdensburg to Montreal. Apparently, even in 1921, large private interests considered the project self-liquidating on power alone.

8. THE SEAWAY AND THE COLD WAR

The foregoing is largely based on a presentation by the author in a debate with Henry Foley, attorney for the Boston Port Authority, before the New England Council on September 12, 1947. In general, recent developments have not weakened the argument. The need for conserving resources is greater; the outlay required for the Seaway in terms of manpower and resources is small. Defense Mobilizer Charles Wilson has said that the amounts of materials and manpower required are so small as to "be negligible in the total mobilization framework." Because it will contribute to the defense of the country, among other reasons, the project now has the support of the Joint Chiefs of Staff, the permanent U. S.-Canadian Joint Board on Defense, the National Security Resources Board, ex-Secretary of Defense George Marshall, Secretary of the Army Frank Pace, Jr., Defense Mobilizer Charles Wilson, Chairman of the Munitions Board John Small, and Chief of U. S. Army Engineers Lieutenant General Lewis Rich.

According to a 1951 estimate of the U. S. Corps of Engineers (February 1951), the cost of the remaining work on the Seaway and the International Rapids powerhouse is $816 million, with the United States' share, $567 million. Of this amount, power would cost this country $192 million, and at 2.5 per cent interest and 50 years' amortization, the annual cost of power would be $11.128 million. The delivered cost of power would be one-half the cost of steam power in this area. The annual cost of the navigation project, with an investment of $433 million (interest and amortization as above) would be $20 million.

If the $492-million estimate of cost of the project is correct for 1947, then a $567-million cost for the United States was low in 1951. In view of the inflation since 1947 and the inflation to be expected in the 6-year period of construction, the costs should be estimated at around $700 million. Inflation will, of course, also affect revenues to be received. In its 1951 *Fact Book on the Seaway*, the Great Lakes-St. Lawrence Association emphasizes especially the large contribution to the Seaway's revenues by the inward movement of iron ore from Labrador.

9. NEW ENGLAND AND THE SEAWAY

It is important to emphasize the significance of the project for the New England economy. Senators Lodge and Saltonstall, the Boston Port, and the New England railroads have been vigorous opponents of the development. Undoubtedly, the Massachusetts senators have been influenced by the interests that are likely to suffer from the Seaway development. The power group has also exercised pressure behind the scenes.

Senator Saltonstall has apparently been disturbed by the project in part because of a legitimate fear that subsidizing other areas injures New England's interests. It is, of course, possible that the project will be self-liquidating. If this does not prove true, then the answer to Senator Saltonstall may well be that, if the project helps the country by opening up cheaper transportation for East-West and West-East trade, this area should not object. Besides, New England might also seek subsidies where there are gains to the country *and* the region.

While much opposition has come from New York City, because of the fear that the New York port would be injured, the statesman-like presentation by the late Mayor Fiorello La Guardia should be recalled:

> The interest of the entire country comes first. That is above the special interest of any one point or port or city. If this provides a cheaper outlet for the Midwest agriculture and industry, they are entitled to have it. I have enough confidence in my state to say that we can take care of ourselves insofar as commerce is concerned, but we do ask help when it comes to the power end of it, because we want to get the electric power into our state and into our city.[2]

New England's opposition is based in part on the argument that we do not need more power. I believe the discussion in the preceding chapters disproves this point. In fact, the addition of St. Lawrence power would not only provide cheaper power, but it would make possible a pooling of resources of great potentialities. It would be necessary, however, to work out an agreement with New York State to assure New England a fair share of the new generating capacity.

[2] Senate Report No. 810, *Great Lakes-St. Lawrence Seaway Project* (January 7, 1948), p. 59.

Our leaders also stress the adverse effects on the Boston Port. Henry Harriman and others have contended that the net effect would be cheaper food and raw materials, a very substantial offset, and also it is not clear that the Boston Port would lose much business. At any rate, the continued losses of the Boston Port and the small part it plays in the economy of the area do not suggest that losses to the Port should count heavily in any appraisal of expediency.

With increased interest in a steel mill in New England, some New England interests may object to the opening of the Seaway on the grounds that this would perpetuate the leadership of the Middle West in iron and steel. Surely cheaper raw materials are a must for the Middle West. Is it wise for New England to fight the Seaway, however, because it would help preserve a dominant industry in an important area of the country?

There are other arguments used by New England opponents. Vulnerability of the Seaway to attack is a point made by Senator Lodge. But on the over-all issue of defense the military authorities are not on his side. The inability of many ships to use a 27-foot canal; the high costs of increasing depth to 30 feet; the unavailability of traffic — are some of the arguments used. But the famous engineers, Cooper and Hoover, the Army engineers, and the Department of Commerce do not support these views.

To the writer the main issue is this: Should New England vested interests block a program which clearly would aid the country, would reduce transportation costs for New England's exports and imports, and would provide more cheap power? Against these substantial gains for the country and region, there are possible losses to the two largest railroads in New England and to the Port of Boston, which plays a declining part in our economy. We cannot afford to be unreceptive to government projects, too large for construction by private interests, and we cannot afford to be unreceptive when the government offers the region cheaper power and transportation.

PART VI

MARKETS, TRANSPORTATION, AND RAW MATERIALS

INTRODUCTION

In the discussion of the New England problem in recent years, the tendency has been to overemphasize the importance of the growth of *distant* markets and to underemphasize the significance of the high costs of raw materials. Almost denuded of raw materials (except for forests, and these are losing ground steadily in relation to other areas), New England's extreme location tends to discourage industries which use heavy raw materials.[1] The large development in machinery industries occurred despite the high cost of the raw materials, and because of the high value relative to raw material costs; the growth of metal fabrication in general rests upon the use of light-weight metals. On top of the distances from sources of raw materials, New England suffers from relatively heavy unit railroad costs (Chapter 23). Against this factor, its tidewater location is likely to be a matter of increasing importance as the country becomes increasingly dependent on foreign sources of raw materials. The case for a New England steel mill rests largely on the need of assured supplies of iron and steel and at reasonable prices (Chapter 24). Because of the help given to other distressed areas and because of the need to stimulate new industries, New England has a special claim on government help in starting a steel mill.

[1] See *Report on the New England Economy,* chap. 8, for further discussion of the raw material problem.

CHAPTER 23

TRANSPORTATION AND LOCATION

In this omnibus chapter, we deal with (1) transportation and location, (2) the basing point issue, and (3) the Boston Port Authority.

1. TRANSPORTATION COSTS AND LOCATION

How significant are transportation costs? According to one estimate, railroad transportation costs average about 4 per cent of all costs. In 1939, freight charges as percentage of wholesale prices were as follows: bituminous coal, 57.4; petroleum oils, 28.2; iron and steel (fifth class), 8.7; cotton in bales, 8.7; fresh meats, 7.5; automobiles, passenger, 3.0; tobacco manufactures, 0.6. (Manufactured products are less costly to transport than suggested by this sample.)

New England suffers from several disadvantages in transportation which result in high unit freight costs: (1) her isolation at one corner of the country; (2) the short hauls (133 miles average in New England and 230 miles in the United States); (3) the semi-monopoly position of two railroads over the richest parts of New England; (4) the subsidies required to cover losses on freight and commuter services; (5) heavy terminal charges, low freight tariff density, and the diversity of routes and diffusion of traffic. A tendency in recent years for the ICC to require charges according to costs, not according to competitive conditions, seems to injure New England's relative position. Finally, New England's imports, requiring about 1⅗ times as many carloads of raw materials moving in as carloads of manufactured goods going out, also increase costs.[1]

---

[1] *Memo of the Boston Reserve Bank*, October 26, 1950; and see especially W. J. Cunningham, "The Railroads in New England," in *New England's Prospect* (1933), pp. 344–361. The evidence of Mr. McCarthy, former Vice-President of the New York, New Haven and Hartford Railroad, before the Council's New England Committee was also helpful.

These disadvantages are offset to some extent by proximity to the Atlantic and the great concentration of population within an area of 500 miles. Unfortunately the rise of labor and other costs has so reduced coastwise traffic in recent years as to deprive New England of a substantial part of the advantages of tidewater location. The proximity to large markets is still a very important matter.[2]

In 1937, the Massachusetts Development and the Industrial Commission drew a 500-mile circle from the center of Massachusetts. This arch encompassed or cut 14 states, the District of Columbia, and four provinces in Canada.

In these states and provinces a total of 56,640,000 persons live, of which 49,421,000 live in the United States. This is 38.7% of the total population of the country.

Within this 500 mile radius there are located 106,175 manufacturing plants employing 4,428,347 industrial workers. In the United States portion there are 85,452 plants, which is 50% of the total for the country and 3,958,617 workers or 53.6% of all employed in industry in the United States.

Included within this 500-mile radius are, of course, the New England States, the Middle Atlantic States, the Northeastern parts of Ohio, West Virginia, and North Carolina, and the eastern half of Virginia. The table on page 257 gives some indication of the wealth of only part of this area.

In that table below, we estimated the absolute and relative rise of population for an area that is closely similar to the above (New England, New York, Pennsylvania, New Jersey, Maryland, District of Columbia, Delaware, and all of Virginia). That table shows that the market (500-mile radius) has grown greatly since 1800: a rise of population from 3.9 to 46.4 million. This area contains, however, but 31.1 per cent of the nation's population as compared with 74.2 per cent in 1800.

But it is especially significant that the rise of population in the last 50 years was virtually as great in this area as in the country. Within this area lies the rich market of New England and the Middle Atlantic States.

These calculations omit the relevant parts of Ohio, Virginia, and North Carolina, and Canada. (The last accounted for about 15 per

[2] Cf. pp. 21–22.

cent of the total population.) The reader should consult a chart in the Report on *The New England Economy* to the President (page 65), which reveals the proportion of income, sales, motor cars, etc., in this region to the national total.

All of this does not mean that New England has not been affected by the movement of the population center away from the Eastern Seaboard. The appearance of shoe centers, for example, in the

Population, Absolute and Relative, for "500-Mile" Radius from Central Massachusetts, 1800, 1850, 1900, 1949

	1800	1850	1900	1949
Absolute (thousands)	3,935	10,774	24,552	46,400
Relative (percentage of U.S.A.)	74.2	46.3	32.3	31.1

Source: Calculated from **Statistical Abstract.**

South and Middle West can be associated with this growth of markets elsewhere. But it is well to note that growing markets offer opportunity for New England products.

Transportation costs are important not only to New England's markets but to raw material supplies. The location of industry is greatly influenced by the location of materials used in manufacturing, and New England's natural resources are meager indeed.

Perhaps forests are the most important natural resource in the area. They support the furniture and lumber products, paper and printing and publishing industries, which account for more than 10 per cent of New England's manufacturing employment. But foreign supplies of lumber and pulp are also essential. From 1889 to 1947 lumber production in New England declined by 25 per cent. Unless strong measures are taken to maintain the forests, including increased plantings, scientific cutting, reformed taxation, and improved roads, the dependence on foreign sources will increase.

In the Report of the *Committee on the New England Economy* it was suggested that cheap water transportation rates favored industries employing 428,000 workers, or 34.3 per cent of all factory workers (page 91). Once the Labrador and Venezuela ore mines become available, New England's tidewater location should be a considerable advantage to developing industries using iron and steel.

The table presented by this Committee should, however, be

interpreted with care. For example, the 245,000 workers in the textile industries are included among those with a location advantage vis-à-vis foreign raw materials. Of the 260,000 production workers in textiles in 1947, 105,000 were in woolens and worsted. Woolen manufacturers in New England and other tidewater locations have lower transportation costs for foreign wool than do inland firms. But for the large supplies of wool produced within the United States, New England is at a locational disadvantage. On the other hand, the use of foreign wool is increasing. In 1936–1939, imports were less than 25 per cent of total domestic production; in 1946–1949, imports were more than 1½ times as much as domestic production.[3] The other major raw materials used in textiles are domestic cotton and rayon, and in these New England is clearly at a locational disadvantage vis-à-vis its strongest competitors.

Some doubts may also be raised concerning the significance of attributing a locational advantage to 99,000 workers in the leather and leather products industry. The leather and shoe industry has moved westward partly to be close to domestic sources of raw material. New England retains an advantage in that a substantial proportion of hides and skins comes from abroad.

When the country is exclusively dependent on foreign sources, the East retains an advantage in transportation costs of raw materials; but when the West or South can obtain domestic sources from nearby locations as cheaply as New England can by sea, the advantage of New England is lost.

Not only is New England at a disadvantage in accessibility to raw materials, but New England's businessmen seem to realize that this is one of the handicaps which must be faced. In response to a questionnaire, they expressed this view.[4] The metal-using industry and cotton textiles are especially aware of this disadvantage.

In summary, New England as a great manufacturing area is probably less blessed with the required raw materials than any other great industrial area. This area has neither coal nor iron; neither wool nor cotton; no hides; scanty food products for processing. Against these deficiencies, New England has one important advantage: relatively low transportation costs for foreign raw materials.

[3] BAE, *Agricultural Outlook Charts* (1951), p. 78.
[4] *Monthly Review*, Federal Reserve Bank of Boston (September 1949).

2. RECENT RATE CHANGES

Over a long period, the East had lower railroad freight rates than other parts of the country, the explanation in part being the greater density and presumably lower costs; and to some extent discrimination. A number of official reports have apparently raised some questions concerning the lower rates in the Northeast. Writing in the *Southern Economic Journal* (July 1949), Mr. Buchanan contends that these were not justified by lower costs.

At any rate, the Interstate Commerce Commission in 1945 announced a 10 per cent increase of rates within the Official Territory (largely Northeast) for *class* commodities and a reduction of rates on *all* commodities for interterritorial traffic. The results can be understood by example. If Boston and New Orleans competed for a Youngstown, Ohio customer, the Southern city's position is now significantly improved. (Youngstown is in Official Territory.) Actually, in a recent year class rates applied only to 14.1 per cent of manufacturing and miscellaneous commodities. They are, obviously, more important in heavily industrialized areas.

This rate increase is a matter of some significance, though perhaps less than it seems — particularly to witnesses before the President's Council's Committee on the New England Economy. It is offset by a reduction of 10 per cent in interterritorial shipments; the increase applies only to 14 per cent of manufactures and miscellaneous; and (in 1944) the South sent only 27.4 per cent of its "manufactures and miscellaneous" to Official Territory; and the Western Trunkline Territory sent only 32.3 per cent into Official Territory; and Mountain-Pacific Territory, only 5.4 per cent.[5]

We conclude that rate discrimination is not nearly so important as many businessmen in New England believe. Analysts of the economic problems of the South, discussing alleged discrimination against the South, have concluded in a similar vein. Incidentally, a recent study by the ICC of freight rates for the various areas confirms this conclusion. Since 1947, the ICC has been sampling 1 per cent of all waybills and from these constructing an index of freight rates. They compare the prices of similar freight services by areas.

[5] All figures from *Regional Shifts in the Postwar Traffic of Class I Railways*, I, 1946.

All Commodities: Five Territory Average = 100

Official = 98.7 (Includes primarily New England, New York, Pennsylvania,
        New Jersey, Virginia, Ohio, Indiana, Illinois, and Michigan)
Southern = 98.5
Western Trunk Line = 100.5
Southwestern = 97.5
Mountain Pacific = 104.5

Source: ICC Comparison of Average Rates Charged on Intraterritorial Carload Freight, ICC (1950).

In assessing the effects of greater remoteness of markets from New England and recent ICC decisions favoring other areas, we should also note that on the whole, in inflationary periods, freight rates *may* not rise as much as other costs. Where overhead is large, as in the railroads, and unit overhead costs decline with increased business in inflationary periods, transportation costs may decline as a percentage of all costs. Freight rates are probably a smaller part of total costs than in 1939, and, therefore, any disadvantages suffered from decisions favoring the South or West are probably more than offset by this advantage: a reduction in the proportion of transport to all costs — particularly important for outlying regions.

3. THE CEMENT CASE AND THE BASING POINT SYSTEM[6]

In the Cement Case the United States Supreme Court recently ruled against the basing point system; and this was followed by the introduction of FOB pricing by the steel industry, that is, the buyer was forced to absorb freight. Since the method of pricing influences the location of industry, it is necessary to discuss the problem briefly here.

Under the basing point system, a seller fixes price on the assumption that the commodity is shipped from a basing point: the freight is added from the basing point. Thus, steel may be shipped from Gary, Indiana to Chicago. With a Pittsburgh basing point, the

[6] See, especially, (1) U. S. Department of Commerce, Technical Release No. 8, *Basing Point Charge and Industrial Location* (1948); (2) New England Council, *The Basing Point Decisions and the New England Economy* (September 18, 1948); (3) Hearings Before a Subcommittee of the Judiciary on S. 1008, *Pricing Practices — Moratorium* (March–April, 1949); (4) Senate Document No. 27, *Study of Federal Trade Commission Pricing Policies* (February 1949); (5) Interstate Commerce Commission, *Regional Shifts in the Postwar Traffic of Class I Railways* (September 1946). F. Machlup, *The Basing Point System*, is the most exhaustive study and, on the whole, is critical of the system.

consumer is charged freight from Pittsburgh to Chicago. The difference between actual freight costs and the much larger freight charged is phantom freight. If the basing point is closer than the place of shipment, then the producer absorbs freight — e.g., steel shipped from Pittsburgh to Bridgeport, with a basing point of Bethlehem, Pennsylvania.

4. EFFECTS OF THE BASING POINT DECISIONS

The Supreme Court decisions have been upsetting, and in New England much concern has been expressed concerning the effects of these decisions upon the New England economy. Recourse to FOB pricing in place of a basing point system is likely to have the following effects:

1. It will make raw materials more expensive to New England manufacturers; for in the past there has been a substantial absorption of freight to outlying areas. The effect may well be a tendency to establish fabrication plants nearer the source of raw materials. Thus, a firm giving employment to a large part of the employable population of an up-state New York town threatens to leave because of the increased cost of raw materials. An advertisement by the Commonwealth of Pennsylvania says: *"Will the FOB Mill Pricing System Make It Necessary for You to Have a Plant in Pennsylvania?* . . . Already a number of companies are looking over the many plant locations of Pennsylvania . . ." On this score, the reader should consult the chapter on an Integrated Steel Mill for New England. The case for the mill rests in part upon the increased costs of the raw materials under FOB pricing.

2. It will jeopardize outlying markets of New England manufacturers. Should the privilege of absorbing freight be denied, then producers nearer the consumers might take away New England markets. In Eastern Pennsylvania, where there is a heavy concentration of cement production, it is estimated that the plants denied rights to absorb freight would lose 98 per cent of their market.

There are, however, some offsets to losses associated with the trend towards FOB pricing. Loss of markets and increased costs of raw materials may stimulate an exodus of firms from New England; but producing firms will tend to establish plants near New England markets both to sell raw materials and to sell finished goods in New England markets. Thus, an Ohio metal fabrication plant, with its

New England market in jeopardy, may well build a plant in New England. Again, in some industries, though not in many, New England will gain because of the proximity to sources of materials — e.g., the paper manufacturer who is close to the paper pulp supply of New England.

The effects of a shift from freight absorption to FOB pricing may not be so large as is sometimes assumed because:

1. Transportation rates as a rule are not a large part of the total costs. Acording to Paul Zeis, head of the Transportation Division of the Office of Domestic Commerce, the average freight rate per ton of freight for miscellaneous products, inclusive of manufactured goods, during the year 1947 was $7.60. This was about 4–5 per cent of the delivered price. For iron and steel, freight was about 10 per cent; for cement, about 30 per cent. In the latter two, transportation is an important item. Again there are offsets. First, because rates may be reduced. Thus, the United States Steel Corporation is already seeking a 40 per cent cut in railroad rates from Pittsburgh to New York. Then, cheaper kinds of transportation will be used, and there will be gains as, with less cross-hauling, the average haul will be less.

2. Buyers will seek supplies nearer to their factories. In the present tight market, this will be difficult. But with the passage of time, there will be an exchange among suppliers and buyers, with the result that average hauls will be reduced.

3. Many industries are geared to their present location for reasons other than transportation. Dr. McLaughlin notes that ship-building, the automobile industry, and the railroad equipment industry, for example, will not change their situs as a result of a change in the amount of freight absorbed.

4. In many industries, FOB pricing is prevalent. For example, this is the practice in apparels. In upper New York, out of 237 answering the question, 81, or slightly more than one-third, replied that they purchased 90 per cent or more of their materials FOB mill; for sales, 116 out of 238 sold FOB. In paper, however, three-quarters of the sales and purchases were under a delivered price system; in primary metals, one-half of purchases and two-thirds of sales were made on a delivered price basis. In New York City the proportion buying and selling on an FOB basis is much higher than in upper New York State.

5. A large proportion of sales are within 500 miles. Thus, the survey by the New York State Department of Commerce revealed that plants in upper New York State sold 13 per cent of their output within 100 miles, 46 per cent between 100 and 500 miles, and 41 per cent over 500 miles. Again, in 1939, 86.9 per cent of the manufacturers and miscellaneous commodities originating in *official* territory (largely Northeast) was destined for the Northeast.

6. Compulsory FOB selling is not required under the Supreme Court decision. Absorption without collusion is still legal.

5. SPECIAL RELEVANCE FOR NEW ENGLAND

The problem of freight absorption is especially important for New England, because the decisions especially affect manufacturing, and New England is primarily a manufacturing area; and also because an area that concentrates heavily on machinery and metallic fabrication and paper products will be greatly affected by a rise in the cost of raw materials; and finally because exports of manufactured goods (value added) amount to about $3000 million, or more than 20 per cent of the income of the area. Any loss of markets is then bound to be a serious matter. According to the New York survey, the business respondents feared much more the effects on markets than on the cost of raw materials.

My conclusion is that the effect of the Basing Point Decisions is likely to be adverse for New England; but not seriously. The result is likely to be a greater decentralization of manufacturing, which is harmful to a heavily industrialized area.

By sending out questionnaires, Mr. Alfred Neal of the Federal Reserve Bank of Boston obtained some information from New England manufacturers on the possible effects of the mandatory shift to FOB mill price system upon the New England economy. On the basis of 445 returns from a mailing list of 2500, Mr. Neal estimated a loss of 32,850 jobs. (The sample is probably biased, because those concerned are more likely to reply.) The major losses were in iron and steel and their products (8800), machinery (6800), paper and allied products (6350), and nonferrous metals and their products (6000). These manufacturers absorb freight to a considerable extent. Of those replying, at least 24 indicated that a straight FOB system would force them to relocate outside New England or establish branch plants outside. Purchasers of iron and steel apparently have to pay more now, though a minority situated closer to the plant than the old basing point pay less.

Mr. Neal believes that the net loss of jobs will be substantially less than 33,000, in part because this survey does not deal with the resulting influx of plants; and in part because freight absorption, and possibly freight equalization, will not be discontinued. Moreover, he sees in the increased cost of iron and steel an additional reason for establishing an integrated iron and steel mill in New England. Items produced in Pittsburgh and sent to central New England which had a Buffalo basing point will now cost $1.50–$2.00 a ton more; those with a Bethlehem basing point, $3.50–$5.00 more; those with a Sparrow's Point basing point, $2.00–$3.00 more.

6. THE BOSTON PORT AUTHORITY

In general, the Boston Port Authority has lost ground over many years. There are many explanations: a reputation for high labor costs which is apparently not justified; a large decline in coastwise trade associated in part with the large relative rise in shipping costs (an important loss for New England); the differential export-freight rates favoring Baltimore, Philadelphia, and Gulf ports; the equalization of ocean freight rates irrespective of distance to foreign ports; the lack of independence of the port authority and other administrative weaknesses; the leadership and initiative shown by other port authorities (e.g., New Orleans); the cumulative effect of a decline once started which brings a decline of sailings and further cuts in use — these are the main explanation of the losses suffered by the Boston port. The decline is especially unfortunate because access to tidewater was one of New England's great advantages in the nineteenth century.

It is no wonder then that Boston, which was second only to New York in 1900, was in 1948 fifth in imports and 48th in exports. Whereas in 1922, Boston accounted for 5.2 million tons of foreign freight, in 1948, with foreign trade much greater, she accounted only for 3.2 million tons. The New York City Port captured 26.3 million tons of foreign traffic; Baltimore, 16.1 million tons; and Philadelphia, 14.0 million tons. Even New England firms found the limited sailings and facilities of the Boston Port a handicap: a sample of New England firms revealed 88 per cent of their exports went out via New York City in 1939 and 81 per cent in 1948.

It seems unfair that, in 1947, freight rates on refrigerators (per 100 pounds) from Chicago and Cincinnati should be $.98 and $.79 to New Orleans, respectively, and $1.10 and $.92 to New York and Boston, respectively, though the latter two are closer, and that ocean freights from Boston to Calcutta and Bordeaux should equal those from New Orleans, although Boston is 1740 miles closer to Calcutta and 1926 miles closer to Bordeaux. New England is deprived of its natural advantage of proximity to foreign ports, and yet Philadelphia, Baltimore, and Gulf Ports receive special favors in discriminatory rates. The ICC claims that these advantageous rates to the latter ports stem from the shorter routes from the Middle West to these ports than to Boston and New York. In 1951, the ICC corrected this situation to some extent.

CHAPTER 24

AN IRON AND STEEL MILL FOR NEW ENGLAND

In the last few years, public-spirited citizens in New England have campaigned vigorously for a steel mill for New England, and in a manner reminiscent of the enthusiasm of an emerging industrial area rather than of a declining economy. This campaign reflects a determination to advance on the economic front which has been sadly lacking at times. The New England Council, the Boston Federal Reserve Bank, and others deserve much credit for the pertinacity with which they have fought for an integrated mill for New England.

Why this sudden enthusiasm for the mill? One explanation is the increased importance of the metal fabrication industries which in 1947 accounted for almost 40 per cent of New England's employment in manufacturing, an increase of 75 per cent over 1939. These industries need raw materials at reasonable prices if they are to flourish, and iron and steel have been scarce for many years now. When a raw material becomes scarce and the seller customarily absorbs part of the freight, there is a tendency to sell to nearby rather than to distant buyers. Consequently, New England's industries are relatively neglected.

This point of view was clearly set forth by A. J. Hazlett of Jones and Laughlin, who testified before a Senate Committee as follows: [1]

SENATOR ELLENDER: How did you make a selection as between customers, if you gave steel to some and not to others, who were your former customers?

MR. HAZLETT: Well, in some cases we exercised our selection on the basis of the profitableness or the prospective profitability of the business and the potentials for the future.

[1] Senate Report No. 44, *Changes in Distribution of Steel, 1940–47* (1949), p. 22.

SENATOR ELLENDER: What do you mean by that, profitableness?

MR. HAZLETT: I mean it is, in some cases, the matter of location. In certain products, that traditionally are not high profit, we felt we could not afford to ship into high absorption territories.

MR. DICKEY: By "high absorption territories" you mean high freight absorption territories?

MR. HAZLETT: Yes, sir.

SENATOR ELLENDER: Your basic price was the same?

MR. HAZLETT: Yes, sir; it was.

SENATOR ELLENDER: So that the additional profits you may have made resulted from lower freight rates?

MR. HAZLETT: That is right, from not having to give to the railroads a part of the revenue from the transaction.

SENATOR ELLENDER: Well, would you be able to say what percentage of your former customers found themselves in that condition?

MR. HAZLETT: Where we didn't give them any steel?

SENATOR ELLENDER: Yes.

MR. HAZLETT: I don't know. I couldn't answer the question. I would say the number would be very small.

. . . . . .

MR. HAZLETT: There are some places that we would sell normally with respect to certain products and not others.

MR. DICKEY: Could you tell us what those places are and what products they are?

MR. HAZLETT: For instance, take the city of Chicago. We cannot afford to send plates and hot-rolled sheets to Chicago, products that normally have a small profit margin and absorb $7.80 a ton freight. I think it is $7.80. Yes, $7.80. On the other hand, we can ship cold drawn bars to Chicago. We can afford to do that.

In the war period, such considerations were particularly important, for changes in pricing method were prohibited and sellers could avoid some of the squeeze of price control by shipping to nearby markets. Priorities and direct controls were necessary to prevent this method of allocating scarce materials.[2] In more recent years, the shift from basing point to FOB pricing has reduced the danger that iron and steel will not be shipped to outlying manufacturers; but, on the other hand, FOB means higher prices to these firms and, therefore, a loss of competitive power and the danger that plants will move closer to sources of raw materials.

The power to govern the distribution of steel is the power of life and death in the economic world. The way in which it is exercised determines which businesses grow and which do not, which industries expand and

[2] See my *Price and Related Controls in the American Economy*, pp. 220–222.

which do not, which states and regions prosper and which do not. Yet despite its overwhelming importance, the power appears to have been exercised, for example, so that the 12 areas which happened to be the major centers of steel production received nearly half as much again as their prewar shipments of hot-rolled-steel sheets, while the amount flowing into the remainder of the country stood practically unchanged, rising only 2.7 per cent.[3]

The Senate Small Business Committee notes also that producing companies purchase fabricating subsidiaries and favor them in allocations; that because the production of cold rolled steel is very profitable, insufficient resources are devoted to the production of hot rolled steel. The Committee does not, however, insist that large customers in Massachusetts and Connecticut have suffered serious deprivations, though smaller producers and firms in the smaller New England states have especially suffered.[4]

A third point is of even greater importance. It is imperative, if New England is to continue as a flourishing community, that new industries replace the soft-goods industries which are losing ground.

The metal fabrication industries are growing, and their development depends upon the continued availability of raw materials at reasonable prices. But the major steel companies have shown little interest in building an integrated steel mill in this area. It is cheaper to increase capacity by enlarging an existing plant than by building a new mill. Is it therefore necessary or wise to subsidize a New England steel plant? There are strong arguments to support such a move.

(1) New England would gain as workers and management, squeezed out of declining industries, find greater outlets in expanding industries. Communities and local services would continue which might otherwise have to be abandoned. Offsetting the outlay of public funds would be large gains in income.

(2) New England is entitled to special consideration because it has transferred large amounts of cash to the Treasury in the past.

[3] Senate Report No. 44, *Changes in Distribution of Steel, 1940–47* (1949), p. 1. Cf., however, Boston Federal Reserve Bank *Monthly Review* (September 1948), pp. 2–3.

[4] Senate Report No. 44, pp. 4–10, 18–31. Cf. The Commonwealth of Massachusetts, Governor and Council, *Report to the Industry on the Site for a Steel Plant in New England* (1950). The emphasis is put on cheap transportation, cheap scrap, large markets, available sites, and plenty of water.

Its present situation as a mature area confronted with serious problems of adjustment seems to merit help from the Treasury.

(3) In the semi-war or war economy of 1951, there is a great need for additional iron and steel capacity. If 17 million tons are added in the early fifties, New England, with about 10 per cent of total employment in the metal fabricating industries and with no steel mill, has a special claim on part of this new capacity.

At the present time, there are also other reasons for supporting a New England steel mill. The Midwest iron ore deposits are rapidly being depleted. Unless a cheap beneficiation process is discovered, it will become necessary to import ore. Brazilian mines, with the largest deposits, are still relatively inaccessible. In Venezuela, high-grade ore reserves estimated at 2 billion tons contrast with the 0.65 billion tons estimated to be available in the Great Lakes regions — approximately twenty years' consumption. And this foreign ore can be shipped into New England at advantageous rates.

There are still, however, obstacles to full exploitation of foreign ores. In Labrador, large investments are required and overhead costs will be high until output increases substantially. Furthermore, it is necessary to provide much new shipping and to go ahead with the St. Lawrence Seaway. With Venezuelan ore, serious transportation problems are still to be solved by the two large companies with exploitation rights. It is of some interest that these two firms are also interested in tidewater steel mills in the United States which would import ore cheaply from these countries.

Another relevant factor is the tendency of the industry to become more market oriented. For many years the large economies in coal required for the production of steel and the increased use of scrap and higher transportation costs for the finished products have tended to increase the importance of markets as against raw materials as the determinant of location. (Scrap has to be transferred from the market to the production point.)

From J. H. Cumberland's Doctorate thesis ("The Locational Structure of the East Coast Steel Industry with Special Reference to the Feasibility of an Integrated New England Steel Mill," Harvard University Library, 1951), I have drawn the following figures:

Transportation costs of coal and iron to Fall River and New London, suggested sites for an integrated mill, are relatively high. But once allowance is made for savings on transportation of the finished product from these cities to (say) Boston, then these locations seem advantageous. A Fall River mill would benefit the Boston market more than it would benefit Southern New England; if that market is to be supplied, New London is the required location. Otherwise, Trenton's competition would be serious for sales in Southern New England.[5]

Transportation Costs on Ore and Coal Required per Net Ton of Steel for Various Cities Serving Boston (Dollars)

	Ore to These Cities	Coal to These Cities	Finished Products to Boston	Total
Fall River — Labrador Ore	4.56	6.01	4.60	15.17
Venezuela Ore	3.68	5.63	4.60	13.91
New London — Labrador Ore	4.56	5.79	6.80	17.15
Venezuela Ore	3.68	5.42	6.80	15.90
Pittsburgh	5.55	1.56	15.20	22.31
Cleveland	3.16	3.85	15.20	22.21
Sparrows Point	4.73	4.26	12.40	21.39
Buffalo	3.16	4.27	12.60	20.03
Trenton	3.68	4.65	10.40	18.73

Source: J. H. Cumberland, "The Locational Structure of the East Coast Steel Industry," p. 133.

Dr. Neal, in evidence before a congressional committee, contended that the New England mill could capture part of the New York and New Jersey market. The careful analysis by Dr. Cumberland seems to show, however, that mills on the Delaware River could sell more cheaply in the New York and New Jersey market than a New England mill. Thus, Dr. Cumberland finds transportation costs of between $17.90 and $20.97 in New York for the New England mill and $13.13 for Trenton.[6]

Power and tax costs may well be higher in some New England cities and may influence the particular site chosen. Because surplus labor is frequently available in textile towns, Fall River might provide the mill with cheap labor, a very significant advantage. But transportation costs would be much lower for New London, which,

[5] Cumberland, p. 134.

[6] Cumberland, pp. 139–140, and also the discussion of the mill in the *Report of the President's Council's Committee on the New England Economy* (pp. 94–100), a part of the report largely contributed by Dr. Neal; and also *Statement by Alfred C. Neal on Behalf of New England Council*, Congressional Record, January 30, 1950.

on the whole, does not have the labor surpluses and reservoir of a city like Fall River. New London also has a tax advantage.

Unfortunately, Dr. Cumberland does not deal adequately with these problems. But he does show that the cost of construction is about $300 per ton as against $50 of existing capacity. Against these high construction costs for new plants a mill would not be feasible unless subsidized by government. Otherwise, the effect would simply be higher prices than prevail today.

Apparently in 1947, consumption of steel in New England was roughly 1.5 million tons. Dr. Cumberland compares minimum economical capacity and net New England consumption exclusive of agglomerative, etc. consumption (see below). The results are substantial deficits in demand for the output of New England mills. (Even these deficits understate the problem because the analyst should consider supply and demand for various types of each class of product. But this information is not available.) Nevertheless, Dr. Cumberland concludes that demand will be adequate. One must consider growth factors, the agglomerative effects (i.e., the association

Mill-Market Relationship

Type of Manufacture	Minimum Economical Capacity	Net New England Consumption	Present New England Market Deficit
1. Sheet and strip	600,000	475,984	124,016
2. Plate	250,000	225,807	24,193
3. Structural	300,000	204,661	95,339
4. Bar	270,000	359,968	−89,968 (Excess demand)
5. Rod	150,000	143,865	6,135

Source: Cumberland, p. 186.

of fabrication with the availability of steel mills) and, finally, the secondary effects — e.g., inter-industry effects. Presently, I shall discuss the agglomerative effects. Cumberland's ingenious discussion is very helpful; but it should be noted that too much can be drawn from past association of growth of metal fabricating industries and location of steel plants. On the basis of a careful analysis, Dr. Cumberland concludes that a steel mill is feasible and could be profitable in New England — but a subsidy would be required for construction. Incidentally, it may be asked why is one being built and another projected by private enterprise in New Jersey and so little interest shown in New England. The answer probably is that the Middle Atlantic market is much larger.

Dr. Cumberland estimates the increment associated with agglomerative effects at 102,451 tons for sheet and strip consumption and 13,392 tons for plate. Even with these additions, demand remains inadequate.[7] Allowing for the growth element (2 per cent a year) and the secondary agglomerative effects, Cumberland concludes that the deficits can be wiped out.[8]

Relying on the Leontief input-output method, Dr. Cumberland finds that the secondary agglomerative effect (inter-industry effects) would be a rise of 40,317 tons in demand.[9] The total demand now is estimated as

> 661,512 tons for steel and strip, and
> 266,628 tons for plate.[10]

These totals include a 10 per cent growth figure for demand since 1947. The reader should note, however, that the assumption is continued full employment, unusual prosperity, and a growth element of a few per cent per year.

In summary, a strong case can be made out for an integrated steel mill for New England. With the increased market orientation of steel-using industries, related in part to altered distribution methods for raw materials; with continued high employment and adequate demand, such a plant appears economically sound. (The case may have been overstated when it has been contended that a New England mill can poach on the New York–New Jersey market.) The big issue is the source of capital. It is obvious that the mill cannot be built at present high construction costs and steel prices without a government subsidy. But New England, with its transitional problems of declining industries, has a special claim on such funds. I do not, however, share the view of some supporters of the mill who want the government to provide $300 million now with

[7] Cumberland, p. 261.
[8] Cumberland, pp. 261–267.
[9] Cumberland, pp. 299–300.
[10] Cumberland, p. 303.

the understanding that later they will sell to private enterprise for $25–$50 million.

In early 1952, the prospects for the New England mill do not seem to be very good. A certificate of necessity has been issued which would give the relevant steel company large tax concessions. Unfortunately, this privilege is useful only to large firms with sufficient profits for accelerated write-offs. The steel companies so far have shown no disposition to accept this subsidy. Hence, an outright government construction of the plant on World War II model offers the best chance of obtaining a New England mill.

PART VII

INDUSTRIAL STRUCTURE

INTRODUCTION

My object in the next two chapters (25 and 26) is to study the trend of New England industries as a guide of future promise and past mistakes. Chapter 25 reveals the importance of outside markets for the declining industries, the handicaps resulting from the high cost of raw materials, the significance of local (sheltered) industries, and the kind of industries that are growing and declining. Chapter 26 is devoted to a study of four industries and occupations as a means of throwing light on some of the perennial problems — e.g., in textiles, the concentration in the South and relative neglect in the North; in shoes, the ease of movement and the pull of the market.

The next two chapters are useful in that they integrate the perennial New England problems with employment trends in New England. It helps to consider the problems from the viewpoint of occupations.

Some readers may, however, prefer to skip these chapters and read the brief conclusion.

CHAPTER 25

EMPLOYMENT OPPORTUNITIES AND ECONOMIC STRUCTURE

1. INTRODUCTION

In earlier chapters we have discussed the major cost items and their relevance for any economic losses suffered by the New England area. In this and in Chapter 26, the objective is to study the trends in important fields of employment and to associate them with cost and other relevant factors. Among the factors that will receive particular attention are proximity to markets, transportation costs, availability of investment. Labor supply, capital, taxes, and power, always relevant factors, will be reviewed briefly.

As has been mentioned before, New England is a heavily industrialized area — in the proportion of factory workers to total workers, it is still the most industrialized area in the nation.

Yet even in New England, employees in manufacturing establishments were a minority:

	1st half 1949	000's
Total employees, nonagricultural		3,150
Employees in manufacturing		1,366
Per cent of manufacturing to total		43

Source: **Handbook of Regional Statistics.**

The proportion of workers in manufacturing varies greatly: from 49.7 per cent for Connecticut to 36.2 per cent for Vermont. Service (tertiary) industries are large in Vermont, Massachusetts, and Maine in contrast to Connecticut, Rhode Island, and New Hampshire. Where Connecticut's tertiary workers are but 45.6 per cent of the total, Massachusetts' and Vermont's are 56.5 and 58.3 per cent of the total. These are provocative figures. Yet Colin Clark and others have held that the proportion of tertiary workers tends to rise in an advancing society: the higher the proportion, the higher the per capita income. High employment in service industries may reflect high productivity in manufacturing and/or agriculture. With reduced demands for labor to produce a given quantity of goods in these industries, surplus purchasing power is shunted more and more into the service industries, which in turn become the profitable and high-paying employments. In fact, many of these employments are directly related to manufacturing — e.g., accountants, efficiency experts, lobbyists.

This theory of a positive correlation between the proportion of tertiary workers and income per capita does not seem to apply to New England. Connecticut is clearly the most prosperous and productive state in New England and yet has the lowest proportion of tertiary workers. Vermont, with the lowest per capita income, has the highest proportion of tertiary employment, perhaps reflecting tourism and recreation. Massachusetts' tertiary industries have developed, at least in part, because of losses in manufacturing rather than gains. Selling, distribution, professional work, and the like are outlets for surplus labor, not only because labor is released as productivity rises, but also because labor is released as Massachusetts suffers from competitive losses. The same argument can be applied to Vermont or Maine. In these instances, however, the losses in agriculture are also relevant.

Earlier (see, e.g., pages 8–9) we discussed the outlets in the tertiary industries. Some of these are of great importance as sources of employment — e.g., insurance, banking, finance, and education. But we should distinguish these tertiary employments as sources of employment from their significance as earners of dollars from the outside. It is not at all clear that education is of great importance as an "export" industry. Dr. Hartland's study, for example, points in that direction, as do my own, presented in part in my *Market for College Graduates*. According to a survey published in the *New England News Letter* (May 1951) by the New England Council, the educational institutions of New England accounted for expenditures of $237 million in 1949–50; and 50,000 students from outside New England brought $85 million into this area. Unfortunately, the Council does not mention the movement in the reverse direction. In contrast to education, Dr. Hartland estimates insurance sales as 80 per cent outside of the region.

One of the most interesting advances in recent years has been that in investment trusts. Just before the war, New England accounted for about one-half the sales of stock by all open-end investment trusts. In 1949, according to *Fortune* (December 1949), the open-end trusts accounted for $1.8 billion, or about two-thirds of all assets held by investment trusts. And the Massachusetts Investors Trust, the largest in the country, held about 15 per cent of the total of investments in open-end trusts. Among the 75 largest investment trusts studied by the SEC (*Interlocking Directorates*, 1951), there are many New England firms. Unfortunately, we do not know how much employment is yielded nor the inflow of dollars for which these investment trusts are responsible.

2. NEW ENGLAND'S INDUSTRIES AND NATIONAL GROWTH

Old industries tend to grow less rapidly and even decline as new tastes and industries develop. Professor Arthur Burns, in his pioneering study of production trends, elaborated this law of retardation in the rate of growth. Ultimately growth may yield to decline. Rapid growth in general accompanies decline in the rate of growth of individual industries. This is the Burns thesis. Furthermore, may I add, an industry in a particular region, and especially an older one, may well grow less rapidly or decline more than the industry in the nation. This is essentially the New England problem, since this area has been so dependent on older industries.

Even in the period covered by Burns, there was evidence that important New England industries were slowing down. From 1870 to 1929, the increase in cotton consumption per year averaged 3.5 per cent and in wool consumption, 1.7 per cent; but from 1885 to 1929, only 3.0 and 1.0 per cent, respectively. From 1885 to 1929, cotton consumption ranked 30th among 57 items in the rate of growth; but for wool the rank for growth was 48.4, or *last*.[1]

From 1919 to 1947, there was a rise of 44 per cent in manufacturing employment for the country. Growth was especially disappointing in the industries in which New England excelled.

1. *Leather and leather products:*
New England's share of employment — 31.7 per cent
National growth of employment, 1919 to 1947 — 4 per cent

[1] A. F. Burns, *Production Trends in the United States since 1870* (1934), pp. xvi, 58, 84–85.

2. *Textiles:*
   New England's share of employment — 23.3 per cent
   National growth of employment, 1919 to 1947 — 7 per cent

3. *Rubber products:*
   New England's share of employment — 17.1 per cent
   National growth of employment, 1919 to 1947 — 20 per cent

Of great significance are the trends in a more recent period: 1939 to 1947, the years of the last two Censuses of Manufactures.

In these eight years, employment of workers in the nation rose by 53 per cent; in New England by 32 per cent. These gains compare with increases in population of 12.2 and 10.3 per cent, respectively, in the years, 1940 to 1949.

The New England record of employment relative to the nation's was especially poor in textiles (6 per cent rise for the nation, no change for New England), and leather and leather products (6 and —8, respectively). The relative deterioration in tobacco products and petroleum was also marked, but total employment in these is small in New England. In rubber and related products, national employment increased 78 per cent; in New England, only 41; in apparels, 29 and 9 per cent; in instruments and related products, 113 and 69 per cent. These are the industries in which New England's gains relative to the nation's were less than the over-all *relative* gains for New England. These industries accounted for 40 per cent of New England's manufacturing employment in 1947. Perhaps the relative losses should not be taken too seriously in rubber and rubber products and in instruments and related products, for New England's gains exceeded the nation's *over-all* percentage improvement in the former and growth in the latter exceeded New England's over-all improvement. The other industries listed in this paragraph, which account for one-third of New England's production workers in manufacturing, are those which bear close scrutiny in the future.

In three industries — furniture and fixtures, paper and products, and printing and publishing, which account for 9 per cent of New England's productive workers, the relative gains roughly equaled those for total New England employment. Against the losses associated with depletion of raw materials, these industries retained important marketing advantages.

There are also industries which grew more rapidly in New England than in the nation and others, of course, which expanded more rapidly than the average for all New England's industries. Especially large gains were made by the following:

Percentage Rise of Production Workers, 1939 to 1947

	U. S.	N. E.
Lumber and lumber products	41	50
Stone, clay, glass, etc.	52	54
Transportation equipment	81	81

These three industries employ 6–7 per cent of the production workers in New England. The first of these industries is likely to suffer in the long run from depletion of forests unless remedial measures are taken. The second is an industry largely sheltered from outside competition.

Then there are the important metal fabricating and machinery industries. These are the industries which may grow to absorb a large part of the slack resulting from deterioration of the older industries. Inclusive of instruments and related products and transportation equipment (both already considered), these industries account for 37 per cent of the production workers in New England. In 1939, they accounted for only 27 per cent.

Their growth in 1939 to 1947 relative to the nation's was as follows: [2]

	Per Cent
Primary metals	80
Fabricated metals	74
Machinery (except electrical)	74
Electrical machinery	74
Transportation equipment	100
Instruments and related products	57

Should we include chemicals and allied products (national growth, 69; New England, 66) and miscellaneous (65 and 59), then the industries which can maintain New England as a healthy economy now provide 47 per cent of the production jobs.

It is interesting that the growing industries — chemicals, metals, machinery — are the ones that are pulling old England out of her quagmire; and as in old England, these industries are replacing

[2] All figures in last few paragraphs calculated from U. S. *Census of Manufactures, 1947*, vol. III, *Statistics by States.*

textiles in part and industries affected by depletion of resources (e.g., coal in England and lumber in New England).

The direction of industrial movements is suggested well by the changes in relative importance of industries in the years 1939 to 1947.

For two groups of industries out of the twenty, the rate of growth in New England exceeded that of the nation. These were lumber and products, except furniture, and stone, clay, and glass products: these industries employed 3.4 per cent of New England's production workers in manufacturing in 1939 and 4.0 per cent in 1947. It should be noted that these are industries which are sheltered to a substantial degree from outside competition, for transportation costs are high.

Growth for ten groups of industries exceeded the average for all industries in New England, but advanced less rapidly than did these industries in the nation. These were primarily the metal and machinery industries and included chemicals, rubber, instruments, transportation equipment, and miscellaneous (jewelry the largest item in the last). In 1939, these industries acounted for 38.3 per cent of production workers in New England and 49.7 per cent in 1947. This relative advance of 30 per cent in eight years is striking indeed and points to the crucial importance of these industries as the ones which can save New England from the transitional pains associated with large declines in important industries.

In these same years, the eight groups of industries which grew less rapidly in New England than in the nation and less than *all* industries in New England, included (the most important) textiles, leather and leather products, apparels, paper and paper products, printing and publishing. In 1939, these industries employed 58.4 per cent of New England's manufacturing production workers. In 1947, they employed only 46.3 per cent, or a decline of more than 20 per cent. The major losses were in textiles and leather and leather products — the relative contribution from these two groups of industries declined by 10.1 percentage points, or 26 per cent. These, of course, are the problem industries which have emphasized the ease of migration and of location elsewhere as major New England difficulties.

One other aspect of these problems should be examined. New England's manufacturing employment is 10 per cent of the nation's total. Yet there are eleven groups of industries in which New

England's employment of production workers is less than 10 per cent of the total. In tobacco, New England contributes but 1 per cent of the nation's production workers; in petroleum, 2 per cent; in stone, clay, etc., 4 per cent; in primary metals and food, 6 per cent; in chemicals, 4 per cent; and in transportation equipment, which employs almost a million manufacturing production workers or 9 per cent of the nation's total, New England's employment is but 4 per cent of the nation's. In all these, the paucity of natural resources in New England is very important, for the largest employment is located near the source of raw materials. Despite its early manufacturing leadership, New England has played a disproportionately small part in the development of the automobile and satellite industries, for, of 600,000 workers in the automobile industry, its share in 1947 was but 5500.

In summary, we stress the point that New England's future growth seems to depend largely on its capacity to find outlets in the growing industries for workers displaced in the declining industries, and for new workers. In a semi-militaristic and full-employment economy, the outlets are likely to be especially in the metal, machinery, chemical, transportation equipment, etc., industries. In competing for employment in these industries, New England suffers from one serious handicap: the material-oriented nature of these industries.

3. THE EXPORT PROBLEM

One of New England's problems is that, in the manufacturing field, its output greatly exceeds the amounts that can be consumed in the region. This is a problem that has already been alluded to in Chapter 9. The relevance here lies mainly in the fact that where the main attraction of an industry is proximity to market, New England faces special difficulties in maintaining its present share of the nation's output. Even favorable labor conditions may give only a temporary support. In such industries as apparels, textiles, leather and leather products, it is difficult to stop the trend towards decentralization and, therefore, the threat to New England lies particularly in the industries in which New England still produces substantially more than its consumption and which move with ease to newer industrial regions. The fact that these industries are market-oriented, that the training of labor is relatively easy, that capital and management migrate freely, and that the optimum or most economical size of the unit is not large and therefore wide dispersion of production is economical — all of these add to the threat to these industries in New England.

For the industries as classified in the United States Census of Manufactures (1947, volume III), I have calculated the excess of value added in New England over the likely consumption in New England (assumed to be 6 per cent for consumption goods, 9 per cent for non-consumption goods, and 7½ per cent for miscellaneous manufactures). The net result is an excess of production over New England consumption of $2478 million. This roughly represents the value added by New England's industry which has to be exported outside of the region. Should we add the excess over 6 or 9 per cent for subindustries within industries which produce less than 6 (or as required 9 per cent of national output), then the required exports are $322 million additional. It is well to note that even today textile exports are $925 million, leather and leather products, $377 million, and paper and allied products, $225 million. These three industries may well be the most vulnerable. They account for more than $1500 million of exports, or more than one-half of all exports, and whereas all exports are more than two-fifths of the total value added, the exports of these three industries are more than one-fifth of the region's total value added.

Since value added is less than one-half of the total value, exports are about twice the exports of value added (given above) but against the exports of non-value added component, we must include a coresponding value of imports.

4. CONCLUSION

New England's losses in manufacturing are offset in part by gains in tertiary (service) employment. Gains in the latter do not always reflect a rising standard of living, as Colin Clark claims, but frequently reflect a deterioration in manufacturing: the small proportion of tertiary workers in Connecticut, the most productive state in the area, and the high proportion in Massachusetts are of some significance.

A few other features of the industrial structure should be stressed. First, New England depends heavily on industries which are vulnerable because they have to sell most of their products outside New England and yet these industries are in part market-oriented. Second, the New England industries with the best comparative record are in part sheltered from outside competition. They account, however, for but 8–9 per cent of manufacturing employment. (In tertiary occupations, the sheltered employment is much more important.) Third, New England depends excessively on industries which in the nation have declined or grown little in the last generation. Finally, note that from 1939 to 1947, the employment of the vulnerable industries in New England declined from 58 to 46 per cent, whereas employment in the growing industries, mainly metal fabricating and chemicals, increased from 38 to 50 per cent. In these industries, as in many others and particularly those in which New England's share is way out of line with its 10 per cent contribution to the nation's manufacturing total, its weakness in no small part stems from an unfavorable position for obtaining raw materials.

CHAPTER 26

TEXTILES, SHOES, AND OTHER EMPLOYMENTS

It is not possible, in the limitations of the space available, to discuss all the industries of New England in detail. But brief comments on textiles and leather and leather products and even briefer comments on education and agriculture may help clarify New England's problems. One crucial point should be noted at the outset. In both textiles and shoes, a large part of costs are fixed in the sense that competitors cannot significantly influence them: notably raw materials in both, and capital charges especially in shoes. The competitive aspects relate especially to labor costs, management, power, and taxes.

1. TEXTILES

In earlier chapters, we have discussed the major difficulties of the New England textile industry. High wages, low work-loads, heavy taxes, obsolescent plant and equipment, high power costs, subsidies in regions seeking new industries, and the over-all decline of demand for textile *workers* are among the reasons considered earlier.

We now propose to elaborate on some of these points and emphasize their significance for the whole economy.

About the decline of the New England textile industry, there can be little doubt. The losses at first were in coarse goods, but gradually the South is encroaching on finer cotton goods. Even before the war, the South had made great progress in the higher counts. From 1 per cent of No. 41 and over (fine) cotton yarn produced in 1900, the South raised its share of the nation's total to 61 per cent by 1935. Its proportion of coarse (No. 20 and under) had risen from 41 to 88 per cent.[1]

By 1947, textile employment had fallen to 283,000 in New

[1] S. L. Wolfbein, *The Decline of a Cotton Textile City* (1944), p. 61.

England, as compared with 440,000 in 1919. It is, of course, a mistake to concentrate on all textiles. For example, the 1947 census national figures reveal a rise of 6 per cent over 1939 for production workers in textiles; but an increase in woolens and worsteds of 12 per cent and a decline for knitting mills of 10 per cent and for hats of 20 per cent. Again, New England employed 60.5 per cent of the workers in woolens and worsteds in 1919 and 63.37 in 1947; but in cotton, rayon, and silk the respective figures were 38.0 and 17.2 per cent.[2] Since the 1947 census, the New England textile situation, and particularly in woolens, once more has reached crisis proportions. I refer to the 1951–52 decline.

One of the unfortunate aspects of the textile situation is the heavy concentration of workers in particular localities. Thus Lawrence accounts for one-quarter of all the woolen workers in Massachusetts, and Lawrence, Lowell, Worcester, and Pittsfield for about two-thirds. Massachusetts employs more than 30 per cent of the nation's workers in woolens and worsteds.[3] In 1907, New Bedford's wage earners in textiles accounted for 85 per cent of all manufacturing employment, and by 1938, only 42 per cent. The latter figure reflected, of course, the difficulties in the twenties and thirties. It is significant that even in the prosperous twenties, the textile industry revealed underlying weakness. Thus, from 1925 to 1929, wage earners in manufacturing rose by 5 per cent in the country, declined by 6 per cent in Massachusetts, and in cotton manufacturing in New Bedford, by 15 per cent.[4] But let us return to the problem of concentration. In Manchester, New Hampshire, the Amoskeag Mills in the early thirties alone employed 18,000 out of a total population of 52,000; a proportion roughly equal to that of total employed to total population in the nation. The effect of the closing of this mill and similar episodes — e.g., Textron in Nashua, New Hampshire — may well be imagined.

The shutting down of mills and migration to the South is an old story. But it is one that works havoc in the communities where heavy concentration of industries prevails. The resulting economic, medi-

[2] *Report of the Committee on the New England Economy.*

[3] The Commonwealth of Massachusetts, *A Report on Compensation Benefit Costs in Massachusetts* (1950), pp. 160, 170.

[4] S. L. Wolfbein, *The Decline of a Cotton Textile City*, pp. 31, 156. The experience in 1949 and early 1950, when 50,000 jobs were lost in textiles in New England, is also relevant.

cal, and sociological problems raised are serious indeed. For Massachusetts alone, the Masachusetts Textile Commission lists 90 plants liquidated or removed from 1923 to 1948. These plants had total capital of $112 million, 6.6 million spindles, 74,347 employees, and paid annually $61 million of wages.[5] The 74,347 employees involved accounted for about 10 per cent of employment in Massachusetts in 1948 and about one-half of total covered employment in textiles in 1948.[6]

In the Textron case, the company had closed plants employing 10,000 workers. In Nashua, New Hampshire, the number of employees involved before Textron acquired the mills was 5000. The bitterness aroused by the Textron case resulted in part from the fact that the mills had operated for more than 100 years, from the fact that Mr. Little, the President, had used the tax-free trust fund as a means of obtaining control over some of his mills, and generally from the impersonal approach of absentee ownership. Outside interests began, during the war period, to buy up mills in New England in order to assure continued supplies of short materials. The new owners frequently planned ultimately to dispose of all liquid assets and then to liquidate. The former owners escaped the burden of trying to survive under less favorable conditions, and sold under unusual conditions, since they received high prices and tax privileges.[7]

Many reasons can be adduced for the losses in textiles. Certainly the ease of movement and the large advantages that the South has in labor supply, wages, power, and taxes are important. But inept management also contributed to the losses in textiles and the rate of loss; and this problem is relevant for all New England industries.

In its report, the Massachusetts Textile Commission stressed the weakness of the industry and, in so doing, emphasized the difficult problems of adjustment for the future.[8] In the middle thirties, Secre-

[5] *Report of the Special Commission Relative to the Textile Industry* (May 12, 1950), pp 9–12.

[6] *A Report on Unemployment Compensation Costs in Massachusetts,* pp. 338–339.

[7] Hearings, Senate Sub-Committee of Interstate and Foreign Commerce, *Investigation of Closing of Nashua, N. H. Mills and Operations of Textron, Incorporated.*

[8] *Report of the Special Commission Relative to the Textile Industry,* pp. 36–37.

tary Wallace had been even more critical when he referred to the "flabbiness of the third and fourth generations."

The charge against management lies in part in the failure to make the most effective use of its profits. Indeed, in 1926–1939, Dr. Bachman estimates losses at $629 million and profits at $796 million.[9] But in the forties, profits had been very large, in both the North and the South. These profits could have been used to improve equipment and plants; but frequently a defeatist attitude resulted in liquidating or moving southward. A frequent complaint has been inadequate depreciation funds and excessive withdrawals by owners. In refusing to lend $2,250,000 to the Hayward-Schuster Woolen Mills, of East Douglas, Massachusetts (later a loan of $1,050,000 was approved with unfortunate results), the RFC commented on the reasons for refusal: " . . . continued losses, unwise use of the funds in the past in payment of salaries and dividends, the depressed state of the wool industry, and the generally poor prospects for the applicant."[10] Profits were indeed higher in the South than in the North: in the years 1922–1939, profits as a percentage of net worth were 1.84 per cent in the North and 5.29 per cent in the South.[11] Prospects have been better in the South. But it is well to take account of the large investments in the North, as well as the probable reduction of advantages of the South over the North as wages and taxes increase in the South.

Inefficiency and lack of enterprise are an old story in some parts of the textile industry. In a study of the New Bedford industry, Dr. Wolfbein explains the problem in part by the concentration of control, with interlocking directors, in relatively few families. Control passed from father to son and to son again. Some experts in the thirties put it as follows:

The cotton business has suffered most because official salaried positions have been given to sons or friends of those who had pull, and whose investments were negligible, without regard to qualifications of any respect. There are many who have been drawing $10,000 to $25,000 a year as

[9] J. Bachman and M. R. Gainsborough, *Economics of the Cotton Textile Industry* (1946).

[10] Senate Hearings, Sub-Committee on Banking and Currency, *Study of Reconstruction Finance Corporation*, I (1950), p. 323.

[11] *Report of the Special Commission Relative to the Textile Industry* (May 12, 1950), p. 38.

officials in the cotton manufacturing business whom I would pension
rather than have them in the employ of the Dartmouth Mfg. Corporation.

. . . . . .

It is not only textiles but many lines of industry that have flown South
and West to escape the results of tradition and managements hiding
behind a large invested capital but represented by a small par value of
capital. . .[12]

No better evidence is needed than the failure of Northern mills
to adopt the great inventions in the industry for which their leaders
were responsible. The Draper automatic loom proved to be much
more popular in the South than in the North. Of 222,000 of these
looms added in the years 1899 to 1914, the South accounted for
153,000. Fear of unemployment resulting from introduction of
automatic machinery and the unwillingness of management to
scrap old equipment contributed to the lag in the North. By 1929,
the South had about 1½ times as large a percentage of plain
automatics and twice as large a percentage of fancy automatics as
the North. In the South also the high-speed spinning frames were
received with enthusiasm.[13]

The Massachusetts Textile Commission, in its 1950 report, well
summarized the management problem as follows: [14]

It has been stated to the Commission that the nature of the textile industry has been substantially affected by the technological changes which
have taken place in fibres, equipment, processes and finishes; by the commercial changes which have resulted in large mergers, the combination
of selling and production interests; by the changes in the system of management, which has become modernized and schooled; and by the methods of merchandising and fabric development. In this new competition,
the management which continues to proceed along older channels and
procedures and is without the advantages of a technically trained staff,
schooled supervision, and full research and control resources is at a
disadvantage.

In the past, fewer Massachusetts manufacturers recognized the nature
of the changes in the production and marketing processes, and the management spent proportionately less on new equipment and the modern-

[12] S. L. Wolfbein, *The Decline of a Cotton Textile City,* pp. 91–98.

[13] The reader will find much information on these problems in J. K. O. Ott,
"The Migration of the New England Textile Industry, 1894–1950"; Honors
Thesis, Harvard University, 1951; also see T. R. Smith, *The Cotton Textile
Industry of Fall River* (1944).

[14] *Report of the Special Commission Relative to the Textile Industry,* pp.
35–37.

ization of their plants than in other areas. The plants which have become modern and are developing fabrics and combing new markets are more than able to keep abreast of conditions, and there are several outstanding examples of successful operations to be found. Technological developments and modernization programs necessarily result in the displacement of workers.

It is represented that the industry is being radically transformed by technological changes affecting the methods of manufacture, the plants and the products. In this connection the most significant fact for New England is that the wool and worsted industry is facing competition from new fibres and new processes. Rayon tropical suitings have definitely established themselves and are now making progress in getting part of the all-year-round market.

Technological developments have not been restricted to the wool and worsted industry. It is only being more radically shaken by them because of its slow technological progress during the last thirty years. The appearance of nylon is fast threatening many established cotton and rayon products. Orlon is on the horizon and promises to make further invasions into the wool and worsted market. Saran is substituting for rayon and cotton duck. Fibre glass has made notable progress in replacing cotton tire cords.

The most sweeping change in mill organization has been the widespread introduction of mechanical conveyance devices and the techniques for the realignment of machinery to eliminate the need for much material handling. Modern mills must have the new automatic winding machinery, and in each branch of the industry, new machinery is being introduced at a rapid rate. New types of products, such as bonded web products and plastics, are coming on to the market. New consumer and industrial demands are scrapping old products and opening up new opportunities.

The textile industry has been relatively slow to feel the impact of current industrial developments. But now precision machinery, electronic controls, quality testing, new lay-outs, labor-saving devices and methods are flowing into it at a rapid rate. The company and plant which wants to keep abreast of this flow must be prepared for the changes and be ready to move ahead to new markets, products, machinery and methods.

It has been represented that a number of management factors have stood in the way of growth; that there has been little concerted effort on the part of top management to promote greater competency in the ranks of supervision; and that there is practically no effort at the present time to arrange technical conferences for supervision such as is found in other areas. The available services for technical guidance of manufacturers are costly and incomplete. The smaller manufacturer is less able to keep abreast of technical changes, unprepared to follow the innovations of a chemical or electronic character, and has little or no access to tested information. There is no facility available which would provide him with adequate overall knowledge on the trends within the industry. He must rely on word of mouth communication and releases through news channels.

There are few resources available for aiding him in trying out new ideas and fabrics, or in studying the opportunities for new markets. Competition has insulated manufacturers from one another so that they are unable to meet the onrush of technical and commercial change.

Textiles are clearly a weak spot in the New England area. Inept management is an important factor in the losses and rate of losses. Our experience vis-à-vis the South has not been unlike England's vis-à-vis the rest of the world. We shall continue to lose and with the beginning of a migration in woolens and worsteds and with the vast technological improvements promised, employment in the textile industry is almost certain to fall — even in a full employment economy. The drift will continue to the more productive metal fabricating industries, to the white-collar employments, and also to some extent to less productive occupations. But vigorous measures might well greatly decelerate the rate of decline.

The importance of some factors in the situation may well be exaggerated. As suggested earlier, tax differentials may play a part. But note that according to the Senate study of 1926, the ratio of taxes to gross sales of cotton textile corporations was 4.33 per cent for the South in 1933, 3.28 per cent for Massachusetts, and 2.91 for the North. In earlier years, however, rates were lower in the South.[15] Much has also been made of the larger investments in the South. Indeed, they have been larger, and New England has lagged. Thus, in 1947, investment per employee in the South was $320.50; in New England, $261.90; in Massachusetts, $256.70.[16] But an expanding industrial area is bound to spend more per employee. The fact is that new plants cost much more than expansion of older plants. This discussion does not deny the advantage of newer plant and equipment for the South. A third factor is of more importance.

Earlier we mentioned the fact that one advantage of the South lies in the greater concentration of the industry in smaller communities, where the cost of living is much less than in the large cities. The importance of this consideration is suggested by the following:

1. Only 13 of the 57 main cotton-spindle counties in the Southeast

[15] Senate Document 126, *Report on the Cotton Textile Industry* (1935), pp. 150–151.

[16] The Commonwealth of Massachusetts, *Report of the Special Commission Relative to the Textile Industry*, p. 39.

employed as many as 10,000 manufacturing wage earners in 1929.[17]
2. Counties in 1930 with

	25,000 wage earners	5,000–10,000 wage earners	10,000–40,000 wage earners	More than 40,000 wage earners
South	36	14	10	0
New England	4	9	11	10

3. Density of population per square mile, 1940, by counties:

	Less than 100	Less than 300	More than 1,000
South	37	5	0
New England	8	15	4

The crucial issue lies in differences in costs. Allow me to summarize the views of two experts. In defending the closing of the Textron Mills in New Hampshire, Mr. Little, its President, compared his costs.

Costs in New England and the South — Textron Corporation

	New England	South
Power — KWH (average of two New England and three Southern) — mills	14.7	6.9
Transportation [a] of raw cotton — cents per 100 weight	90	30
Compensation insurance [b]	100	44
Pay-roll taxes [b]	100	73
Fixed taxes per spindle — cents	253	43
Take-home pay [c]	110	100
Productivity as measured by output of muslin sheeting (pounds)	5.37	9.62

[a] Note that this disadvantage is largely offset by savings on transportation for finishing and marketing.
[b] Rhode Island = 100.
[c] South = 100.
Source: Hearings, Subcommittee on Interstate and Foreign Commerce, Part I, **Investigation of Closing of Nashua, N. H. Mills and Operations of Textron, Incorporated** (1948), pp. 12–35.

In the discussions of labor-management relations in the Southern textile industry in 1951, Mr. Stanton, of the Hathaway Manufacturing Company, presented some interesting evidence to a Senate Committee. His major points were that wages were much higher in New England; that work-loads were much lower; and that non-unionization was a strong advantage for the South. In his view, New

[17] R. B. Vance, *All These People* (1945), pp. 303–305.

England would never recoup the jobs lost in the 1948–49 recession; and in part because, in response to declining demand, the South reduces wages and prices and the North does not. As a result of such wage differences and a greater rise in the South recently, Mr. Stanton estimated wages in New England about 19½ cents above the minimum on government contracts set under the Walsh-Healey Act. Actual wage differences amounted to 11.6 cents per hour plus a fringe differential of 9.145. Total wage differences would then be $20 million per year for New England's 70,000 cotton textile workers. As a result of these differences, Mr. Stanton expected the loss of New England's one remaining profitable field of operation, the combed goods industry. His major recommendation was a national rise of minimum wages from 75 cents to 1.06½ cents per hour, thus removing wage differentials.

In reply to Mr. Stanton's statement, Mr. Solomon Barkin, representing the Textile Workers of America, insisted that differences in work-loads reflected in part differences in working conditions; and that wage rates adjusted to the kind of product turned out varied much less than Mr. Stanton had suggested. The basic wage difference between unionized mills in the South and North was, in Barkin's view, but 3 cents per hour; between Northern unionized and Southern non-unionized, 6.5 cents. Variations in fringe items were also held to be smaller than indicated by Mr. Stanton. Mr. Barkin also emphasizes the failure of management rather than wage differentials. First, there was the desertion of mills by New Englanders who wanted to get money out and obtain the advantages of being taxed under a capital gain rather than an income tax. Second, there were the older operators who were not prepared to deal with revolutionary technical changes. Finally, the national chains tended to concentrate in the South. New England firms, in Barkin's views, have not kept abreast of technological advances.[18]

In conclusion, the textile industry is confronted with a serious crisis, the effects of which are felt especially in the textile towns but also by the entire economy. Management is in part to blame although there are many brilliant and venturesome executives; labor with its

[18] Hearings, Senate Sub-Committee on Labor and Public Welfare, *Labor-Management Relations in the Southern Textile Industry*, Part 2 (1950), pp. 32–71.

unwillingness to adapt itself to the changing situation is also partly responsible; and government and the communities are just beginning to be aroused to taking corrective measures.

The migration to the South is in part the result of genuine advantages there; but it is also in part the result of unfair competition which can be treated. Governor Dever's proposal in January 1952 for a state financed corporation to sponsor new plants is a step in the right direction, as is the appointment by the Conference of New England Governors of a Committee on the New England Textile Industry.

2. A BRIEF COMMENT ON WOOLENS AND WORSTEDS

For what follows, I am especially indebted to Dr. Morris for an enlightening study of the "Woolen and Worsted Industry in the Southern Piedmont States" (Ph.D. Thesis, 1951, deposited in the Widener Library, Harvard University).

Governor Ellis Arnall, in his *Shores Dimly Seen*, has predicted that the South would capture the woolen and worsted industry. In 1950, the South's share in woolens and worsteds, 6–7 per cent of total output, was about equal to its position in cotton textiles in 1890. Since 1939, the major plants built have been in the South: the number of woolen plants in the Piedmont (the major producing area) increased from 21 to 29 in 1950, while worsted plants numbered seven in 1939 and 29 in 1950. In contrast to the cotton development, Northern capital is making a much larger contribution. In 1939, there were five branch plants of Northern firms, in 1950, 25; while locally owned or independent plants rose from 23 to 33. In general, Southern plants are larger than those in New England, but there are few giant plants. These are not flexible and are risky in case of stoppages.

The advantages of the South are the usual ones: community spirit, newer plant, cheap construction costs, lower taxes. (Dr. Morris says the last is relatively unimportant, for taxes account only for 1.6 per cent of the total costs.) In wages, the hourly difference is almost 20 per cent, though this is partly offset by higher productivity in New England. According to the author, the Northern worker is better trained, but the Southern worker is more flexible. Building costs seem to be about 20–25 per cent less in the South than in Lawrence, Massachusetts and Pawtucket, Rhode Island: a

Southern plant saved $50,000 a year on coal as compared to its New England costs. Power costs for three shifts in 6000-loom factories were about one-half in the TVA area compared to New England.

In woolens and worsteds, New England has two important advantages that are not available in cotton: the first is proximity to markets (New York City sells 43 per cent of men's and boys' clothing and 70 per cent of women's, misses' and junior outerwear); the second is better location relative to raw materials.

Nevertheless, the South offers a real threat. Unless New England is on its toes, the woolen and worsted industry may vanish as cotton textiles have — though not so fast. The *Boston Herald*, in an editorial of December 2, 1948, was sufficiently agitated to take South Carolina to task for making exaggerated claims for its woolen and worsted industry.

3. LEATHER AND LEATHER PRODUCTS [19]

I shall discuss this industry, a very important one for this region, more briefly than the textile industry. In 1919, the industry provided 155,000 jobs in New England; in 1947, 109,000. The decline for the country was much smaller — from 399,000 to 383,000 or 4 per cent, as compared with almost 30 per cent for New England. From 1925 to 1949, however, New England's share of shoe production dropped only from 33.2 to 31.6 per cent, though the year 1947 was a bad one. The proportionate decline for New York and Missouri in the last 25 years has been substantially more than in New England. In Pennsylvania, the expansion from 1925 to 1949 was from 5.3 to 10.1 per cent and for "all others" (exclusive of New England, New York, Pennsylvania, Illinois, Wisconsin, and Ohio), the growth was from 6.6 to 15.3 per cent.[20] These figures point to decentralizing tenden-

---

[19] I have depended especially on E. M. Hoover, Jr., *Location Theory and the Shoe and Leather Industry* (1937); BLS, Bulletin No. 360, *Time and Labor Costs in Manufacturing 100 Pairs of Shoes, 1923* (1924), and *Trends in Man-Hours Expended Per Unit, Selected Postwar–1948; Monthly Bulletin of Boston Reserve Bank,* especially November 1948, August and September 1949, and October 1950. Also see the *Report of the President's Council's Committee on the New England Economy*; the Commonwealth of Massachusetts, *A Report on Unemployment Compensation Benefit Costs in the United States* (1950), pp. 176–189.

[20] Based on figures in *Monthly Review of Federal Reserve Bank of Boston.*

cies, which appear even in New England. From 1919 to 1947, employment in Massachusetts dropped from 38.8 to 28.4 per cent of the total, whereas New Hampshire and Maine increased their proportion from 7.4 per cent to 9.3 per cent.

In comparison with textiles, New England's producers of leather and leather products are maintaining their position better, and particularly in the last 25 years. New England's share of national output is still larger than its textiles as a share of the nation's. In one respect, the stronger competitive position of New England in leather and leather products is surprising. The system of renting factories, sites, and machinery reduces the amount of capital required and makes technical secrets equally accessible to all, with the result that entry is relatively easy. In charging rentals at a uniform unit amount, the United Shoe Machinery Company denies to the large factory an important economy of scale.

New England's capacity to retain a substantial part of the leather and leather product industries may be partly explained.

1. A skilled labor force is still essential, probably more so than in textiles. As Dr. Hoover contends in his excellent book on *Location Theory and the Shoe and Leather Industry*, though many of the operations have been reduced to simple ones using unskilled workers, the high skills are still a requisite in the industry.

2. Migration seems to have taken the form largely of movement within regions rather than across regional lines. In part the migration has been from large to small communities, where cheap labor is of some importance for the production of staple items. This migration towards smaller communities prevails in New England as well as in the Middle West.

3. On the whole, the development of these industries outside of New England has been in large cities or in smaller communities in the Middle Atlantic and Middle Western states. Although in some instances these centers of shoe manufacturing have important advantages in transportation costs, they do not profit from the large wage differentials vis-à-vis New England as have the Southern textile states vis-à-vis New England. In areas outside of New England, the leather and shoe industry has had to compete much more with other employments than have textiles in the South. Organizational differences (i.e., trade unionism) have not been so great interregionally as in textiles, and wage rates have been more nearly

equal. The large differences in wage rates have been between large and small population centers and have been related in part to organizational diffrences, to variations in the cost of living, and to the kind of labor and type of shoes produced.

4. It may well be that technological changes have been bunched much more in the past in shoes than in textiles and, therefore, that current employment prospects are better in the former. Thus, according to the BLS, time cost of labor per pair of shoes declined from 18.32 hours in 1863 (hand labor) to 2.36 hours in 1895 and 1.07 hours in 1923. It is, however, a fact that advances still continue in the shoe industry. From 1926 to 1946, according to the BLS, man-hour output increased by 75 per cent more. These technological advances, both in textiles and shoes, reduce the labor demand in the industry.

Despite the more favorable position of New England's shoe industry compared to its textiles, the region faces serious problems in this industry. First, just because the region's participation exceeds the contribution in textiles, the export problem is very serious. At least 75 per cent of the output has to be sold outside the region. Yet the fact is that outside sales become increasingly difficult as access to the industry is facilitated and the manufacture of shoes becomes more and more oriented towards markets. Of outside sales of $400 million, about $250 million represented imported materials. The net exports are then of the order of $150 million.

There are other problems also. Technical experts find that the New England factories, in contrast with Middle Western, are too small to operate at minimum unit costs; that there are signs of managerial inefficiency (recall the failure to adapt production to postwar changes in age distribution); that marketing methods, with excessive retail outlets, accentuate instability. Again, although this is primarily an industry of small units, the very large units are becoming more important — 5 units control more than 70 per cent of men's low-priced shoes. These large units operate primarily outside of New England. It is not surprising, then, that New England's manufacturers express great concern over future prospects in this important industry which accounted for 8 per cent of all production workers in New England in 1947 (the corresponding figure for textiles was 21 per cent).

4. EDUCATION[21]

The major importance of education lies in its contribution to an improved citizenry, which in turn contributes towards high economic productivity. New England, a pioneering region in education, still retains certain important advantages. Outlays per student are still large relative to important industrial rivals, though the difference is related to some extent to the higher cost of living in New England and though in recent years New England's relative position has deteriorated. Public education strains the economies of Southern states much more than it does the New England economy, even though the latter spends about three times as much per student-day. In the proportion of its population benefiting by public education, New England is in a more favorable position than the South.

In higher education, New England's investments are large; but she is gradually losing leadership here and in the proportion of the adult population with higher education her position is roughly equal to the nation's. The Mountain States and the Pacific States register a much greater educational achievement today, that is, in man-years of college completed, than New England. Since the latter is so greatly dependent on private institutions, now in vulnerable financial position, New England is likely to continue to lose ground unless help is had from government.

In one respect, New England's contribution is sadly lacking. Many of her major institutions are national in outlook and hence they do not interest themselves in regional problems of research, management, and the like. Institutions of higher learning in other regions, particularly in the South and West, contribute much more to the economic development of their regions.[22]

5. AGRICULTURE

A brief word about agriculture (Professor Black in two recent books has largely exhausted this problem). With about 2½ per cent

[21] See especially the Council of State Governments, *The Forty-Eight State School Systems* (Chicago, 1949); *The Report of the President's Commission on Higher Education, Higher Education for American Democracy,* 1947, vol. 6; T. L. Hungate, *Financing the Future of Higher Education* (1946); S. E. Harris, *The Market for College Graduates* (1949).

[22] For references and more extended discussion of the problems of education, see the section written by the author in the relevant section in the *Report of the President's Council's Committee on the New England Economy.*

of her income from agriculture, New England's dependence on agriculture is disproportionately small. Agriculture is a declining industry in New England, as it is almost everywhere in this country. But it is worth noting that the long-term trend has been reversed in the last generation. With the growth of large concentrations of population, the high demand for dairy products, vegetables, etc. contributed to the recent maintenance of agriculture in New England. How long New England will be able to postpone further declines will depend largely on training of manpower, scientific advances, and the continued protection offered by high transportation costs and perishability to certain types of output, e.g., dairy products.

In relation to national averages, the following deserve comment: New England's agriculture is much more intensive than the nation's, with larger outlays per acre of capital, labor, and fertilizers. (In each instance three to four times the national average per acre.) In numerous instances this intensive farming shows up in high yields: potatoes per acre, milk per cow, and egg output per hen.[23]

This region has also received much less support from the federal government relative to her participation in the nation's agriculture than the country generally.

6. CONCLUSION

Unfortunately, space precludes a discussion of all employments, one by one. Textiles and leather and leather products, as the two especially vulnerable industries, deserve special mention; old industries, they suffer from defects in management. They are vulnerable in part because entry is relatively easy. Losses to the South in textiles stem from the peculiar advantages for nurturing textiles there, with the result that the South can concentrate on capturing this industry in a manner that a more industrialized area cannot. In the Middle Atlantic and Central States, the leather and leather products industries are encroaching on New England's domination. But in these other areas the shoe and related industries have to compete with other industries for labor and other factors of production. Again, management deficiencies here seem to be accelerat-

---

[23] See the section contributed by the writer in the above report on agriculture where a fuller discussion is presented. Above all, see the valuable book by J. D. Black, *The Rural Economy of New England* (1950).

ing New England's relative losses; and unlike the textile industries, differentials in wage costs do not seem to be a vital factor. Both textiles and shoes and leather depend greatly on sales outside; and since the industries are largely market-oriented, the dependence on exports is a threat to the health of these industries. Even in education, which is much more a production factor affecting all employments than a source of either employment or of dollars, New England's early advantages are being lost.

CHAPTER 27

CONCLUDING REMARKS

1. PRESCRIPTIONS

It is not necessary to summarize the main analytical points made in the body of this book. Chapter 1 offers a quick summary. Any careful reader of the book will also find many recommendations widely distributed between the covers of the volume. Admitting that diagnosis is easier than therapy, I nevertheless present in summary form the most important prescriptions.

1. It is the responsibility of the federal government to impose uniform standards of hours, working conditions, social security, minimum wages, and, in so far as possible, equitable taxation among business, labor, and agriculture. Only in this way can we stop the economic war between states and regions, which results in *excessive* migrations of industry, competition to keep social security and related standards as low as possible, and unforgivable wastage of resources in older industrial areas. As the federal government's outlays relative to those of states and local governments continue to increase, as social security becomes federalized, as minimum wages rise, etc., the dangers of the new civil war will be reduced.

2. New England will have to reconsider its attitude towards federal government. If it does not accept a stronger federal government and seek a fair share of federal outlays, it will suffer continued drains of cash, which will be used in part to strengthen the competitive position of areas attracting our industries, capital, and managerial talent. It is refreshing to learn that businessmen replying to a New England Council questionnaire overwhelmingly approved the recommendations of the Committee on the New England economy to the President, inclusive of greater receptiveness to federal aid. Possibly businessmen are occasionally misrepresented by their associations. (See the *Boston Globe*, October 19, 1951.)

3. New England's interest in federal policy is not confined to the

legislation suggested in (1) and (2). Thus, New England would gain greatly from lower prices for food and raw materials, and might therefore press for lower tariffs on these products, an elimination of quotas, and modifications in farm policy. The region would profit from more rapid amortization for tax purposes as a special spur to get rid of old plant.

4. It is easy to blame management and easy to say that New England needs twenty-first-century management, not nineteenth-century. In fact, no one conversant with its problems can be blind to many of the weaknesses of New England's management, evident for example, in the failure of New England manufacturers to adopt improvements as rapidly as those in other areas; in their ancient plants; in their penchant for security; in their excessive fear of government.

There are, of course, important exceptions. In fact, New England has thousands of outstanding businessmen. But we need less nepotism; more use of the unusually rich research facilities of the region; less blaming of government and more concern with managements' own weaknesses; use of more profits to modernize plant rather than to buy bonds or export capital; greater concern for New England's problems rather than exportation of cash and talent elsewhere; more spirited coöperation both among businessmen and with local and state governments; more effective use of all racial stocks.

5. Labor is not without fault either. Productivity depends on labor as well as on management. In the light of the serious competition confronting New England, labor's frequent attitude towards higher productivity is all the more to be lamented. Labor tends to adhere to old work-loads too rigidly, and in general shows a high degree of inflexibility. Management and labor are both responsible in part for New England's problems.

Improvements in productivity are indispensable, if, at current relative wages in New England, this region is to achieve high levels of employment. It is well to note that not only must New England absorb displaced workers, but over the next generation this region may have to provide 400,000 new jobs, or about 10 per cent of the current total. New plant and machinery, enlightened management, coöperative labor, and active *support* of state and local governments are all ingredients of the full employment and prosperity prescription.

6. It is scarcely necessary to add that the policies of the federal government are of crucial importance. New England's relative losses may be consistent with high or low employment and with high or low income, depending upon the effects of national policy on employment and productivity.

7. Much has been said about a favorable business climate — only in part relevant. Should the economic war between states be stopped or greatly reduced as suggested in (1) above, then a halt might be called on current discussion. For the unfavorable "climate" in (say) Massachusetts stems largely from the excessive incentives offered by aggressive states elsewhere. Federal action can reduce this evil; and more aggressive management in New England can help. I am not convinced that the way to meet Southern competition is to give Massachusetts a sales tax rather than a corporate income tax, to reëstablish the three-shift system, to reduce unemployment benefits to $15 a week, etc.

I do not, however, wish to give the impression that in some states taxes on business may not be too heavy or that government spending may not be excessive. There is a problem here, but its proportions are often exaggerated; and the proposed solutions are not the best ones. Should corrective measures be taken as suggested here and in the body of the book, then the new industries required to replace declining ones will be found. At any rate the more standards improve in the South, the less positive government action will be required in New England.

2. PERSPECTIVE

As has been said, the opening chapter provides a useful summary as well as an introduction. But for the reader who insists on abtaining a perspective at the end, let me add a few points for emphasis.

1. *A great deal depends on the federal government.* Thus with a prosperous economy, the weaknesses of the New England economy become of greatly reduced significance. Note the many problems dealt with in this book which federal policy touches or even determines the solutions of: taxation, inclusive of the net outflow of cash on Treasury account; foreign trade (as a substitute for losses of interregional trade); river and power development; the policy towards dispersion of plants, and depreciation; the New England steel mill; the prices paid for food and raw materials; minimum

standards of social security, and labor and working conditions. Federal policies touching these matters greatly influence New England's position.

2. *Then there is the problem of costs.* Federal policy is, of course, relevant here. New England's problems are high labor costs in the declining industries (fortunately offset by favorable labor costs in the expanding industries). Where labor costs are high, the explanation is in part higher wage rates, related in turn to the concentration of industry in high-cost cities, to the restricted flow of labor compared to other regions and also to rigid work-loads, old plants, and less than adequate management.

3. Labor costs are not the only problem of costs. The distance from raw materials is a factor of first-rate importance. The survey of industrial trends (Chapters 25 and 26) reveals the importance of this factor.

I am not convinced that taxes are as important as is generally assumed. They are only in part costs; and the *differences* among states are not a substantial item. High cost of fuel and power is also not a major factor but is probably more important than taxes.

4. *Especially significant are the interregional problems.* Dependent on manufacturing and especially on soft goods industries, the New England states are especially vulnerable to the long-run changes in employment trends (manufacturing tends to become less important and particularly in the soft goods industries). Yet New England "exports" about one-half its manufacturing product, of which exports textiles, shoes and leather account for one-half. Yet these are the very industries which are easily captured by other areas. With federal policies tending to raise prices of raw materials and food, the decline of the "export" industries raises serious problems for New England.

5. Older regions everywhere face similar problems. But it has also been suggested here that older regions need not decline relatively (e.g., cf. New York) and the rate of relative decline can be slowed down. On this score, a comparison of declines of Northern New England since 1800 with the much smaller relative decline of Southern New England is of interest, as well as a comparison of Massachusetts' trend with that of Connecticut, with the latter maintaining its position well in the last generation.

Economic arteriosclerosis is evident in labor and management attitudes, in old plants, in the frequent adaptation of older business units to a $50 billion economy instead of to a $300 billion economy which it is, in a concentration on nonassembly-line industries.

3. A CHEERFUL NOTE

Finally, let me end on a note of optimism. I quote from an optimistic report of the New England Council, 1951, *The Rising Tide Lifts All the Boats*.[1]

1. New England, with 6.4 per cent of the nation's population, owns 13 per cent of the savings deposits, 10 per cent of the capital resources in banks, and 8 per cent of the life insurance in force.

2. "By 1960, if the present upward trend is maintained, New England's income (in terms of 1935–1939 dollars) will be $10 billion a year, as compared to $4 billion in 1920. Its labor force will have increased by 32,500 a year, to 4,500,000, and its retail sales by $91 million a year to $5.5 billion, as compared to $3 billion in 1929."

3. From New England's 20,000 manufacturing establishments, products worth $14 billion come annually.

4. With 8.4 per cent of the country's manufacturing establishments, New England has 15 per cent of the industrial research laboratories.

5. Its per capita income is above the national average.

6. New England's earnings from tourists jumped from $400 million in 1935 to $850 million in 1949.

7. New England grows 27 per cent of the country's potatoes, 42 per cent of the maple syrup, and 60 per cent of its cranberries.

Then the Council suggests what remains to be done: more finance, new equipment, efficiency and economy in government, build more industries on the basis of raw materials from abroad, import natural gas, improve tourist facilities and land utilization, develop new uses for food fibers, etc. But, interestingly enough, not a word about federal government. "Maintain vigorously the rights of the *states* to control the development of their natural resources . . . " (my italics).

[1] In quoting this report, I am not endorsing it without reservations.

INDEX

Adams, Henry, 56, 57
Adams, James Truslow, 58
Advantages of New England, listed, 53–54
Agriculture, workers in, 134; industrial structure of, 301–302
Aiken, Sen. George D., 242, 244, 247
American Enka Corporation, 77
American Falcon Company, 54
American Regionalism, quoted, 76
American Woolen Company, 49
Amoskeag Mills, 289
Anti-trust policy, effects, 116
Anti-union activity in South, 171–176
Apparel industry, 29, 43, 137; wage differentials, 141; effects of FOB pricing, 262
Arnall, Ellis, 297
Athol, Mass., 54
Axelrod, Joseph, 50

Bachman, J., 291
Balance of payments, 56, 90
Baltimore, Md., differential freight rates, 264–265
Barkin, Solomon, 152–154, 296
Basing point system, 28, 260–264
Benton, Sen. William, 53
Beverly, Mass., 192
Black, John D., 65, 301–302
Blanchard Report, The, 204
Borg-Warner Corporation, 80
Boston, Mass., 59, 73; taxation problem, 25–26, 192, 194–195, 200, 213–216, 217; wage rates and hourly earnings, 43, 137, 140–142; manufacturing employment, 44; accumulations of capital, 93; cost of living index, 157; power costs, 236; attitude on St. Lawrence Seaway, 242–243, 249–250; advantages of integrated steel mill, 270
Boston banks, conservatism, 33
Boston City Club, 242, 244
Boston Edison Company, 48

Boston Port Authority, objections to St. Lawrence Seaway, 27, 248; reasons for decline, 264–265
Bowles, Chester, 35
Bradford, Governor William, 55
Bridgeport, Conn., decline of employment, 72; taxation, 200
Bright, Arthur A., Jr., 231, 232
Brockton, Mass., 74
Brooks, Van Wyck, 61
Bureau of Labor Statistics (U. S. Department of Labor), wage differentials, 140; cost of living index, 157; textile mill migrations, 163; shoe industry data, 300
Burlington Mills, 173
Burns, A. F., 281
Business climate, importance of, 306
Business taxes, trends in Massachusetts, 209–213
Businessmen, views on tax burden, 196–198

Calumet and Hecla Consolidated Copper Company, 78
Canadian government, attitude on St. Lawrence Seaway, 245
Capital, migration from New England of, 21; imports of, 101
Capital costs of industry, 128–131
Capital investment, state and local differences, 69–70
Celanese Corporation, 77
Cement Case (U. S. Supreme Court), 260–261
Chatham, Mass., 73
Channing, William Ellery, 55, 58
Chelsea, Mass., 54
Chemicals and allied industries, growth, 29; wage differentials, 142; power costs, 235; employment, 283
Cheney Company, 49
Chicopee, Mass., 192
Clark, Colin, 279, 286
Clay industry, 28